LAND UPRISING

SIMÓN VENTURA TRUJILLO

LAND UPRISING

Native Story Power and the Insurgent Horizons of Latinx Indigeneity

THE UNIVERSITY OF
ARIZONA PRESS
TUCSON

The University of Arizona Press
www.uapress.arizona.edu

We respectfully acknowledge the University of Arizona is on the land and territories of Indigenous peoples. Today, Arizona is home to twenty-two federally recognized tribes, with Tucson being home to the O'odham and the Yaqui. Committed to diversity and inclusion, the University strives to build sustainable relationships with sovereign Native Nations and Indigenous communities through education offerings, partnerships, and community service.

First paperback edition 2022

ISBN-13: 978-0-8165-4018-1 (cloth)
ISBN-13: 978-0-8165-4694-7 (paper)

Cover design by Leigh McDonald
Cover art: *Under Clouds of New Shape* by Marla Allison
Map design by Once-Future Office

Unless otherwise noted, all photos are by the author.

Publication of this book is made possible in part by the proceeds of a permanent endowment created with the assistance of a Challenge Grant from the National Endowment for the Humanities, a federal agency.

Library of Congress Cataloging-in-Publication Data
Names: Trujillo, Simón Ventura, author.
Title: Land uprising : Native story power and the insurgent horizons of Latinx indigeneity / Simón Ventura Trujillo.
Description: Tucson : The University of Arizona Press, 2020. | Includes bibliographical references and index.
Identifiers: LCCN 2019036753 | ISBN 9780816540181 (hardback)
Subjects: LCSH: Alianza Federal de las Mercedes. | Mestizos—New Mexico—History. | Right of property—New Mexico. | Mexican Americans—Land tenure—New Mexico.
Classification: LCC F801.2 .T78 2020 | DDC 978.9/0046872—dc23
LC record available at https://lccn.loc.gov/2019036753

Printed in the United States of America
♾ This paper meets the requirements of ANSI/NISO Z39.48–1992 (Permanence of Paper).

For Ventura Chávez

Cruzita Chávez

Gail B. Fox

Jesse O. Baros

CONTENTS

ILLUSTRATIONS

FIGURES

MAP

NOTE ON TERMS, OR X MARKS A SUTURE

This book is an attempt to reconceptualize the place of the New Mexican land grant struggle and its significance in the fields of Indigenous, Latin American, Chicanx, and Latinx studies. As these movement-driven fields of study attest, terms and nomenclatures of identification are sites and signs of material struggle. In the struggle to determine an apt nomenclature for the multiple indigeneities and *mestizajes* studied this book, I have turned to the Latinx nomenclature. I use Latinx not to supplant the specificity of Chicanx but rather to address the social and cultural heterogeneity within and beyond the Chicanx movement. Latinx offers a provisional third term to name the ways Chicanx operated in tandem and tension with Indohispanx. I therefore use Latinx to hold open the politics of insurgent naming of the Chicanx movement to speak to the multiple trajectories of Latin American identifications and namings that are currently transforming the politics and scope of Chicanx and Latinx studies. As is also apparent in my usage, I have turned to the X for similar reasons. Alan Pelaez Lopez marks the X in the emergent articulation of Latinx nomenclature as a wound "that trans and gender-nonconforming Latin Americans wear as we navigate a Latinidad that has yet to love us."[1] He identifies the X as signifying four paradigmatic wounds in the experience and study of Latinx life, theory, narrative, and culture derived from colonization: settlement, antiblackness, feminicides, and inarticulation. In my use of the X, I approach the wounds with a difference. Because X marks the wound that has historically carried the imperiled promise for premature death under dueling regimes of white patriarchal supremacy, I invoke the X as a suture. Indeed the very alphabetic graphic of the X evokes the image of a stitch, an act of weaving, an intersection, and a crossing over. As a suture, the X signifies a wound. But, with the attention to land reclamation explored in the following pages, I also use it to mark a wound that has been identified for devotional care and regenerational time and energy. That said, when quoting or situating the ensemble of Latinx nomenclatures in their historically localized usage, I have retained their original formulation. Yet across *my* descriptive usages of the various nomenclatures of Chicanx, Latinx, Genízarx, Indohispanx, and Latin Americanx identification and study, I have employed the X.

ACKNOWLEDGMENTS

This book is the product of labors, struggles, and insurrections from a wide range of people and beings from before and beyond my time. It is an honor to be able to acknowledge and offer gratitude for the inspiration, guidance, and support that I have received in making this project come alive.

I first would like to thank my mother, Gail B. Fox; my grandparents, Ventura and Cruzita Chávez; and my sister, Michelle Trujillo. My mother taught me and my sister the strength, optimism, and vitality of wholehearted love. She and my grandparents lived through many of the stories that I write about, and this book would not be possible without their hard, tireless, and dignified work. Michelle continues to be a source of generosity and humor, and I am in awe of her dedication to her work as a nurse and to *el pueblo salvadoreño*. I would like to thank my stepfather, Robert Fox, for the care and many, many jokes he has brought to our family. My late, great uncle Jesse O. Baros selflessly helped to nurture, finance, and support my and my sister's education and livelihoods in moments when we needed support the most. I miss his questions about my travels and work, but I hope that he is able to read what he helped make possible wherever he may be in the universe. My father, Pedro Trujillo, has provided invaluable love and support during my graduate school career and beyond. I thank him and his wife, Margie Trujillo, for their care, warmth, and kindness.

I would not have made it to graduate school without the guidance and support of my mentors at the University of New Mexico: Edward DeSantis and

Hector Torres. As my first intellectual mentor, DeSantis played a formative role in fostering my curiosity about and study of the written word. He is responsible for allowing me to believe that I could do this work. I miss our long discussions about politics, literature, film, the university, and the mysticism of faith. I remain forever grateful for his patience, wisdom, hospitality, and generosity of spirit. I met Hector during my last semester at UNM, and he completely upended my intellectual world. He taught me what it means to think in the face of death, how to live when confronted with unrelenting absence. He was a friend, ally, troublemaker, and tireless advisor in the labor of deconstruction. He was taken too quickly from this world, but his spirit permeates every word here. During her brief time at UNM, I took a cultural studies class with Catherine Sue Ramírez that radically changed and challenged my outlook on cultural work and the world. I continue to draw from the lessons learned in that course.

While at the University of Washington (UW), I was fortunate to be a part of a cohort of students, faculty, and community members who provided me with a decolonial education that surpassed the disciplinary trappings of schooling. My dissertation advisor, Eva Cherniavsky, was a model mentor. Her generosity, intellectual rigor, and commitment to critical practice provided an example that I strive to emulate daily in my own work. Chandan Reddy's brilliance is the reason I decided to attend UW for graduate school. His radiant, expansive intellect, warmth, and deep commitment to antiracist intellectual work has made a lifelong impression on my thinking. Ileana Rodríguez-Silva brought a vibrant dedication to anti-imperialist historiography to my studies. I remain grateful for the conversations I had with Lauro Flores on the bounty and unpredictability of genealogical investigation.

During my time at UW I was also blessed to work with an amazing cohort of graduate students. The cultural organizing I participated in with the Race/Knowledge Project taught me two treasured lessons: the personal is political, and the university is ours for the dismantling. I remain grateful for the love and critical intimacy I encountered with Kate Boyd, Christian Ravela, Sydney Fonteyn Lewis, Jed Murr, Sooja Kelsey, Suzanne Schmidt, Jason Morse, and Pacharee Sudhinaraset. I want to thank Andrew Rose and Curtis Hisayasu for their repeated engagement with my writing. I would also like to thank Sergio Casillas and Mike Viola for their friendship and critical interlocution. During my last year of graduate school, I was lucky to be a part of an emergent cohort of borderlands scholars from a variety of disciplines, thanks largely to the work of María Elena García and José Antonio Lucero. Their imaginative dedication to interfacing Latinx, Latin American, and Indigenous studies in the Mellon-Sawyer Seminar, "B/ordering Violence: Boundaries, Indigeneity, and Gender in the Americas," remains a key source of inspiration for my work. The community that they fostered played an indelible role in allowing me to finish my degree, and I would like to thank Marisa Duarte, Miranda Belarde-Lewis, Raj Chetty, Allen Baros, Melanie Hernández, Molly Todd, Dian Million, Michelle Habell-Pallán, and Juan Guerra.

My colleagues at New York University have provided invaluable support, guidance, and friendship throughout the process of conceptualizing and manifesting this project into book form. I would like to thank the faculty, staff, and students of the English Department. My faculty colleagues in the English Department have been an incredible inspiration and source of critical exchange. I would like extend my deep gratitude to Elizabeth McHenry, Phillip Brian Harper, Crystal Parikh, Sonya Posmentier, John M. Archer, Patrick Deer, Nicholas Boggs, Elaine Freedgood, Toral Gajarawala, Thomas Augst, Josephine Hendin, Jennifer Baker, Julia Jarcho, Patricia Crain, Wendy Lee, Juliet Fleming, Maureen McLane, Peter Nicholls, Urayoán Noel, Dara Regaignon, Lytle Shaw, Greg Vargo, Christopher Cannon, Una Chaudhuri, Rajeswari Sunder Rajan, and Jini Kim Watson. I would also like to thank the staff of the English Department for their community-building work: Alyssa Leál, Lissette Florez, Patricia Okoh-Esene, and Mary Mezzano. Nikhil Pal Singh, Paula Chakravarty, and Kim Phillips-Fein made indelible impressions to my work and life in New York City. My colleagues in Latinx and Native studies continue to bring new, challenging, and vibrant horizons to my work. I wish to thank Arlene Davila, María Josefina Saldaña-Portillo, Cristina Beltrán, Urayoán Noel, Cecilia Márquez, Renato Rosaldo, Jane Anderson, and Elizabeth Ellis. In the 2017–18 school year, I was awarded a fellowship through the NYU Center for the Humanities, which enabled me to learn from and share my work with an interdisciplinary cohort of faculty and graduate students. I would like to thank Gwynneth Malin, Ulrich Baer, Gabriela Basterra, Heather Lee, Greg Vargo, Joan Flores-Villalobos, Wendi Muse, Ayasha Guerin, MC Hyland, Cécile Bishop, Kaitlin Noss, Wendy Muñiz, Christine Mladic, Kaitlin Noss, and Hannah Zeavin for offering a critically rigorous and hospitable environment for the development of this project at a critical stage. Dean Itsuji Saranillio and Sharon Heijin Lee have made New York City feel like home in the most generous and caring ways imaginable. As a friend and cosmic kin, Dean's incisive and expansive work on settler colonialism in Hawai'i has taught me so much, and I continue to be inspired by our conversations on Indigenous knowledge, fatherhood, and the politics of intellectual and activist work.

Over the years, I have had the privilege of sharing portions of this book in a number of different venues. The Colloquium for the Study of Latina/o/x Culture and Theory at the Graduate Center of the City University of New York provided invaluable feedback to the project in its early stages, and I would like to thank William Orchard, Inmaculada Lara-Bonilla, and Dalia Kandiyoti. In fall 2016, Jason Oliver Chang graciously invited me to share my work with students and faculty at the University of Connecticut. I wish to thank Jason and Fred Lee for their critical engagement. On the fiftieth anniversary of the Tierra Amarilla courthouse raid, I participated in a commemorative event at the Center for Contemporary Arts in Santa Fe. For sharing their insight and their dialogue, I would like to thank Alex Rivera, Lorena Oropeza, David Correia, Larry Calloway, and Robert Martínez. In spring 2018, my department invited Mary Pat Brady and Arturo Aldama to participate in a manuscript workshop. I remain astounded by the depth and warmth of their critical engagement. They each provided scrupulous written commentary on the manuscript and offered thoughtful support about the publication process and the profession in general. The Postcolonial, Race, and Diaspora Colloquium in NYU's English Department generously invited me to share portions of this work in the fall of 2018, and I remain grateful for the warm and incisive feedback I received from the organizers and those in attendance. I would also like to thank the graduate students who I have the privilege of working and learning with: Nicole Eitzen-Delgado, Alex Ramos, Mercedes Trigos, Nicholas Duron, Yollotl López, Sarah Proo, John Linstrom, Saronik Bosu, and Marcela DiBlasi. The conversations fostered by a number of scholarly organizations have been decisive in providing forums in which I have been able to share my work and learn from others. The National Association of Chicano and Chicana Studies, the Latina/o Studies Association, the American Studies Association, the Latin American Studies Association, and the Native American and Indigenous Studies Association have all provided hospitable and pedagogical spaces for critical dialogue.

For the support and instructive dialogue across these different sites, I wish to thank Patricia Trujillo, Ramón Gutiérrez, Raúl Coronado, Chela Sandoval, Jennie Luna, Brian McNeill, Lorena Oropeza, Melissa Moreno, Alicia Arrizón, John Alba Cutler, Agustín Palacios, Lorna Perez, and Marta E. Sánchez.

The Historical Society of New Mexico and the Office of the State Historian of New Mexico provided financial support for archival research while this project was in the early dissertation stage. The archivists and librarians at the University of New Mexico's Center for Southwest Research provided invaluable support, and I would like to thank Nancy Brown-Martínez, Cindy Abel Morris, and Samuel Sisneros.

Of course, there is the camaraderie of friends old and new. Andrés Aceves, Ben Jimenez, Benjamin S. Rogerson, Sean Tollison, Kathy Fletcher-Tollison, Clay Holtzman, Justin Parks, Manuela Mondloch, and Grant Schauer ground me in the necessity of humor, play, and adventure for the serious work in our moment and to come. The New York City cousin crew has been vital for survival in the wilderness of the Big Apple. My deep gratitude goes to Dungjai Pungauthaikan, Christopher Lee, Mina Panichpakdee, Niti Poosomboon, Nikki Chung, and Doug Daniels for the food and festivity throughout the years. May Sudhinaraset and Kenny Kong; Amy Sudhinaraset and Mike Tsui; Vacharee and Michael Oberbeck; Tanya Panichpakdee and Miah Cook—thank you for the care, love, and support throughout the years.

In 2012, while completing my degree at the UW, I was fortunate to visit Reies López Tijerina and his wife Esperanza Tijerina at their home in El Paso. It is an honor to build upon the unfinished legacy of Reies's work, and I would like to extend my deep gratitude to him and Esperanza for opening their home to me and my family. In addition, I would like to thank Mary Gladys Mendoza and Roberto Tijerina for their help in making that visit happen and for their continued support for my work on La Alianza.

Kristen Buckles at the University of Arizona Press has been an ideal editor, and she is backed up with a remarkable editorial team. I would like to thank the two anonymous readers from UA press for their probing, critical, and astute feedback. I wish to thank Sonya Manes for her thorough and scrupulous copyediting, and Amanda Krause, Sara Thaxton, and Stacey Wujcik for their hard, behind-the-scenes work in compiling together all of the elements of this book. I am so honored that Marla Allison's stunning painting *Under Clouds of New Shape* graces the cover, and I wish to thank Leigh McDonald for pairing it with such a beautiful and powerful design. I remain grateful to Nikki Chung, Nick Fogarty, and Dungjai Pungauthaikan at Once-Future Office for translating my barely legible scribbles into the radiant map that prefaces this study.

My partner and best friend, Pacharee Sudhinaraset, continues to teach me the multidimensional interconnectedness of love, work, passion, and laughter.

I've learned so much from the dignity, dedication, and deep love she brings to her family, friends, work, and our daughters, Belén and Nara. Her luminosity enriches all aspects of my life in ways that continue to surprise and inspire. Her parents, Jitlada and Sirivat Sudhinaraset, provide selfless love and support for our family in ways that I strive to emulate for our own children. Belén and Nara, you two have brought extraordinary joy and wonder to my life. Being your parent remains my most fantastic and challenging accomplishment. I am so honored to witness the magnificent transformations that you bring to the world.

LAND UPRISING

Land Uprising

Horizons for Indigenous Reclamation

Spanish and Mexican land grants were instrumental features in the European invasion of the Americas. Indigenous alliances have always refused, interrupted, and remade their imposition with work on story, the power of memory, and kinship with land.

↑ Standing Rock
Chicago
Mannahatta
Story Power
Settler colonialism has long relied on books and maps to sanction its violence and destruction. Stories precede and outlive their arrest in parchments and paper. Stories subvert the documents that certify the settler impulse to destroy. Stories disintegrate the pages written in defense of stolen land.
Taos Pueblo
ANA CASTILLO
Tesuque Pueblo
NICOLÁS CATUA &
PEDRO OMTUA
PO'PAY
Ohkay Owingeh Pueblo
San Cristóbal
Comanchería
Barrio de Analco
Cuervo
Santa Rosa
PABLO MONTOYA LAND GRANT
EL VIEJO
Sandia Pueblo
ANTON CHICO LAND GRANT
Albuquerque
ELIZABETH "BETITA" MARTÍNEZ
SNCC Headquarters
TOMÉ LAND GRANT
The Genízarx Continuum
Millions of Native men, women, and children were taken captive by the Spanish and Mexican colonial orders. The captivity of Native life has never ended in the Americas. Escape from the confinements of colonial occupation continues to this day.
BELÉN LAND GRANT
Trinity Site
La Malogra
BARBED WIRE
WALL
ATLANTIC OCEAN
CUBA
AYITI
BORIKÉN
Rebel Zapatista Autonomous Municipalities
SUP MARCOS
Chiapas

PROLOGUE

THE LONG, WONDROUS LIFE OF VENTURA CHÁVEZ, 1926–2013

Corncobs and husks, the rinds and stalks of animal bones were not regarded by the ancient people as filth or garbage. The remains were merely resting at a midpoint in their journey back to dust. Human remains are not so different.

—LESLIE MARMON SILKO, "INTERIOR AND EXTERIOR LANDSCAPES: THE PUEBLO MIGRATION STORIES"

Makers pose a danger to those who fear. Because revolutions begin with love. Campesino wars begin with love. Art begins with love. Love is inspired by art. We makers have nothing to lose and nothing to hide. We are fearless, fearless. We are born, we love, we die, and there is not much more that really matters in the end. And so we pass the rope, not thinking about what will happen to us once we collide with the earth, force the ash to rise. And trust you can withstand the fire in your hands.

—HELENA MARÍA VIRAMONTES, "THE WRITES OFRENDA"

Family, friends, and all of our relatives.[1]

Hello, *bienvenidos*, and good evening.

Thank you for convening here to read this book.

It begins with a eulogy on the life and work of my grandfather Ventura Chávez.

I used to call him El Viejo.

At the age of eighty-six, after a three-year struggle with Alzheimer's disease, El Viejo returned to the land at his home in Albuquerque, surrounded by family, on March 11, 2013.

The *Oxford English Dictionary* defines a eulogy as "a set oration in honour of a deceased person."[2] As an oration dedicated to El Viejo's long and wondrous life, however, I want to put the eulogy form to a different kind of work to frame the connections between genealogies of land grant tenure and dispossession, the colonial legacies of racialized and gendered labor, and the politics of land and organic radicalism in New Mexico that are explored in the following pages. This means violating certain narrative precepts of the eulogy form. Rather than stressing the exceptional trajectory of El Viejo's life in individual terms, I'm telling his story to constellate a broader network of Indigenous memory and endurance within occupied New Mexico. Rather than equating El Viejo's death with finitude, this eulogy is about coming to terms with the fact that the dead never stay still—that, as Raymond Williams writes, "the dead may be reduced to fixed forms, though their surviving records are against it."[3]

As some of you may know, in the 1960s and early 1970s El Viejo and Cruzita Chávez, my grandmother, were active members of La Alianza Federal de Mercedes, the renowned and pivotal New Mexican land grant movement of the mid-twentieth century. For more than a decade, I have been researching and writing about La Alianza's cultural politics as a way of rethinking the questions of land, race, and indigeneity within the formation and dispossession of Spanish

FIGURE 1 Ventura Chávez in the late 1990s.

and Mexican land grants in New Mexico. El Viejo's eulogy, then, also unfolds a story of how I came to this work. Or, rather, it is a story of how this work contacted me—how I came to inherit this work from my grandparents and what it means to remake it in our present moment.

In addition to being a grandfather, parent, husband, son, and brother, El Viejo was one of the sharpest social critics I've ever met. For someone who only attended school up until the age of thirteen, he possessed a wisdom that came from way before and beyond his time. He found lifelong inspiration from the stories of our Indigenous and settler ancestors. Despite his limited formal schooling, he was an avid reader of New Mexican history and culture. His personal library was an eclectic mix of Spanish and Mexican land grant historiography, Chicanx borderland history, Native American philosophy, Christian mystical literature, and Western fiction. On a single, overflowing bookshelf in his room, titles such as David Weber's *Foreigners in Their Native Land* and Vine Deloria Jr.'s *Behind the Trail of Broken Treaties* sat next to a vast collection of Louis L'Amour novels. Frank Waters's *Book of the Hopi*, Fabiola Cabeza de Baca's *We Fed Them Cactus*, and Fray Angelico Chávez's *My Penitente Land* resided alongside work on prophecy and interplanetary influence by Edgar Cayce. As an organic radical intellectual, his embrace of the power of storytelling upended the social and disciplinary boundaries between myth, history, science, and fiction. He had learned somewhere that stories are not only the way that we make this life meaningful in the face of death, but that they overflow their established generic containers. He knew that stories perform a power that connects us to the land. He knew that without our stories, we are nothing. In short, among being a cowboy, a railroad worker, a sailor, an aircraft painter, and a radical civil rights activist, El Viejo was a storyteller.

Here is a story about the storyteller.

El Viejo was born on October 30, 1926, on a small ranch a few miles outside of Cuervo, New Mexico—a small village east of Santa Rosa that was reduced to a virtual ghost town by the construction of Interstate 40 in the middle of the twentieth century. He was the youngest of thirteen children born to Mariana Maestas and Manuel Chávez. Mariana was the granddaughter of a woman of Cherokee descent who was adopted as a servant for the Lucero family in New Mexico.[4] Manuel was a sheepherder who worked for the Bond and Weist Company on land that was formerly the Anton Chico and Pablo Montoya Land Grants, which itself was terrain that hosted a complex network of Kiowa, Comanche, and Apache tribes before that.

FIGURE 2 Ventura Chávez, early school years, ca. 1930.

With instruction from his father, *tíos* (uncles), and older siblings, El Viejo learned how to ride horses, herd sheep, and work as a vaquero. When El Viejo was thirteen, his father froze to death after getting caught in a blizzard while returning home one night from Anton Chico. When he was sixteen, El Viejo lied about his age and joined the Navy. After training in San Diego, he was stationed in Okinawa, Japan, and served as a gunner on a battleship during World War II. While in the Navy, he met a professional fighter from New Orleans named Earhardt who taught him how to box, a skill that would serve him well in subsequent years.

After the war, El Viejo returned to New Mexico for a while, picked up work as a cowboy, and helped at a gas station that he had built with Procopio, his older brother. Later, with assistance from the GI Bill, he moved to Kansas City, Missouri, and attended a trade school for paint and body work on cars and airplanes. When he completed school, he returned to New Mexico and met Cruzita, or as her grandchildren call her, Nana. They married in 1957 and together had five children.

Sometime in the early 1960s, El Viejo attended a meeting of a newly formed organization in New Mexico called La Alianza Federal de Mercedes (the Federal Alliance of Land Grants). While there, he met its president, Reies López Tijerina. As part of its initial settler occupation of New Mexico, U.S. agents and colonists considered the Native and Mestizx New Mexicans they dispossessed who were poor and landless as culturally backward from not being able to speak English, from not knowing how to "develop" the land properly, and from being a "degenerate" mixture of Indian and Spanish. This is a formative narrative of land usurpation, and it continues to this day in the U.S. government and media; many still believe it. Yet with members such as Nana and El Viejo, La Alianza provided a way of speaking back to these misrepresentations proffered by the U.S. government and our national culture. La Alianza challenged the idea that being mixed Indian and Spanish was a marker of shame. They refused the idea that the poverty endured by Pueblo Indian and Indohispanx peoples is a result of a so-called backward, insular nature. Rather, they linked our distinct yet overlapping racialized poverty to

FIGURE 3 El Viejo the day before departing for the Navy. On the back of this photograph there is a handwritten note from him that says, "This picture was taken the year of 1943 June 21 Benny Chavez at S.R. N.M. After Tomorrow what will I do."

centuries of land theft by the U.S. government, the national forest service, and a number of cattle, mining, and timber corporations.

As a descendant of captive Indian servants living on land grant land that would ultimately be taken from his family, El Viejo had a memory that powerfully resonated with La Alianza's work. El Viejo was part of a pivotal generation of people of Mexican, Indigenous, and Mestizx descent who went abroad to fight for the United States, only to return and discover ongoing exclusion from the basic rights and protections of U.S. citizenship. This realization prompted a tireless, everyday devotion to the movement for years by Nana and El Viejo. It would also catalyze, for El Viejo, his participation in one of the most renowned events in New Mexican history: the armed raid of the Tierra Amarilla Courthouse on June 5, 1967. Along with twenty other Aliancistas, El Viejo attempted to place then–New Mexico district attorney Alfonso Sánchez under citizen's arrest for violating La Alianza's right to peacefully assemble. As I grew up, I encountered El Viejo's courthouse raid story as one of his most guarded yet cherished stories.

We were scouring the place
looking for Sanchez
and anyone else who was hiding out.
When we got upstairs, we found a door that was closed
locked from the inside.
I knocked once and
gunshots tore through the door.
They just barely missed my head.
Now that pissed me off.
Reies and I were carrying machine guns.
Together we blasted the door open.
The jailer just stood there
holding his gun, looking scared.
He dropped it right away
When he saw us.

I walked over to him
punched him right in the face
split his cheek open.

I was fortunate enough to know El Viejo not only as a grandparent, but as a father figure who ferociously worked to feed, shelter, care for, and educate me and my sister, Michelle. Indeed, the memories I have of El Viejo as a storyteller are inseparable from memories of him picking us up from school, of him taking me to buy toys when I was little, of sharing meals, of road trips, of him working in his garden, of him cleaning beans for supper. His story of the courthouse raid was tied to a bundle of other stories, jokes, and observations he would tell over the years that existed atmospherically in our Albuquerque home. Because they were El Viejo's stories, they surrounded everything. Yet I knew nothing about from where they came; I knew even less about what it could mean to listen.

One evening El Viejo is chopping onions for dinner. He stops and looks at me.

Our People, the Indohispano,
need to become educated
because an education is
the one thing
they cannot take away from you.

El Viejo pulls his hand back quickly.
I nicked my finger
he says.
Blood trickles down.
He gets up to wash his hands.
Over the sound of running water
he jokes
There goes the Iberian part of me.

In 2002, a worker from the U.S. Census Bureau visited our home in the Westside of Albuquerque. I was twenty-two and completing my last year of undergraduate study at the University of New Mexico (UNM). The census worker began his interview with El Viejo by asking questions about his work and recent retirement. He then asked about El Viejo's racial status.

Are you Hispanic, sir?
Hispanic?

El Viejo laughed as if
he heard
the punchline of a joke.
No.

We are Indohispanos.
We are mixed
Half Native American and half Iberian
mostly Jewish.
We are not Hispanic.

The census worker smiled
with confusion
and looked at me.
He didn't know what to do.
Neither did I.
El Viejo did not relent.

Our people are Indohispano.
We are not "Spanish."
"Spain" was not a sovereign country when Columbus came here.
And we are not only Iberian.
My great-great grandmother was half Apache and half Cherokee.
She became a slave to the Spaniards
and was named Dolores Lucero.
We are mixed.

The Census worker sits up
adjusts his glasses and says
Sir, that is fascinating.
Under race, you may want to fill in
the "other" box.

I had heard this story many times before without knowing from where it came. I did not know how to listen to his stories. I was always called "Hispanic" in school. I heard it everywhere on the local and national news. I had seen it on applications for schools and on doctor's forms. I had even heard of "Chicano" from some faculty and Movimiento Estudiantil Chicanx de Aztlán (MECHA) programs in high school. But *Indohispano*? I had only heard El Viejo talk that way. No other member of my immediate or distant family had ever really talked that way. As an English and philosophy major at the University of New Mexico, I was able to nurture my ongoing love of reading and inquiry. At the same time, these disciplines surreptitiously primed me to accept the coloniality of textual authority over knowledge, being, and the imagination. From this acquired vantage, world-historical events happened elsewhere, and New Mexico was mired in the solitude of an antiquated time. Bereft of an ear for his stories and the surrounding oral cultures of land grant struggle in New Mexico, I took the encounter as yet another example of El Viejo's "eccentric" historical worldview and nothing more.

I moved to Seattle in 2005 to begin the PhD program in the Department of English at the University of Washington (UW). During my second year, I became interested in Black cultural politics and the ways in which Black radical intellectuals critiqued the racist underpinnings of liberal forms of emancipation and capitalist modes of production. In graduate seminars and reading groups, I encountered work by W. E. B. Du Bois, Cedric Robinson, Robin Kelly, Angela Davis, and C. L. R. James. Together, they taught me that contemporary iterations of capitalism, nationalism, state power, and citizenship—that is, the hallmarks of Euroamerican modernity—were not self-originating and self-perfecting concepts and political structures borne out of the grandeur of European civilization. Rather, I learned how the political, cultural, and economic structures of modernity remain financed and organized through antiblackness and the captivity of Black life—in forms that ranged from chattel slavery to segregation and into our contemporary nightmare of mass incarceration. W. E. B. Du Bois's *Darkwater*, for example, connected the U.S. racial doctrines of white patriarchal supremacy to a global structure of European capitalist imperialism: "The World War," he writes, "was primarily the jealous and avaricious struggle for the largest share in exploiting darker races."[5] Reading Cedric Robinson's *Black Marxism* and his theory of racial capitalism in particular exposed how antiblack racism structures capitalist and nationalist social formations, yet remains irreducible to Marxist conceptions of class struggle. In doing so, Robinson showed me the powerful and perennially challenged role that the Black Radical Tradition played in formulating a materialist theory of race that enabled "opposition to the alienation of labor and the ordering of social life according to the dictates of private property."[6] By virtue of these critiques, I was starting to consider the ways in which Black writers and cultural workers manifested acts of what Fred Moten and Stefano Harney call "fugitive enlightenment"—that is, a "ruptural and enraptured disclosure of the commons" enacted by "the life stolen by enlightenment and stolen back."[7]

Black fugitivity cleared the path that led me back to El Viejo's stories. One evening in the summer of 2007, I was browsing the Black Studies section in Magus Books, a small independent bookstore close to UW. While scanning the titles, I came across a book edited by Angela Davis titled *If They Come in the Morning: Voices of Resistance*. The book is a collection of writings by and about imprisoned radical intellectuals during the freedom and decolonization struggles of the '60s and '70s. I pulled it off the shelf and opened it at random, thinking I was going to find something written by George Jackson, James Baldwin, or any of the other authors listed on the back cover whom I wanted to read.

Instead, I encountered an entry on "Reies Tijerina."

Reies Tijerina?

That name struck an uncanny chord with me. I had heard it before, but couldn't place it at the moment. I read the beginning of the entry.

> Since the Treaty of Guadalupe Hidalgo between Mexico and the United States in 1848, Mexican-Americans have lost over 4,000,000 acres of land-grant territory in the Southwest. The Chicano demand for lands illegally wrested from their ancestors received militant expression as early as 1963 in the *Alianza Federal de Mercedes*. This mass movement, deeply rooted in the rural population in northern New Mexico, was headed by Reies Tijerina. In 1966, it was estimated that the organization had a membership of over 14,000 families.[8]

El Viejo's stories of the courthouse raid slowly resurfaced. I continued reading.

> The day before the *Alianza's* national conference was scheduled to take place in June 1967, it was arbitrarily pronounced an unlawful assembly by the local District Attorney, who threated to arrest all the participants. That same day he rounded up 18 *Alianzans* on charges which were clearly fabricated. The District Attorney's actions, undisguised violations of the *Alianzans'* constitutional rights, prompted other members to plan a citizen's arrest. Twenty armed men, deputized by the People's Republic of San Joaquin, descended up on Tierra Amarrilo [*sic*] courthouse and seeking the District Attorney, whom they never located, held it for 90 minutes. In the course of the raid, a policeman went for his gun and he and the local jailer were wounded. An undersheriff and a reporter were escorted away from the scene, but later released. Ten *Alianzans* were brought up on charges.[9]

I read the entire entry over and over in the middle of the bookstore. I was stunned, disoriented. A set of people, events, and keywords pivotal to the history of New Mexico and the Chicanx movement began to find their connective threads to stories that I had grown up with, yet somehow and some way had never really thought carefully about: Reies López Tijerina, the courthouse raid, the People's Republic of San Joaquín, the Treaty of Guadalupe Hidalgo, and the land grants.

I called him the next morning.

Hey Viejo
I have a question for you.
Were you a member of La Alianza?
Did you know Reies López Tijerina?
Were you a part of the Courthouse Raid?

There was a pause on his end of the line.

What the hell
do you think
I've been telling you?

The stun redoubled. The ground shifted beneath my feet. A disassembled puzzle that apparently had always surrounded my life began to take shape. Only now was I beginning to recognize it as a puzzle that required a particular discernment to recognize the shape of its pieces and the depths of its logic.

That moment sparked an itinerant quest to learn everything I could about La Alianza and the land grants. I flew home in between terms at school to record El Viejo's long monologues about the land grants, La Alianza, Tijerina, and Indo-hispanx mestizaje. I researched accounts of the movement in Chicanx, Latinx, and Native American, and Indigenous studies. I pursued narratives of land grant formation and dispossession in the sociology, history, and anthropology of the U.S.-Mexico borderlands. I sought examples of decolonial intellectual labor from work on subaltern movements and Indigenous racialization in South Asian and Latin American studies. And I began to research the surviving records of La Alianza that are housed in numerous archival sites in New Mexico.

In the process of learning about the overlaid colonization of New Mexico, I began to see how the political economy of Spanish and Mexican land dispossession offered a distinct yet complementary genealogy of slavery, property, nationalism, patriarchy, race, and revolution that Cedric Robinson and other Black radical thinkers traced in the reverberations of the modern transatlantic slave trade. That is, while Black radical intellectuals attuned me to the theft of

Black life and labor that sustained legal and cultural logics of private property, I began to see how La Alianza connected the freedom of individual and corporate ownership of land as alienable property to a massive racialized and gendered process of land dispossession under U.S. sovereignty that dismantled the land grant communities' subsistent and communal mode of occupancy. As the racialized effect of land grant dispossession ironically worked to legally validate Pueblo Indian landholdings due to their racialization as "wards of the state," it also reframed generations of Mexican and Genízarx land grant subjects—that is, La Alianza's constituency—with a "Spanish-American" identity that excised the Mestizx and Indigenous pasts of the land grants from public knowledge. Robinson gifted a language, in other words, that allowed me to reframe Genízarx Indians not as the assimilated forebears of a settler Spanish American political class but rather as a diasporic network of detribalized Native relations that continues to resurge and regenerate our contemporary moment.

In this way, I learned that El Viejo's stories about La Alianza were not motivated by nostalgia but, rather, were stoked by a decolonial desire for land. That is, as I began to actively listen to his stories, it became clear that he was less interested in telling me how it really was as an Aliancista. He was telling me how the land was stolen and how he tried to take it back, and he wanted to know why my work mattered for such a labor.

El Viejo's demand for the land compounded the urgency and oddity of my research. On the one hand, I often marveled at the fortuitous conditions for learning and research that my graduate training offered for tracing the history of La Alianza and land grant struggle. On the other, El Viejo's continuous demand for land put my politics of reading La Alianza's writing and listening to his stories into crisis. Why would I simultaneously desire to recover La Alianza's history yet presume the question of the land grants as settled? What politics of knowledge would sanction a study on La Alianza while also sanctioning the impossibility of land reclamation? What modes of violence are brought to La Alianza's archive by a reading practice that presumes U.S. sovereignty as a settled state? These questions reframed the movement and the land grant political economy as a landscape inhabited with multiple scales of violence, erasure, silence, mystery, and absence. I began to see how these overlaid colonial scales of violence and silence resonated in my inability to listen to El Viejo's stories. Although my inability to listen found expression in the everyday dynamics of my family, I was beginning to see its reflection in a systematic politics of opacity

FIGURE 4 Ventura Chávez in a political announcement for the Partido Constitucional Popular (PCP) in *El Grito del Norte* 1, no. 4 (October 31, 1968), Peter Nabokov Papers, MSS 93 BC, Special Collections and Center for Southwest Research, University of New Mexico Libraries.

and motivated amnesia of Native and Mexican land usurpation that attends the imposition of colonial modernity in the Americas.

This discovery was undeniably transformative, and yet it came in hand with a rather terrible loss. In the spring of 2011, El Viejo began to show the first signs of what would become a long and painful descent into dementia. For the following two years until his death, my family cared for him in our house in Albuquerque. While his loyal, selfless, and feisty emotional core remained intact, we witnessed the slow yet unpredictable disappearance of El Viejo's memories of his family and friends. He lost his senses of place and time and a sense of continuity between the days and nights. He frequently forgot that he spoke English and would be unable to remember that our house in Albuquerque had been his home for more than thirty years. On those days, he would ask us in Spanish if we could take him back to his home out on the Cuervo *llano* (plains). His family would be worried about him, he would explain, and they needed him to work. Not long after, his ability to hear and tell stories would ultimately disappear. Like so many others before and after him, El Viejo put his life on the line to challenge the systemic forgetting of settler colonialism. To witness the last years of his life succumb to the physiological disintegration of memory remains an irony of astonishing cruelty.

In a remarkable stroke of foresight and resistance before his diagnosis, El Viejo began to write his life story. On a bundle of two spiral notebooks, he hand-wrote memories from his childhood, his service in the Navy during World War II, and his work as a cowboy in eastern New Mexico. Written in the eclipse of memory, the notebooks stage his life story as a prism for a set of critical ruminations on the racial politics of New Mexican land grant tenure and U.S. sovereignty. On the inside cover, he wrote:

Ventura Chávez.
Life Story
I live under the Treaty of Guadalupe Hidalgo

El Viejo does not state that he lives under the United States. Rather, by living under the "Treaty of Guadalupe Hidalgo," he is insisting that he lives in occupied conditions under alien landlords. As his memory vanished, I transcribed his writings onto my computer. During the many sleepless nights that I faced during his illness, I would return to his notebooks again and again in a frantic search for some definitive truth in the fragments. I yearned to uncover suppressed truths about the land grants, our family's detribalized indigeneity, and an elsewhere from the open-air penitentiary of private property. However, rather than confirming a stable past, his notebooks proliferated fragments upon and within fragments. Rather than making History, the notebooks performed the very limits of text-based historical knowledge.

And yet, paradoxically due to his work on language, the disappearance of El Viejo's memory did not devolve into a totalizing loss. Its fragmental composition also performed a power of signification within an unstoppable chain of other stories of land, storytelling, memory, labor, and the mystic vitality of Indigenous insurgency that crosshatches Chicanx, Latinx, Native American, and Latin American literature and social movement practice. Tracing the discontinuous and itinerant linkages of this chain of land-based stories and movements is the undertaking of this book. Below, I share El Viejo's writings in rewoven form because they signify an ongoing and active formation of rebellious Indigenous storytelling in the present moment. In the following pages, I am calling this formation Native Story Power. As a nexus of Native Story Power, El Viejo's notebooks connect to the land in a way that situates Native life as a precondition for the future of decolonization. In doing so, they provide a footing for a way of being humble and reverent to the exponentially continuous vitality of Native and Indigenous lifeways and knowledge systems—they beckon us to desire knowledge in a way that recognizes our limited capacity to know under modernity. I share them as one pathway to recognizing a more diffuse account of life and stories that can equip us to dismantle the global dictatorship of private property and activate a future attuned to the instructions of the land and its first peoples.

The last word belongs to El Viejo.

In August 15,
Kearny stood in the plaza in Las Vegas
to tell those he had just conquered
that he was among them for their benefit,
not their injury.
"We come as your friends
to better your condition.
I am your governor, look to me for protection.
We are your friends."

Seems to me that our friends are not our friends.
We have fought in all wars—
the Civil War, World War I and II.
And we'll fight in every war that comes
always the orphans in this land
to support the good USA.

Then a man came from Texas
and started to teach about the Treaty of Guadalupe Hidalgo.
We are here under their treaty.
We belonged to two grants: Anton Chico and Pablo Montoya.
My grandmother was born in the Pablo Montoya grant.
My great-grandmother is buried in that grant.
My great-grandmother helped the whites control the Pablo Montoya grant
because she was half Apache, half Cherokee.
They married her with a white man named Barney Gare.
Her name was Dolores Lucero.
The Luceros adopted her.
My great-grandma had three daughters.
Juanita, Chonita, and Ascensión.
The Apache and Comanche liked to hunt buffalo there,
and they left the land grant because
I guess she had pull with the Indians.
But they got pushed off the Pablo Montoya Grant.
Because now it is Anglo law.

The land that was our father's, grandfather's, and great-grandfather's was stolen.
Anybody who tried to help us was branded a bandit.
We were secondhand.
With World War II, they started calling on our people
and then we were suddenly
Americans.
But our land grants are not ours.
They were given to white people.
But we had nothing. Our people fight in all wars.
Our people have to defend this land,
but we have no land grants.

We are the Indohispanos of this country.
We were raised in New Mexico.
Since we are 85 percent Indian,
I feel bad.
I miss what I feel they went through.
I belong to the Anton Chico Grant, but I can't be there.
My dad would tell me
how he loved his ancestors.
They had other bosses and
heard a different language.

I was in World War II.
Seems now like we are prisoners of war.
We are free but can't speak our own tongues.
And then it hit me:
We are being used here.
They are only in charge of this land.
They don't own it.
The white people are under order of
the government of the USA.
The white people are only holding the land
from the brown and red people.
They can never own it.
I am eighty-four years old. I haven't gotten my land grant back.
What is the United States?
We need to tell the people some stories
like the ones we've heard
a long time ago.
Give it all back
Take it all back.

INTRODUCTION

INSURGENT HORIZONS

Native Stories are Power. They create people.
They author tribes. America is a tribal creation story.
—LEANNE HOWE, "THE STORY OF AMERICA: A TRIBALOGRAPHY"

I write in a contemporary moment marked by escalating ecological crises, ascendant transnational unions of fascism, white supremacy, and hyperfinancialization, and a heightened, depraved assault on the sovereignty of Native people and migrants across the Americas. It is a moment of mass, overmediated cynicism regarding the planetary survival of humanity, one that aspires to annihilate the plausibility of any meaningful alternative to the cascading catastrophes unfolding within the intersections of capitalism, racism, militarism, heteronormativity, patriarchy, and nationalism. As such, it is also a moment in which Native American and Indigenous movements uprise for land reclamation and to generate vitally urgent and proactively responsive visions of anticapitalist futurity and continuance beyond colonial modernity. These agile visions of deep Indigenous wisdom—from the Standing Rock Sioux's defiance against neocolonial, underground oil pipelining, to the Kānaka Maoli defense of Mauna Kea from the destructive imposition of the Thirty Meter Telescope, and to the ongoing Zapatista autonomy project in Chiapas, Mexico—incite the demand for Native land reclamation not as a reinscription of private property and settler sovereignty but as a radically open convening of a global array of Native sovereignty movements and decolonial alliances. It is a moment, in other words, marked by proliferating, state-sanctioned besiegements of migrant life in which Native and Indigenous insurgency impresses a particular urgency for Chicanx and Latinx studies to radically rethink their connections with land.

This predicament calls for a regenerated analytic power for the study of Latinx culture, literature, and politics in dialogue with the instructions of Native, Indigenous, and feminist decolonization. It calls for analysis that can simultaneously nullify the settler colonial assault on migrant life and Native lands across the Americas while cooperating with the surrounding exuberance of Indigenous sovereign endurance. In this moment, as modern statecraft spirals into multicriminal formations, the horizon of migrant dignity becomes abundantly connected to a question about the ways in which Chicanx and Latinx writing can speak with movements to reclaim the Americas as Indigenous land.[1] *Land Uprising* actions the cultural politics of the New Mexican land grant movement, La Alianza Federal de Mercedes, to reckon with Native land reclamation as the horizon for the future of Chicanx and Latinx life and study.

A formative organization of the Chicanx movement of the 1960s and '70s, La Alianza formed to revitalize the cultural and political rights of Spanish and Mexican land grants—communal property formations in New Mexico stemming from seventeenth-century Spanish rule—that had been dispossessed in the wake of the Mexican-American War and the U.S. colonization of northern Mexico in the mid-nineteenth century. According to the movement's founding constitution, La Alianza mobilized the disparately located and impoverished New Mexican land grant heirs in order to "recuperate all of [their] lands and their culture" and to "demand compliance of the Treaty of Guadalupe Hidalgo from the two governments that signed it."[2] Prior to the U.S. invasion, Spanish and Mexican land grants were the dominant form of usurping Pueblo and Plains Indian land and administering the violence of territorial and civic rights in New Mexico. Imposed in New Mexico during the late sixteenth century, the land grant system bestowed land to various settler castes as a reward for expanding the empire of the Iberian Peninsula's Catholic monarchy.[3] For roughly the first century of its imposition, the land grant system was entrenched in the Spanish empire's cruel campaign of racialized and gendered labor exploitation and religious persecution that mediated its colonial settlement on Pueblo Indian lands. When the Pueblo Indians organized a multitribal and cross-caste alliance to stage an anticolonial revolt in 1680, the Spanish were ousted from their settlements on Pueblo lands as the Native and detribalized Mestizx rebels destroyed colonial property titles and Catholic objects of devotion.

As Spain began to recolonize New Mexico in 1693, land grants became places where detribalized Indigenous captives and slaves, known as Genízaro and Genízara Indians, obtained burdened emancipation by settling on large common property tracts on the borders between the colonial interior, Pueblo Indian homelands, and the terrains dominated by Ute, Diné, Comanche, and Apache peoples.[4] Throughout the eighteenth century and into the period of Mexican independence, Genízarx subjects inhabited a specific form of communal land grant known as the *ejido*. The ejido patterned the settlement of land grant villages away from the racialized labor exploitation of Pueblo Indian subjects and instead placed legal and cultural emphasis on subsistent agriculture and ranching supplemented by a cross-cultural economy of Native captivity.[5] The ejidos integrated communal tenure on land by detribalized settlers for grazing, timber, and irrigation within complex trading and raiding relations with many Plains Indian tribes at the crossroads of Spanish settlements and Pueblo Indian homelands. The liberal reforms that subsequently marked Mexican independence at once abolished the *casta* system and institutionalized land grants as the privileged mechanism for an emergent regime of property privatization. Rather than abating the colonial logics of land usurpation negotiated by Pueblo Indian and Genízarx communities, the ascent of liberal governance spawned an outbreak of non-Indian claims seeking to privatize Pueblo Indian lands and other communal land holdings.[6]

In 1846, enthralled by doctrines of manifest destiny, the U.S. military exacerbated the catastrophe summoned by private land claims when it invaded Mexico with aims to expand the slaveholding empire of the United States.[7] Two years later, the terms to end the Mexican-American War and the annexation of nearly half of Mexico's sovereign territory by the United States became drafted in the Treaty of Guadalupe Hidalgo. Around thirty-five million acres of the land occupied by the United States after the Mexican-American War in 1848 were in the form of a Spanish or Mexican land grant.[8] By 1910, despite the Treaty of Guadalupe Hidalgo's mandate to honor Mexican land rights, 70 percent of that land would be usurped through a series of legal obfuscations, U.S. property tax impositions, political maneuverings, mistranslations, and outright thieveries within the land grant adjudication process.[9] The subsequent U.S. colonization of New Mexico privileged individual and corporate ownership of land as an alienable commodity by imposing legal and cultural logics of private property.

The fanatical devotion to private property that marked U.S. settler sovereignty in New Mexico would require the destruction of the alliance of subsistent livelihood differentially shared by Pueblo Indians, Plains tribes, and their interwoven cluster of detribalized land grant communities.

Initially modeled on the already existing Abiquiú Corporation in New Mexico, La Alianza was an iteration of a long history of underground and popular forms of insurrection that continuously rebuked processes of land grant usurpation. In the late nineteenth century, Las Gorras Blancas (the White Caps) formed as a shadow movement that protested the U.S. enclosure of land grant commons. Known for its mobilization of armed horseback riders covered with white sheets who would burn fences, kill livestock, and destroy railroad tracks at night, Las Gorras Blancas gained some political momentum in San Miguel County yet dissolved after the incarceration of key members.[10] Struggles over the control of the Tierra Amarilla grant between its residents and U.S. settler Thomas Catron in the early twentieth century manifested La Mano Negra, another shadow organization that sabotaged efforts at large-scale fencing in the area.[11] These acts of guerrilla insurgency occurred alongside concurrent and subsequent litigation surrounding a number of grants. Together they brought about a push by New Mexico's state government in the 1920s to formalize land grants with boards of trustees and rules for townships. While providing a mechanism for patenting community grants and establishing communal control of the land, these measures also enabled certain forms of intensified privatization. They permitted board members to sell individual plots at will and constrained "who counted as an heir for a given grant based on lineage to original settlers."[12] A number of subsequent organizations on the Abiquiú, Tierra Amarilla, and San Joaquín del Río del Chama land grants combined recovery efforts to include legal challenges, fence cutting, barn burning, and the issuance of eviction notices to Anglo individuals and corporations who were settling on dispossessed common lands.

When La Alianza emerged publicly on February 2, 1963, the anniversary of the signing of the Treaty of Guadalupe Hidalgo, it immediately struck a number of novelties within the history of land grant organizing. Instead of a New Mexican land grant heir, La Alianza came into formation with an itinerant, excommunicated Pentecostal preacher from Texas named Reies López Tijerina as its president and main public figure. Prior to Tijerina's work with La Alianza, he and his family were fleeing a disbanded project of religious communalism called El Valle de Paz (The Valley of Peace) that they and a cohort of Mexican

American families established in 1956 just north of the Tohono O'odham homeland in Arizona. Motivated in part by a divine vision he experienced about New Mexico's land grant struggle, Tijerina arrived in New Mexico with his first wife, María Escobar, and their three children while on the run from the Arizona police for attempting to break his brother Margarito out from the Pinal County Jail. In New Mexico, families from the Abiquiú, Tierra Amarilla, and San Joaquín del Río del Chama land grants not only provided sanctuary for Tijerina and his family but also shared deeply influential stories of land grant dispossession. Tijerina recalls how during this nearly ten-year period, "everyone gave us a long, sordid, violent history of what had happened to them in New Mexico since the loss of their properties, their communal lands, *ejidos*."[13] In this same period, Tijerina maintained a number of connections with Elijah Muhammad and the Nation of Islam and was deeply influenced by the tactics of civil disobedience employed by Dr. Martin Luther King Jr. and the Southern Christian Leadership Conference.[14] In this way, Tijerina's presence enabled La Alianza to cohere through a coalitional framework that sidestepped the pursuit of land rights through the historically established channels of individual or familial litigation against the state. Instead, the movement fashioned itself as a "federal alliance of land grants" whose purpose "shall be a permanent organization and government for the perpetual protection of Heirs."[15] La Alianza's first convention in October 1963 circulated one of its first publications—a flyer of the Treaty of Guadalupe Hidalgo—and drew representatives from fourteen land grants, setting into motion a series of efforts to publicize land grant history and garner membership.

A key component to the labor of alliance that constituted La Alianza's movement was the reclaimed nomenclature of "Indo-Hispano" mestizaje. Alternately deployed as "Indohispano," "Indo-Hispano," or "Indiohispano," the nomenclature was recalled from Tijerina's encounter with the story power of Genízarx land grant memory and a fugitive engagement with a transnational range of colonial archives. In addition to combing archival collections in Albuquerque and Santa Fe, Tijerina visited the National Archives in Mexico, where he became acquainted with *La Recopilación de leyes de Los Reynos de las Indias*—known in English as "The Laws of the Indies"—colonial documents outlining the parameters of ownership of the New Mexican land grants.[16] Later, La Alianza's membership would finance Tijerina's travels to Spain, where he performed archival research, met with governmental officials over the dispossession of New Mexican land grants, and was interviewed by a number of media outlets. This research would inform the production of a multiform, unbounded collection of texts that include local, national, and transnational print journalism; radio and television programs; testimonial literature; public flyers, posters, pamphlets, and other ephemera; letters to state, federal, and international politicians; *corridos* (border ballads); internal position papers; grant applications; and "direct action" planning documents. In these documents, the Laws of the Indies are often invoked as the legitimating legal framework for the international recognition of land grants as sovereign "free city-states" whose rights remain violated by the U.S. nonenforcement of the Treaty of Guadalupe Hidalgo.[17]

This strategy for the reclamation of land and the protection of cultural rights would empower La Alianza to manifest an explosive repertoire of protest against the settler politics of U.S. sovereignty. Land grant activist Valentina Valdez recalls, "if the Huelga [the United Farmworker's Strike tied to Cesar Chavez] gave Raza a sense of pride, then the Alianza gave it a sense of power."[18] In fall 1966, the group mobilized a symbolic mass occupation of the Echo Amphitheater in Carson National Forest, land in northern New Mexico that was formerly part of the San Joaquín del Río de Chama land grant. Decades of judicial and extralegal maneuverings by the U.S. courts throughout the late nineteenth century eventually facilitated the appropriation of nearly the entire grant to the Forest Service in 1908. As part of the occupation, the group proclaimed the land grant a republic governed by a Pueblo council who issued eviction notices to the U.S. Forest Service and impounded Forest Ranger vehicles. The following year, La Alianza publicized plans for an international convention in Coyote, New Mexico, on the weekend of June 4 to assert the sovereignty of Spanish and Mexican land grants under international law. A few days prior, New Mexico district attorney Alfonso Sánchez authorized the preemptive arrest of eleven members. A vocal critic of the movement who repeatedly dismissed La Alianza as a communist threat to the United States, Sánchez declared over the radio his intent to arrest anyone attempting to attend the convention. On June 5, 1967, Aliancistas responded by storming the Rio Arriba County Courthouse in the village of Tierra Amarilla to liberate their members and place Sánchez under citizen's arrest for violating their constitutional right to peaceful assembly. The Tierra Amarilla Courthouse raid, as it is colloquially remembered and institutionally inscribed in Chicanx studies, transformed Tijerina's public image from a religious eccentric to a revolutionary bandit–cum–civil rights leader.[19] In the process, La Alianza's project of land grant reclamation began to speak to the concerns of an emergent Chicanx movement as well as a U.S. civil rights movement that was transforming into a multiplicity of power movements across North America. The discovery of land reclamation as a labor of alliance would also prompt La Alianza to engender multiple coalitions with movements for Black Power, Native Sovereignty, and Puerto Rican Independence.[20] The significance of La Alianza's demands, as Juan Gómez-Quiñones and Irene Vásquez note, "did much to shape the character of the cultural agenda of [the Chicanx] movement leadership and to historicize for activists their association with the land."[21]

Indeed, the power of La Alianza's movement remains in the ways its struggle for land reclamation integrated militancy and coalitional movement to unsettle the normalization of U.S. sovereignty over what is now the U.S. Southwest. At the same time, this power amplifies the fact that land grant communities in New Mexico remain built on the ancestral homelands of multiple Pueblo Indian tribes and a surrounding matrix of Diné, Apache, Ute, and Comanche land claims and migratory pathways. As the labor of an urbanized, proletarianized, and unevenly assimilated network of detribalized Indigenous subjects, La Alianza's movement and conditions of emergence encapsulate the paradoxes of simultaneous settler, migrant, and Native relationality that continue to pattern and puzzle Latinx claims to indigeneity under a hemispheric nexus of Indigenous representation and Mestizx racialization. Native land highlights the paradoxical ways in which the Indigenous ancestry and ongoing connection with Native sovereignty that constitute many Latinx indigeneities occur with simultaneous complicity with multiple settler regimes of occupation in the Americas. This paradox requires a critical distinction between *Indigenous people* and *indigeneity*.[22] I use the referent *Indigenous people* to indicate the original inhabitants of what is temporarily called the Americas and to emphasize their endurance as sovereign nations and autonomous territories in distinction to the elimination that nation-state sovereignties impose through minority or ethnic identity categories. Drawing from R. Aida Hernandez Castillo, I use *indigeneity* as a "field of power" to indicate a mode of being in connection to place, one that evokes a constellation of rights, associations, and critiques for disempowered social subjects to mobilize for continuity and autonomy over governance, economy, and community.[23] While maintaining this difference remains a key factor in the protection and continuation of the sovereignty of Indigenous peoples from continual colonial encroachment, the couplet Latinx Indigeneity also indexes historical contradictions and critical paradoxes in this distinction that result from the subjection of *Indigenous people* to manifold European colonial invasions.[24] To name this conundrum as a paradox is to avow that both poles are true to and a part of the modern world and that neither can be denied. Native land exposes a series of relationships for Latinx indigeneity that remains irreconcilable in capitalist modes of exchange, in courts of settler law, and in the industrial complexes of modern media and academia. These paradoxical relationships of Latinx indigeneity set in stark relief the ways in which Native land remains a source of ongoing life, an incalculable debt, and a site of unlegislatable justice for the modern colonial world system at the planetary scale.

For María Josefina Saldaña-Portillo and María Cotera, the psychoanalytic language of loss provides a critical lens through which to grapple with this paradoxical condition. Saldaña-Portillo and Cotera argue that the land grant communities in New Mexico represent a paradigmatic example of Chicanx indigeneity not as an enactment of a settler fantasy but as a condition of "mestizo mourning" born out of the "loss of a historically *filial* relationship with indigenous peoples forged over centuries of interaction, intermarriage, collaboration, and alliance."[25] As Mestizo mourning, Saldaña-Portillo and Cotera position Indigenous ancestry as the "lost object of Mexican American and Chicana/o melancholic incorporation."[26] The critical utility of loss, David Kazanjian and David Eng argue, reveals "melancholia's persistent struggle with its lost objects not simply a 'grasping' and 'holding' on to a fixed notion of the past but rather a continuous engagement with loss and its remains. This engagement generates sites for memory and history, for the rewriting of the past as well as the reimagining of the future."[27] Thus for Cotera and Saldaña-Portillo, Mestizo mourning represents a deeply ambivalent "psychic restoration" that attaches "recuperative decolonial meanings to a search for indigeneity that manifests itself in a variety of cultural, political, and intellectual projects, from mythopoetical invocations of Aztlán as a 'lost land' to . . . Chicana feminist and queer recuperations of indigenous foremothers and gendered ways of knowing."[28] By reformulating a recurring trope of Chicanx historical consciousness—loss—through the psychoanalytic lexicon of melancholia, Saldaña-Portillo and Cotera reinvigorate a "dialogue about the ways in which divergent settler colonial imaginaries have shaped social and political interactions between descendants of indigenous people in the Americas."[29]

Just as the work on loss has been important to the interrogation of the impasses between Chicanx indigeneities and Native sovereignties in North America, Maylei Blackwell, Floridalma Boj Lopez, and Luis Urrieta Jr. cultivate the concept of critical Latinx indigeneities "to examine how Indigenous migrants from Latin America are transforming notions of Latinidad and indigeneity in the US."[30] For these authors, critical Latinx indigeneities critiques the ways in which Chicanx studies has confused *indigenismo* for indigeneity and roots that confusion firmly in the ways the "Chicano Movement recycled Mexican state notions of indigenismo through an Aztec-centric celebration of the Indigenous past of the nation."[31] The intervention of critical Latinx indigeneities joins a number of critiques of Chicanx attachments to indigenismo and the work that attachment performs in the structural complicity with settler colonialism by appropriating, eliminating, and degrading the Native land and life under the hemispheric apparatus of Mestizo political modernity.[32] Of paramount importance to its critical work is the continuation of the political integrity of North American tribal sovereignties by calling on "all migrants and nonmigrants to acknowledge settler status on Indigenous lands and to respect the unique political relationship of US tribal sovereignty."[33] In doing so, the concept carves space to consider "the complex, multilayered, and multi-vocal ways of being Indigenous, especially those being recognized, developed, deployed, and negotiated across national (colonial and Indigenous) borders through overlapping colonialities and settler states and within migrant transregions, which often cross multiple ethnoracial structures."[34] As a multiscalar approach, critical Latinx indigeneities thus analyzes "Indigenous-to-Indigenous relationships, including shared alliances, social structures, and practices that take place within the boundaries of Indigenous nationhood, including through migration, and that do not re(center) the settler state."[35]

Together, the concepts of Mestizo mourning and critical Latinx indigeneities affirm the ways in which Chicanx and Latinx studies remains decisive as a critical, social movement–driven space to consider the multiple racial geographies of settler colonial domination that regulate the co-imbrication of Mestizx, Native North American, and Indigenous Latin American racialization in the Americas. My study builds on this vibrant critical work by interrogating the way in which the questions and relations of Native land can further amplify and unsettle the decolonial urgency of our analytic paradigms. From this vantage, Native land opens the psychoanalytic underpinning of Mestizo mourning to a conceptual universe in which Indigenous kinship is not limited to filial relations. As David Johnson notes, "the general focus of Freud's inquiry ultimately predisposes him to establish a hierarchy of loss, which elevates the loss of 'a loved person' above all possible substitute love-objects, including land."[36] Native lands therefore unsettle the hierarchy of systems of loss that privilege the explanatory codes by which the anthropocentrism of modern psychoanalytic knowledge defines human community under the duress of colonial occupation. Because, Johnson continues, "theories of loss emerge in tension with their contexts," the concept of loss so central to the project of Mestizo mourning requires the further labor of actively engaging *land* as a distinct decolonial referent in the ruptured Native filial relations that constitute Chicanx and Latinx indigeneities.[37]

Here, the diasporic indigeneity of New Mexico's Genízarx peoples that would conjure La Alianza is especially relevant for such a task. While entrapped in the Spanish-Anglo coalition's valorization of pure Spanish ancestry as predicate for U.S. citizenship, the Genízarx diaspora has long mobilized identities through kinship terminologies with land that unsettle the status quo of borders and property.[38] According to Tomás Atencio, this relation to land for "the traditional Spanish-American is not a legal, economic factor. Land is not a commodity that is sold by the owner when he wishes to enter the real estate market for economic gain. Land is directly related to his own being, his life. Hence, Land is home, and yet more to some; it is part of body and soul."[39] Despite their settler relations, the dispersed but continued Genízarx relationship with land resonates profoundly with the kinship networks associated with Native and Indigenous communities across the Americas. Glen Coulthard and Leanne Betasamosake Simpson have named this form of kinship for Native peoples "grounded normativity," a repertoire of "practices and procedures . . . based on deep reciprocity, that are inherently informed by an intimate relation with place."[40] This relationship with land reveals how Native forms of kinship extend the domains of filial relations to include broader horizons of more-than-human life—a definition that has been clearly mandated by the United Nations Declarations on the Rights of Indigenous Peoples.[41] Such kinship relations remain vital for rekindling a dialogue over the ancestral losses that have separated Chicanx and Latinx indigeneities from Indigenous peoples across multiple borderlands on both sides of the U.S.-Mexico border.

The extended kinship network of the Genízarx diaspora also hones a focus on the ways Native land can build out the study of Indigenous movement and migrancy under critical Latinx indigeneities. A crucial point of intervention in the concept is how it identifies the ways in which analyses that gesture to the "entire hemisphere [as] Indigenous land" or illuminate the endurance of "precolonial routes and relations that predate nation-state borders" can occlude respect toward the "unique political relationship of US tribal sovereignty."[42] The kinship with land and water articulated by New Mexico's Genízarx diaspora speaks to this impasse by indexing trajectories of Indigenous migrancy and displacement that remain illegible to the territorial borders of the nation-state and the regimes of tribal recognition under U.S. law. The illegibility of the Genízarx diaspora to sovereign borders therefore provides an occasion to produce a critical distinction between *territory* and *land* as a horizon of decolonial activity. Territory, according to Alyosha Goldstein, derives not from *terra*, which implies "land, earth, nourishment," but rather from *terrere*, which signifies terror and that which is frightful and terrible. "To occupy territory," he writes, "is to receive sustenance and to exercise violence. Territory is land occupied by violence."[43] Territory not only implies, in Mary Pat Brady's words, "the primacy of abstracted space" enforced by violence but also connotes a logic of possession and control across geological spaces and cultures.[44] The Genízarx diaspora shows that when land is made territory, our political imaginaries become restricted to a universe graphed by the dominance of settler frameworks of sovereignty, property, ownership, and the possessive individualism of liberalism across the Americas. At the same time, the Genízarx diaspora also enacts a distinct trajectory of Indigenous movement in which the strictures of settler territory concede to kinship networks connected with land and cooperative relations with Pueblo and Plains Indian tribes that continue to this very moment. Disarticulating land from territory therefore clears a different epistemic framework to approach Latinx Indigenous movement in dialogue with Native and Indigenous storytelling knowledge and their distinct struggles against extant North American settler states.

Land Uprising extends the critical study of Indigenous movement for the interrogation of Latinx studies by honoring Native land as the gift of survival for Spanish and Mexican land grant forms and movements. To acknowledge Native land as a gift is not to say it was or is willingly conceded to colonial occupation. To consider Native land a gift is to honor the radical hospitality that the original inhabitants of the Americas and the Caribbean initially extended European invaders and to interrupt the criminal ways in which that hospitality continues to be forgotten, exploited, and degraded under capitalist regimes of settler modernity. To acknowledge Native land as a gift is to avow the vitality of Indigenous epistemes, which, as Rauna Kuokkanen points out, mark a landscape of exchange that "entails an active relationship between the human and natural worlds [and] extends beyond interpersonal relationships to 'all my relations' [in] recognition that gifts cannot be taken for granted or regarded as commodities."[45] As a gift, Native lands are "characterized by reciprocity, a sense of collective responsibility, and reverence."[46] Merely acknowledging Native land as a gift cannot rescind the paradoxes of Latinx Indigeneity. As Mary Louise Pratt points out, "at the heart of the social formations that develop out of this historical genesis [of settler colonialism] lies a debt, a wrong that—and this is important—can be addressed but never righted."[47] Gifts therefore open up different epistemological and material pathways for regenerating and rebuilding relations fractured by the usurpations and alienations imposed by settler colonialism.

Land Uprising reactivates a gift exchange among Latinx indigeneities and Native sovereignties by excavating La Alianza's repertoire of insurgency as a resource for naming the ways in which land grant forms speak with labors of reclaiming Indigenous land from settler colonial occupation. In an offering of alliance with Indigenous autonomy and sovereignty across the Americas, I illuminate La Alianza within a distinct horizon of literary and social movement cultural production that includes the writings of Leslie Marmon Silko, Paula Gunn Allen, Ana Castillo, Simon Ortiz, and the Zapatista Uprising in Chiapas, Mexico. In my work, I study the ways in which these writers and movements frame New Mexican land grant struggle within noncontiguous horizons of Native insurgency and Mestizx-Indigenous coalition and conflict—a terrain that encompasses the cultural politics of Pueblo Indian continuance, Chicana feminist critique, and the Indigenous autonomy of Zapatismo and the Ejército Zapatista de Liberación Nacional (EZLN). Thus, while grounded in what is now called New Mexico, this book traces a different type of constellation among Indigenous and Latinx Americas that hopscotches colonial, national, and neoliberal periodicities and weaves together lexicons and genealogies of disparately placed anticolonial and anticapitalist insurgency.

In doing so, I cultivate the concept of Native Story Power to shift the plane of analysis of Latinx Indigeneity from loss to land. To move from loss to land, to be clear, is not a downplay of the cruel and grotesquely violent means by which U.S. and Mexican settler colonial regimes have actively proliferated through the usurpation of Native land and destruction of Native filial relations. Native Story Power rather uprises land as a *concept-metaphor* to name horizons of insurgent transformation materialized by movements for Indigenous land reclamation. As Native and Indigenous peoples, movements, and studies attest, storytelling is an indelible component to the way land is made meaningful as place, and placemaking is a vital component of Native sovereignties.[48] For Native and Indigenous knowledge, stories perform the power to connect land to place in acts of political, cultural, visual, and intellectual sovereignty rooted in motion, movement, reverence, and reciprocity with webs of surrounding life.[49] As Vine Deloria Jr. demonstrates in his profoundly radical *God Is Red: A Native View of Religion*, the "vast majority of Indian tribal religions . . . have a sacred center at a particular place, be it a river, a mountain, a plateau, valley, or other natural feature. This center enables the people to look out along the four dimensions and locate their lands, to relate all historical events within the confines of this particular land, and to accept responsibility for it. Regardless of what subsequently happens to the people, the sacred lands remain as permanent fixtures in their cultural or religious understanding."[50]

Coulthard magnifies the radical relationality called forth by Native place-making by arguing that "Indigenous struggles against capitalist imperialism are best understood as struggles oriented around the question of *land*—struggles not only *for* land" as an object of possession, "but also deeply *informed* by what the land as a mode of reciprocal *relationship* (which is itself informed by place-based practices and associated forms of knowledge) ought to teach us about living our lives in relation to one another and our surroundings in a respectful and nonexploitative way."[51] For these reasons, land arises, in Mishuana Goeman's terms, as "a meaning-making process rather than a claimed object," a process that signifies connection to relations, places, spirits, and conjunctures of life that exceed anthropocentric genealogies of power and settler regimes of modern possession.[52] Enactments and studies of Native and Indigenous narrative have likewise long named the ways in which tribal storytellings resist disappearance in colonial scripts and endure as a structuring, signifying force of modern Indigenous cultural production.[53] The creation enacted by Simon Ortiz's work is but one example of the ways in which colonial structures and languages become recalled and transformed by the "speaking-writing" of Indigenous narrative. In doing so, Ortiz transforms what is arguably a restrictive category of nationalism into "a dynamic model . . . that is not based on notions of nativism or binary oppositions between insider and outsider, self and other; a nationalism that does not root itself in an idealization of any pre-Contact past, but rather relies on the multifaceted, lived experiences of families who gather in particular places."[54] Ortiz's invocation of families gathering in particular places is illuminating as a framework that avows language and stories themselves as part of kin groupings.

The overflow of Native and Indigenous storytelling wisdom into critical ethnic studies has resurged *land* as a keyword that circulates in concert with the decolonial call for Indigenous rematriation—a call to honor all existing treaties that uphold the sovereignty of Native peoples alongside labors that cancel the legitimacy of the settler state as a sovereign authority and capitalism as mediating economy.[55] In this vein, Eve Tuck and Wayne Yang have confronted the paradoxes of settler colonial occupation to argue that "decolonization is not a metaphor"—that is, a substitute for anything but the reclamation of Native land relations and the dismantling of the colonial equation of Blackness with antihuman nonbeing without recourse to sovereignty. For settler capitalist economies across the earth, they argue, land "is what is most valuable, contested, required. This is both because the settlers make Indigenous land their new home and source of capital, and also because the disruption of Indigenous relationships to land represents a profound epistemic, ontological, cosmological violence. This violence is not temporally contained in the arrival of the settler but is reasserted each day of occupation."[56] Settler colonial land usurpation in this account operates jointly as a process of eliminating Indigenous kinship structures and conscripting Indigenous people from across the planet into systems of coercive, feudal labor exploitation. This resurgence therefore has enabled an analytic that integrates a critique of the antiblackness and heteropatriarchy that operate in the colonial logics of Indigenous elimination that sanction settler occupation of Native land.[57] For Tuck and Yang, the "metaphorization" of decolonization operates as a "settler move to innocence" that seeks to deflect accountability for complicity with the continued violence required by colonial occupation.[58]

Land as a concept-metaphor, however, signifies counterintuitively to this critical upsurge. Concept-metaphors do not work in the way that Tuck and Yang critique metaphor *as only* substitution or reversal of positions between settler, Native, and slave within the geopolitics of colonial modernity.[59] Concept-metaphors are instead meaning-making processes that avow the roles that language and story play in materializing knowledge of decolonial transformation. Stuart Hall argues that concept-metaphors, or "metaphors of transformation . . . must do at least two things. They allow us to imagine what it would be like when prevailing cultural values are challenged and transformed, the old social hierarchies are overthrown, old standards and norms disappear . . . and new meanings and values, social and cultural configurations, begin to appear. However, such metaphors must also have analytic value. They must somehow provide ways of thinking about the relation between the social and symbolic domains in this process of transformation."[60] In this way, concept-metaphors avow that our conceptual capacity to *know* transformation dwells within the metaphoricity of the language we use to *name* transformation. Concept-metaphors thus bare an unresolvable dialectic between material space, representational figures, and the politics of knowledge, a dialectic that permits us to think "relations between the 'social' and the 'symbolic'" in a "non-reductionist" way and illuminates horizons of decolonial intellectual work that dwell within yet exceed the linguistic trappings and traps of settler colonialism. For these reasons, land as concept-metaphor avows the epistemic and material power embodied in Native and Indigenous storytelling practices. It operates akin to Leanne Simpson's incisive formulation regarding the freedom summoned by the resurgence of Indigenous land relations: instead of substituting *self-possession* as the antidote for *dispossession*, land as concept-metaphor proliferates epistemologies of "deep, reciprocal, consensual *attachment*" to multiple layers and formations of life.[61]

As such, Native Story Power activates land as a concept metaphor to introduce a paradigm of insurgent horizons in the prevailing territorial borders that mark the study and life forms of Latinx indigeneity.[62] Horizons emit the light by which land, in Goeman's terms, signifies "as a storied site of human interaction" and "provides meaning well beyond jurisdictional legal values."[63] Horizons illuminate the ways in which land uprises boundaries and dividing lines among regions of being and knowing that are indeed marked by territorial violence yet not restricted to the abstractions of settler modernity. Horizons, typically understood as the line where land sets the sky in relief, emplace perception. Horizons offer direction and instruction, and they calibrate motion within cyclical patterns. Horizons situate knowledge of place in a way that balances finite vistas and inexorable flux. For these reasons, horizons are not necessarily crossable in the ways that remain customarily associated with territorial borders and partitions. That is, while horizons offer orientation and perspective, they are not in themselves definitive places of arrival or knowledge. Horizons, in the words of Vincent Crapazano, "mark a change in ontological register. They postulate a beyond that is, by its very nature, unreachable in fact and in representation."[64] The moment at which one arrives at a horizon, one immediately encounters hinterlands and elsewheres. By at once upholding and undermining the stability of geographical knowledge, horizons also index incommensurable temporal frames, untranslatable linguistic networks, and irreconcilable epistemic differences.

At the same time, horizons indicate desire, relationality, interconnection, and hope in the paradox of intersubjective encounter. The critical use of horizons is historically associated with the phenomenological hermeneutics of Edmund Husserl, George Gadamer, and Paul Ricoeur. Gadamer in particular uses the phrase "fusion of horizons" to name the ways in which the historical sediments of linguistically mediated perception are not confined within set boundaries but can rather expand and "fuse" with other horizons of meaning.[65] That said, my use of horizons is not a direct engagement with or reliance upon phenomenology. It, rather, speaks with the power in which Native storytelling activates land as a matrix of decolonial signification, a power with unstoppable motion across and between distinctive disciplinary formations of modern knowledge. "In a horizon," according to Ernesto Laclau, "the signifier signifies something different from its usual signified—i.e. it signifies the ultimate impossibility on which the process of signification is based."[66] From this, he concludes, "any term is ultimately *figural* [my emphasis] because the differentiality which constitutes its meaning depends, in the last instance, on naming something which is, strictly speaking, unnamable."[67] In modern astrophysics, the analytic potential of horizons as an opening and limit to knowledge is amplified by the usage of the term *event horizon*. Commonly known as the border line of light that encircles a black hole from which there is no return, astrophysics uses event horizon to name the boundary limit to what can be known, observed, and moved toward at a given space and time. More pointedly, according to Helmut Satz, "the existence of the event horizon means our contact with the world around us is a question of space and time. . . . It is the event horizon that forms the border between future and elsewhere."[68] Horizons, in other words, concede that land can never be fully explained or contained by settler occupation.

These various mobilizations of horizons clearly do not exhaust its meanings but rather grant insight into the myriad ways Native homelands manifest since time immemorial as storied relations of reverence, reciprocity, and interdependence that interconnect geologic, anatomic, and celestial scales of being and knowing. Horizons therefore reframe land not merely as a passive surface for human consumption, nor as the backdrop against which humans accumulate history and partition territory in universal progressive time. Horizons instead avow the ways land signifies as an active material and symbolic network of water, elements, creatures, geothermal dynamics, and atmospheric forces with multiple and unknown states of consciousness, creative power, and scales of animacy necessary for human survival. Horizons reframe land from a fungible object to one in line with what Robert Nichols elaborates as "an intermediary concept—situated between labour and nature, between activity and object." "The land," Nichols continues, "mediates laboring activity through a set of spatial relations which are not themselves the product of human will, but rather a set of worldly circumstances in which we find ourselves. This is why it functions as a mediator; it retains something of the natural world."[69] Significantly, this concept of the "natural world" is not some static, "eternally selfsame" surface but rather itself the horizon of previous generations of creaturely activity.[70] Humans from this horizon move as provisionally bounded forms of life and memory emplaced by stories within other forms of life and memory with elusive origins and trajectories. "Storytellers," Goeman continues, inhabit a particularly potent role in constellating horizons from land because they "in all informal and formal forms, make space come alive by imparting an anticolonial knowledge that travels and connects to other knowledge systems."[71]

Based on this instruction, I use the concept of insurgent horizons to offer a different approach to the study of Spanish and Mexican land grants. On one level, horizons allow me to trace the ways in which land grants represent pivotal civic, economic, military, and political institutions of colonial modernity forged in the crucible of Indigenous land usurpation and racial slavery. Land grants were instrumental to the paralleled emergence of racialized labor and the privatization of land as property across different formations of mestizaje, whiteness, patriarchy, and capital. In this way, land grants remain imbricated in the racialized historical narratives and institutional formations of property that rationalize the uneven and incomplete imposition of nation-state sovereignties and differentiated capitalisms in the Americas. As such, their historic presence demonstrates how the pervasive violence of racialized patriarchy under modernity secures the continuity of property across successive and distinct regimes of colonial domination and capitalist accumulation.

At the same time, the use of horizons provides an optic to read for the ways in which land grants remain latticed by an unbounded network of Indigenous insurgency that operates before, within, and in excess of settler modernity. From the perspective of insurgent horizons, we can read for the ways in which La Alianza, Leslie Marmon Silko, Ana Castillo, Paula Gunn Allen, Simon Ortiz, and the EZLN uprise land-based storytelling networks in modern textual forms to depose land grant territoriality from settler formations of whiteness, patriarchy, property, and knowledge. Situating the territory of land grants within insurgent horizons avows storytelling as a generative labor of anticapitalist decolonization, one that fashions a set of pathways through which the multiplicity of unevenly recognized Indigenous life may flourish in the ruins of settler territories and economies. Insurgency, to borrow the words of Nancy Adajania and Ranjit Hoskote, "returns us to the potency of the horizon as the perennial and renewable site of the not-yet. It is, in the final analysis, not an ontological guarantee of a retrievable selfhood . . . nor a staging of the confrontation between binaries. . . . Rather it is a provocation to constantly destabilize and re-imagine ourselves beyond our provisional locations, to converse beyond our presuppositions about belonging and alienation."[72]

As I demonstrate in each chapter, the concept of Native Story Power names land reclamation as an insurgent horizon that creates autonomous spaces and temporalities to connect Latinx indigeneities and migrant sovereignties that transgress or confound state recognition to the ongoing struggle for Indigenous liberation. Insurgent horizons thus index the power of language *as* story and land as a dynamically inalienable dimension of human kinship. Horizons avow land as the matrix whereby language speaks *as kin*, reframing the Native and tribal kinship of Latinx indigeneities not as lost racial objects but as disappeared life relations whose connection continues in storytelling dialectics of presence and absence. To embrace Indigenous kinship relations as the structuring absence of Latinx indigeneities is not a retreat into text-based meaning nor is it a reiteration of the myth of Indigenous extinction. Rather, it means avowing the sovereign, continuous, and contemporary presence of Native peoples across the Americas as a constitutive, determining life force in the stories Latinx and Chicanx peoples have invented in movements to survive elimination, captivity, and assimilation into settler regimes of occupation. Thus, while situated in New Mexico, my study refuses to regionalize New Mexico as a place contained within nationalist, colonialist, or capitialist grids of intelligibility. The result is an inquiry that situates La Alianza not as a delimiting movement but rather as a grounding formation from which to read a multitemporal and heterogeneous field of Indigenous, borderland, and feminist texts and movements for land reclamation.

Chapter 1, "Revolt Is a Story, Not an Event: Anticapitalism and Pueblo Indian Endurance," elaborates the concept of Native Story Power by placing the legal history of Pueblo Indian racialization and land tenure under Spanish, Mexican, and U.S. colonial rule in conversation with literary work on and by Pueblo peoples. In particular, I turn to Simon Ortiz's *Fight Back: For the Sake of the People, For the Sake of the Land*, Paula Gunn Allen's *The Sacred Hoop*, and Leslie Marmon Silko's *Almanac of the Dead* and literary criticism to elucidate the anticapitalist valences to Native Story Power as well as the ways in which Pueblo Indian continuance has been staked on a subversion of Spanish and Mexican land grant law. As Joe Sando notes, the Pueblo Indian sovereignties legible to the U.S. state are "welded [to] the legal and international ramifications of the Pueblo relationship with the Spanish and Mexican governments, and these have weight even today because of various international treaties, land grants, and court decisions."[73] Through this analysis, I explore how the Pueblo Peoples' endurance of successive colonial regimes manifests a story power that translates colonial law and modern literature into what Alfonso Ortiz describes as "another means of assisting them in their cultural survival and continued revitalization."[74] It is with the network of Pueblo peoples in New Mexico where we see the ways in which land grant forms operate not merely as objects of possession through rights-based claims but as cojunctural mediums of Native continuance with profound ramifications for antisettler colonial/capitalist struggle.

The second chapter, "The Mexican-American War Has Never Ended: Escape Stories and the Genízarx Diaspora in New Mexico," exercises Pueblo Indian Story Power to resituate the Genízarx diaspora in New Mexico in a way that unsettles theories and critiques of mestizaje within Chicanx, Latinx, and Latin American studies. In doing so, I explicate a theory of escape derived from a reading of Silko's *Almanac of the Dead*. Through *Almanac*, I situate escape stories as a different horizon for translating land grant mestizaje into uncanny, place-centered, and Indigenous temporalities that subvert the sovereignty of settler states in the Americas. I reveal how the contemporary critique of Indigenous representation in Chicanx mestizaje as a recycling of indigenismo remains dominated by a monolithic account of the heterogeneity of the Chicanx movement. I show how Genízarx diasporic indigeneity allows a critical disarticulation of Chicanx mestizaje from Mexican nationalism and speaks with a distinct genealogy of Indigenous Chicanx thought that includes figures such as Jack D. Forbes, Reid Gómez, and Gilberto Benito Córdova.

Chapter 3, "The Cricket and the Lion: The Experimental History of Indohispanx Mestizaje," analyzes a vast array of La Alianza cultural production in order to reappraise the discursive logic of Indohispanx, the movement's articulation of mestizaje deployed in the service of land grant reclamation. By analyzing the movement's turn to public culture—its expansive collection of public flyers and pamphlets, its radio and television programs, and Tijerina's testimonial text, *Mi lucha por la tierra* (1978)—I reconsider Indohispanx as an experiment in collective history writing animated by the Native Story Power of the Genízarx diaspora. As a result, I show how Indohispanx mestizaje translates the diaspora of Genízarx Indians into a discourse of coalitional indigeneity that disobeyed the racialized logics of U.S. and Mexican state power and articulated land as an inalienable cultural and territorial right.

Chapter 4, "Remember the Women Who Did the Building: Land Grant Cooperativity and the Folk Base of Chicana Feminism," reconsiders the gendered and sexual politics of land grants as a submerged condition of possibility for the emergence of Chicana feminist critique. In particular, it takes up the call made by Maylei Blackwell to situate the "hidden gender insurgencies" of Chicana feminism as a disparately placed political movement within localized genealogies of colonial power. By investigating the localized conditions of relations between land grant politics and Chicana feminist critique, this chapter reads the independent newspaper tied to La Alianza, *El Grito del Norte*, alongside and against Ana Castillo's magical realist novel *So Far from God*. This chapter contributes to Chicana feminist critiques of nationalist imaginaries by analyzing the ways both textual sites converge in a critique of the heterosexual family as the basis of racial collectivity and property ownership across successive and overlapping colonial formations. In addition, I argue that the land grant moorings of Chicana feminism also unleash an alternative "cooperative mode of power" by which to storytell queer and feminist modes of collectivity and land tenure unbound to the familial inscription of private property.

Chapter 5, "Between the Word and the Land: Zapatismo as a Quantum Theory of Indigenous Rebellion," transnationalizes the political economy of Spanish and Mexican land grants by examining the Indigenous cultural politics of the EZLN. As one of the more vibrant Indigenous movements against the neoliberal world order in the contemporary moment, the Zapatistas have received much scholarly and public attention since its armed uprising against the Mexican state in January 1994. The majority of this attention concentrates on the movement's militant emergence on the eve of the implementation of the North American Free Trade Agreement, its critiques of the neoliberal evisceration of the Americas, and the public persona of Subcomandante Marcos. Yet often relegated as local context to the movement's emergence is its connection to the political economy of ejido land grants in Mexico. In this chapter I reexamine the story power of Zapatismo as an insurgent horizon that provides an optics for a quantum theory of Indigenous rebellion. In modern physics, quantum theory grapples with the ways in which the smallest measurable units of matter disobey Newtonian object-based laws of motion. Drawing from dialogues between Euroamerican scientists and Native elders on the intersections between Indigenous storytelling and quantum physics, I argue that Zapatismo manifests a particular quality of light that illuminates a shared horizon of struggle with New Mexican land grant formations. At stake is a reconceptualization of Chicanx Indigeneity's land reclamation through a transnational genealogy of ejido land grant activism.

In the coda I reflect on a visit my family and I paid to Reies López Tijerina in the winter of 2012 to meditate on the politics of secretarial labor. A position that Tijerina was tasked with upholding through supernatural encounters, the secretary is both a scribe and keeper of secrets. Secretaries open up distinct corridors of insurgent labor by which Native storytelling power outpours a place for knowledge between the colonial politics of ethnographic capture and the presumed boundedness of modern alphabetic knowledge. Their labor therefore pulls together the connective threads of this book by providing the means by which Latinx indigeneities may participate in the reclamation of the Americas for the future of Native and Indigenous peoples—a future, in other words, that offers instruction for refusing the peril of impending human extinction.

I therefore use the phrase Native Story Power to activate the insight that has been a perennial horizon of insurgent work for so many Native, Indigenous, Chicanx, and Latinx activists, writers, artists, and cultural workers—that the scripts of settler colonialism can be reinvented to sabotage settler life—that the invaders in Chicanx and Latinx genealogies will be sent home in their own words.[75] In this way, my analysis draws on critical lexicons versed in literary tropes and techniques to critique the colonial limits of sociological, humanist, and historicist knowledge. As Native, Indigenous, and Chicanx literary production attests, this is not about enshrining literary taxonomies as a higher, more universal form of knowledge that transcends other domains of study. Rather, dwelling in the lexicons of literary expression offers horizons into networks of insurgent labor that disobey the compulsive textuality that constitutes modern knowledge. My study thus discloses the oral persistence of storytelling not only in Chicanx and Latinx literature *but also in* the movement-based historiographies and print cultures that have facilitated their institutional study. This land-based approach to language and narrative practices activates an understanding of Chicanx and Latinx literary and historiographical archives as life sustained through intertextual, intersubjective, and intermedial storytelling relations with Native peoples in distinct places across disparate temporalities. In Raymond Williams's words, Native Story Power is a "cultural hypothesis" that proposes land reclamation as insurgent work with language that breaks down the abstract divisions between religion, history, politics, economy, and culture to nullify settler sovereignty.

Native Story Power illuminates multiple paths of insurgent transformation through the discursivity of land grant settlement and uncoils an anticapitalist dialectics from the unstoppable play of meaning in land-based significations. Through insurgency we can name how stories overtake their means of capture in discourse by installing an unresolvable dialectic of symbolic and material presence in representational space. Insurgency allows us to frame story power as means of escaping invasion and building Indigenous worlds that endure the genocidal disappearances upon which modern politics and knowledge are predicated. The "resiliency to (dis)orient," Goeman reminds us, "is crucial to indigenous scholarship on land."[76] Native Story Power proposes a labor on language that subverts the epistemic, perceptual, and governing practices of colonial occupation such that their limits signify the threshold to an unrelenting heterogeneity of Indigenous life and relations. Native Story Power makes a place for colonial languages to work for Indigenous futurity. Land as a keyword for Latinx Indigeneity holds open the possibility of resurgence and regeneration in destroyed and disappeared relations. Land holds the possibility, to paraphrase Subcomandante Marcos, that what is missing is still pending.[77]

CHAPTER ONE

REVOLT IS A STORY, NOT AN EVENT

Anticapitalism and Pueblo Indian Endurance

Colonialism was, in part, an image of imperialism, a particular realization of the imperial imagination. It was also, in part, an image of the future nation it would become. In this image lie images of the Other.

—LINDA TUHIWAI SMITH, *DECOLONIZING METHODOLOGIES*

Today, most of the pueblos still commemorate the arrival of Coronado's party, portraying him on their feast days as a figure on a dancing horse, holding a sword in his right hand. Another figure plays the snare drum, and the horseman dances to the tune of the drum. In some villages, the horseman is called "Santiago," who appears to be the conquistador's patron saint. Thus, do the Pueblo people work their history into living ceremonies. In this way, they gain a wry revenge upon their persecutors. One waits to see what the role of the Anglo in Pueblo historic observances will be.

—JOE SANDO, *PUEBLO NATIONS: EIGHT CENTURIES OF PUEBLO INDIAN HISTORY*

I became a runner, but I'm not afraid.

—KELIS, "RUNNIN'"

On the tercentenary of the 1680 Pueblo Indian Revolt in New Mexico, Acoma poet and scholar Simon Ortiz published *Fight Back: For the Sake of the People, For the Sake of the Land*. Bound in a deep red cover that simultaneously evokes movements for Native self-determination and proletariat liberation, *Fight Back* consists of poetry and lyric stories that expansively critique the capitalist resource extraction and labor exploitation tied to several legacies of colonial rule in what is now the U.S. Southwest. The cover for its initial publication contains an image by Acoma Pueblo artist and activist Maurus Chino of a miner hunched down before a jagged cave backdrop, an image that weaves the genealogies of Ancestral Puebloan petroglyphs and aboriginal cave paintings with abstract expressionist aesthetics. Roxanne Dunbar-Ortiz's preface for this issue elaborates the book's articulation of Native sovereignty and proletariat struggle by reminding its readers of the legacy of Indigenous labor exploitation that attends the European colonization of the Americas. "For centuries," she writes, "the indigenous peoples of the western hemisphere have worked for various masters." She continues:

> for the Spanish church and state officials; for English planters, traders, and industries; for French fur merchants; for Portuguese colonialists; and for the wealthy of the United States, Canada, Columbia, Peru, Guatemala, Bolivia. In tin mines, silver mines, gold mines, copper mines and lately in uranium and coal mines, they have labored. Stooped, picking the produce of agribusiness, they migrate with the crops. As cowpunchers, domestic servants, maids, cooks, janitors, steel walkers, lumberjacks, in canneries, electronics plants, in radiation labs, offices, as hod-carriers, roofers, welders, and on the railroads, they have worked long, hard hours—lifetimes. Last hired and first fired, they experience the highest unemployment rates and lowest pay in the United States economy.[1]

By mapping the hemispheric sites, sectors, trajectories, and industries of the alienated and coercive labor that attend Native life under colonial capitalist modernity, Dunbar-Ortiz remarkably upends the presumptions of Native elimination that circulate within multiple regimes of settler colonial power. "How is it then," she asks, "that Indians are rarely viewed as workers?"[2] Her question forcefully challenges the cross-colonial representational schema of Native Americans as "wasteful/wasted" labor that María Josefina Saldaña-Portillo identifies as "performing crucial labor for settler colonialism and early capitalist development, contributing to the representation of the American landscape as vacant or vacating, as *res nullius*."[3]

By virtue of this challenge, the text asserts work as a "basis of unity" that "Indians have . . . with non-Indians." While *Fight Back* most immediately grapples with the scales of capitalist dependency and destruction embedded in the Uranium mining industry, Dunbar-Ortiz situates the Pueblo Indian Revolt of 1680 as a distinct horizon for an anticapitalist genealogy of Indigenous struggle "against enslavement and oppression." In doing so, she moves the causality of the revolt from the plane of religious persecution—which dominates many academic accounts—to one of class/caste-based inequality grounded in "the forced labor required by the Spanish officials, clergy, and ranchers." For Dunbar-Ortiz, this helps explain why the revolt, while "organized and led by Pueblos," necessarily took the form of a multitribal and cross-racial alliance "joined by mestizos, mulattoes, by captive Indians from many Tribes, by the Mexican Indians brought by the Spanish to New Mexico as servants, by Navajos and Apaches who were hunted down by Spanish slave merchants." This Pueblo-led anticolonial alliance to oust the practices of labor exploitation, religious persecution, and land usurpation that the Spanish formalized with their arrival serves Dunbar-Ortiz as a "reminder that the Revolt left a legacy of resistance [that] continues in the mines, in the fields, in the factories."[4]

This chapter takes up *Fight Back*'s call to activate the 1680 Pueblo Revolt and narratives of Pueblo Indian endurance across successive and overlapping colonial regimes in New Mexico to reframe land grant territoriality through the register of Indigenous anticapitalist critique and alliance-making—a register that, Reginald Dyck notes, combines "issues of identity and tradition common to much contemporary Native literature" with "a structural critique of economic relations and work culture."[5] That this is routed through the specific genealogies of Pueblo Indian continuance is significant, for while the nineteen contemporary Pueblo Indian tribes federally recognized in New Mexico remain irreducibly distinct at the linguistic, cultural, and geographic level, they nonetheless share, in the words of Alfonso Ortiz, "one non-social structural and non-cultural factor": they have "never been displaced from their homelands."[6]

This remarkable fact also sets in relief the incongruous yet overlapping regimes of settler colonial occupation that the Pueblo people continue to endure and outlast. In a schematically historicist fashion, we may think of these regimes as Spanish colonialism (1598–1680)—interceded by Pueblo Indian Liberation (1680–93)—followed by Spanish accommodation (1693–1821), Mexican liberalism (1821–46), and the U.S. invasion (1848–now). Chronologically, the extractive logic of Spanish settlement in New Mexico challenged by the Pueblo Indian Revolt indeed predates the formation of what many theorize as fully developed capitalism in the uneven emergence of liberal nation-states across the hemisphere. *Fight Back*, however, asks us to suspend what Robert Nichols calls the "stadial interpretation" of capitalist accumulation—that is, the interpretation of "primitive accumulation as a historical stage, overtaken and superseded by the true, mature, general law of accumulation once a full and complete capitalist system is in place" under (neo)liberal nation-states.[7] In this way, *Fight Back* activates the revolt to illuminate an intersecting set of ritualized dispossessive and exploitative logics central to Spanish settlement that continue to structure capitalist accumulation under late U.S. modernity.

While the continuous residence of Pueblo peoples on their homelands has been noted extensively in the modern disciplines of anthropology and history, it is often in the turn to literary practice and theory where Pueblo Indian continuance manifests an explicitly anticapitalist valence. Indeed, *Fight Back* is not alone in this regard. Leslie Marmon Silko's engagement with Marxism in *Almanac of the Dead* recasts Marx as a tribal Jewish storyteller who feverishly works to record the stories of maimed, exploited, and destroyed laborers under capitalism. In the novel, the character Angelita La Escapía—the Mayan commander of the "Army of Redistribution and Justice"—reads *Das Kapital* for the first time in a Cuban communist school that she and her anticapitalist alliance are infiltrating for resources. "Marx," she notes, "had never forgotten the indigenous people of the Americas, or of Africa. Marx had recited the crimes of slaughter and slavery committed by the European colonials who had been sent by their capitalist slave-masters to secure the raw materials of capitalism—human flesh and blood. With the wealth of the New World, the European slave masters and monarchs had been able to buy weapons and armies to keep down the uprisings of the landless people all across Europe."[8]

In dialogue with Ortiz and Silko, Paula Gunn Allen's corpus of poetry and literary criticism deals with the patriarchal valences of alienation that arise from the capitalist displacement and destruction of what she terms Native "gynecratic" sociospiritual systems in the hemisphere. A member of the Laguna Pueblo and the Cubero land grant communities, Allen was a prolific poet, critic, and novelist until her crossing over to the other side in 2008. In her book of critical and personal essays *The Sacred Hoop: Recovering the Feminine in American Indian Traditions*, Allen defines gynocracies as "woman-centered tribal societies in which matrilocality, matrifocality, matrilinearity, maternal control of household goods and resources, and female deities of the magnitude of the Christian God were and are present and active features of traditional tribal life."[9] As a tradition, gynocracies are not static repositories of ritual knowledge based on a rigid male/female gender binary or a reductive embrace of heterosexual reproduction. Rather, the term offers an active, fluid, and contemporaneous mode of power that shifts the axis in American Indian literature to "become centered on continuance rather than extinction." In "The Coloniality of Gender," Maria

Lugones argues that Allen's theory of gynecratic power helps us to "understand the place of gender in pre-colonial societies [in order to understand] the nature and scope of changes in the social structure that the processes constituting colonial/modern Eurocentered capitalism imposed."[10]

Ortiz, Silko, and Allen each in their own way offer distinct and probing critiques of capitalist dispossession in which Indigenous land tenure and reclamation articulate with a critique of racialized and gendered labor exploitation. Their diverse production of literary narratives and theory also radically challenges the modern/colonial separation of land and labor embedded in racialized and gendered capitalist relations and the concomitant series of dispossessions, alienations, and destructions that such a separation necessitates for settler occupation. Their writings illuminate dispossession as a dialectic of land usurpation and labor exploitation for the sustenance of modern settler colonial formations. In doing so, their writing names "a distinct logic of capitalist development grounded in the appropriation and monopolization of the productive powers of the natural world in a manner that orders (but does not directly determine) social pathologies related to dislocation, class stratification and/or exploitation, while simultaneously converting the planet into a homogenous and universal means of production."[11] Pondering the political economy of Pueblo Indian racialization and dispossession across Spanish, Mexican, and U.S. colonial rule through literary representation allows me to locate the separation of land and labor not only in the production of racial capitalist value but also in the lettered modalities of governance and worship inscribed in settler law and religion.

What I'm calling Native Story Power is an attempt at naming the ways in which the Pueblo endurance of overlaid colonial regimes manifests anticapitalist alliances from a storytelling labor that translates the tyrannical textual complex of settler law, institutional religion, public history, wage labor, and modern literature into technologies of Pueblo revitalization. Alliancing here is not only a political practice in the conventional sense of uniting for a common purpose or mutual benefit against capitalist domination. To the processes of labor alienation, resource extraction, and land usurpation that attend racial capitalist dominance under settler modernity, Pueblo Indian Story Power counters with literary narratives that perform alliances predicated on a multiplicity of kinship relations to the land that, in the words of Eric Cheyfitz, are "absolutely inalienable, as literal family, as part of an ongoing and inviolable ceremonial relationship."[12]

RACISMS OF THE LAND/LABOR DIVIDE

The modern separation of land and labor in the formation of U.S. settler colonialism is conventionally understood as a structure of invasion that cohabitates Native elimination for land and Black slavery for labor in the production of white property rights vested in the sovereign authority of a British monarch or the bureaucratic scripts of the nation-state.[13] The operations of Spanish colonialism and of its afterlives in Latin American postcolonial nationalisms has often been cloistered off from the purview of North American settler colonial theory. However, as M. Bianet Castellanos notes, the "logics of dispossession and elimination, which are key tenets of a settler colonial model, were not isolated to British imperialism; they were also central to Spanish and Portuguese imperial projects."[14] In arguing for the relevance of settler colonial theory in Latin America in which Natives, Asian migrants, and creolized Blacks were conscripted into the process of dispossessing Native land, she cautions against "efforts to distinguish regimes of colonialism in the Americas by their method of dispossession, as rooted in *either* land or labor expropriation." Thus analyses that confuse rigid taxonomization for specificity inevitably reproduce, in Castellanos's terms, "binaries (land/labor, settler/Native, Latinx / Latin American) that mask articulations spanning imperial and colonial regimes."[15]

Étienne Balibar offers a useful detour around the land/labor binary with a focus on the "racisms of extermination" and "racisms of oppression" that arise from and structure modern nationalism. For Balibar, racisms of extermination "aim to purify the social body of the stain or danger the inferior races may represent," while racisms of oppression seek to "hierarchize and partition society." Of importance, Balibar undermines a binaristic logic attached to this distinction, arguing that they "identify historical trajectories" rather than "classify types of behavior." As historical trajectories, however, they do not linearly unfold but instead form "a broad, open spectrum of situations . . . with no fixed frontiers." In this way, he notes how "colonial imperialisms have practiced both forced labour, the establishment of caste regimes, ethnic segregation, and 'genocides' or the systematic massacre of populations."[16] Through this engagement, Ortiz, Silko, and Allen animate the modern separation of land and labor in a manner resonant with Shannon Speed's insight that "European settler colonialism was the catalyst of capitalism's expansion and continues to structure life under capitalism as it moves through different phases. Capitalism's current iteration—neoliberalism—continues to be shaped by the settler colonial imperative of dispossession/extraction/elimination justified by racialized and gendered logics that while shifting continue to emerge from that imperative."[17]

Almanac of the Dead conjures an Indigenous horizon of anticapitalist insurgency that deposes the overlapping antiblack and settler colonial logics of dispossession in the Americas. In the early 1980s, Silko moved just outside of Tucson, Arizona, to begin the writing that would become *Almanac*. The move initiates for Silko an encounter with the binational lands of the Tohono O'odham and the Yoeme (Yaqui) peoples. Indeed, one notable feature of *Almanac* remains its sustained engagement with the legacy of Yoeme recalcitrance to Spanish and Mexican settler colonial violence. "Rather than being subdued by the Spanish," Felipe S. Molina and David Delgado Shorter write, "the Yoemem defeated the conquistadors repeatedly. Rather than being missionized by force, the Yoemem villages invited Jesuits into their communities to help learn agricultural technologies and to develop governmental structures."[18] At the same time, *Almanac* as a form borrows from what Kimberly Roppolo describes as the "visual/holistic recording of knowledge" embedded within Mayan codices. Through the register of Laguna Pueblo networked story power, *Almanac* is able to at once draw upon the past of Mayan "semipermanent visual recording of knowledge" while also foretelling the Zapatista uprising among the multitude of Mayan tribes in the Mexican state of Chiapas.[19] The result is a comparative analytic of borderland Indigenous insurgence and alliance that performs as an unbounded bundle of cross- and intertribal storytelling.

In this web of "intertribal metanarrative," *Almanac*'s engagement with Marxism is one of the more frequently explored motifs in the book.[20] Much of the criticism centers on the character La Escapía and her Army of Justice and Redistribution. Within *Almanac*, however, Angelita's translation of Marx finds complementary critical energy in the character Clinton, a Black homeless Vietnam veteran living in Tucson who organizes the city's homeless people into the "Army of the Homeless." Clinton "swears he is no Marxist" because "African and other tribal people had shared food and wealth in common for thousands of years before the white man Marx came along."[21] Clinton, however, uncannily interweaves anticapitalist insights from Black radical thinkers such as Cedric Robinson, C. L. R. James, Sylvia Wynter, and Julie Dash. Clinton stages *Almanac*'s rejection of anticapitalist analytics that erase Native thought as an occasion to unleash a concomitant dismissal of modern antiblack racisms embedded in the blood quantum politics of U.S. tribal recognition and in narratives of mestizaje that excise African genealogies from their logic of multiracial hybridity.

In the novel, before Clinton began his organizing work, he took Black studies classes at the University of New Mexico, where he began to formulate a historical materialism that simultaneously inventories the constitutive violences of plantation chattel slavery while activating Indigenous transformation released from Black escape and fugitivity.

While studying the suppressed yet formative role that the captivity of Black life plays in financing and organizing the political, economic, and cultural structures of modernity, Clinton "had not agreed with Garvey and the others who wanted to go back to Africa . . . because blacks had been Americans for centuries now, and Clinton could feel the connection the people had, a connection so deep it ran in his blood."[22] Locating Black indigeneity as an effect of Black fugitivity, Clinton studies how from "the beginning" of the "Spanish plantations and mines of Hispaniola," "Africans had escaped and hid in the mountains where they met up with survivors of indigenous tribes hiding in remote strongholds. In the mountains the Africans had discovered a wonderful thing: certain of the African gods had located themselves in the Americas as well as Africa. . . . Right then the magic had happened: great American and great African tribal cultures had come together to create a powerful consciousness within all people."[23] Clinton's analysis serves as an important feature in *Almanac* that rethinks the racisms embedded in the land/labor divide by rebuking the ongoing presumption of Black social death and Native elimination under settler colonial modernity.

This challenge to modernity's constitutive racisms reveals, in the words of Nelson Maldonado-Torres, how "secularism legitimates colonial structures of meaning and institutions . . . by taking on certain aspects of religiosities," in particular the "constant purification of the public space from nonnational, noncivilized, and alien interventions."[24] As a result, Maldonado-Torres argues, "Western societies have come to rapidly recognize the religious element in non-Western or colonial societies, but not the emergence of particularly theoretical or philosophical productions."[25] In this way, Clinton's fugitive organizing and study are notably tied to modalities of subaltern writing and publicity. Whole sections of *Almanac* are composed of Clinton's notebooks and scripts of radio broadcasts that depict the spiritual agency informing slave revolutions in the Americas, revolts that "joined forever the histories of the tribal people of the Americas with the histories of the tribal people of Africa."[26] Clinton upends the secular fundaments of power that underwrite disparately located strains of Marxist philosophy, liberal governance, and Black studies. In the process, *Almanac* locates the horizon of a Black-Native anticapitalist alliance on a spiritual plane that is translocally grounded in an intercontinental network of land-based relations.

COLONIAL SETTLEMENT AS MYSTIFICATION

In 1992, *Fight Back* would be reprinted in *Woven Stone*, a collection of poetry and poetic stories written by Ortiz that include the texts "Going for the Rain" and "A Good Journey." Upon first glance, the revolt appears absent in the exigency of *Fight Back*'s republication. Missing in this version is the 1980 version's prefatory inscription, which explicitly signals the book "In commemoration of the Pueblo Revolt of 1680 and our warrior Grandmothers and Grandfathers."[27] Also missing is the critical preface penned by Dunbar-Ortiz. Nevertheless, in *Woven Stone*'s introduction, Simon Ortiz situates *Fight Back* as a "literary work intended to be a political statement about what has happening to our land and lives in the Acoma-Grants-Laguna region where the uranium industry was most active. I had looked back three hundred years at the Pueblo Revolt of 1680 when the dispossessed, oppressed poor led by the Pueblo Indian people rose up against the civil, religious, and military rule of the Spanish."[28] And now, he points out, the "same conditions" of land theft, "slave labor, religious persecution, and unjust tribute demands" animate "a modern-day American society and the uranium industry."[29]

From this vantage, *Fight Back* engages with the pluricolonial racisms of oppression and elimination inscribed in the industries of uranium extraction. Indeed, that both versions of *Fight Back* invoke the 1680 Pueblo Revolt to stage its critique of racialized wage labor, resource extraction, and land usurpation under modern U.S. capitalism opens new horizons to the continuities and disjuncts in colonial accumulation through Native dispossession between 1680 and 1980. It does so, however, by also unearthing the deep power of Pueblo Indian storytelling as an analytic framework for naming and nullifying the devivifying work that colonial languages perform under modern capitalism. Notably, Ortiz uses *mystification*, a vexed term in Marxist philosophy, to situate the revolt's relation to *Fight Back*. He notes that his work as "a writer, teacher, and storyteller is to *demystify* language."[30] For Ortiz, mystification is a process wherein the "European urge for domination, compounded by capitalism's quest for profit, overwhelmed and submerged everything and everyone not only with language, philosophy, behavior, economy, government, but with violence and brute force when rhetorical persuasion failed."[31]

As the first successful anticolonial uprising in the hemisphere, the 1680 Pueblo Indian Revolt radically unsettled the colonial order that the Spanish had established for nearly a century. In the years preceding the official Spanish invasion by Juan de Oñate in 1598, the Pueblo people had already had fleeting and violent encounters with Francisco Coronado's expedition in 1540. On his hapless quest for the Seven Gold Cities of Cíbola, Coronado's expedition would decimate the Tiguex Peoples and invade the Zuni and Hopi Pueblos before returning to Mexico two years later and having his expedition publicly labeled a failure by the Spanish viceroy. After Oñate established San Gabriel, New Mexico's first capitol across from the pueblo of Ohkay Owingeh, the Spanish clergy, civic officials, and military unleashed a brutal campaign of religious conversion, land appropriation, and feudal labor and resource extraction.

The procedure known as the *requerimiento* (requirement) provided a convenient mechanism for congealing these imperialist acts into Spanish settlement. The requerimiento was a written ultimatum read aloud to Native tribes informing them that they would face "war everywhere and however," as one version put it, if they did not submit to the "church as lord and superior of the universal world" as administered by the agents of the "Catholic Kings of Spain."[32] While those who resisted faced total warfare, others who acquiesced were given nominal protection from enslavement while nonetheless facing strict tribute obligations. A pivotal tactic legitimating the Spanish invasion of the Americas, the requerimiento converged textual authority, divine imperative, exploitative taxation, "state-run population surveys," and total warfare as fundaments of colonial occupation.[33]

By the time the Spanish reached the Pueblo people, the requerimiento's ritualized attempt to subordinate Natives to Spanish religious and civil control had been reworked in the Ordinances for New Discoveries of 1573. According to Malcolm Ebright, Rick Hendricks, and Richard Hughes, these "acts of obedience and vassalage" were first put into place at Santo Domingo Pueblo on July 7, 1598.[34] On this day, the leaders of a number of Pueblos convened with Oñate, where he beckoned their submission to King Phillip of Spain and therefore to Christianity, promising justice and peace. Alfonso Ortiz notes that, after conferring with one another, a number of Pueblo elders and leaders, with the exception of the Hopi, agreed. Soon after, Oñate sanctioned mining and proselyting excursions and subsequently divided the villages into seven missionary districts with clergy and civic authorities assigned to each. In this way, the requerimiento predicated the subsequent imposition of the *encomienda* and the *repartimiento* (see below) as systems that formalized the feudal labor exploitation and religious persecution of Pueblo peoples.

A key element of Spanish colonial settlement, encomiendas were formalized titles to Indian labor that accompanied the land granted to conquistadors as either reward or incentive for service to the Crown. A European transplant from the religious warfare of the Reconquista of the Iberian Peninsula, the encomienda and its subsequent replacement with the repartimiento contractualized indentured labor relations and routinized a tribute system that nourished the Spanish and their transported slaves from central and southern Mexico. Regardless of the requerimiento's enunciation, Simon Ortiz reminds us how initial European settlement across the Americas "would have likely perished" without "native help and knowledge." At the same time, he asserts that "Native American people were mystified and probably enchanted" by the "persistence, fortitude, and dogmatism" that accompanied the colonizer's "obvious helplessness and ineptitude."[35] At once extractive, enchanting, and vigorously myopic, the text-based authority shared by the Christian and civic institutions of Spanish empire mediated the sustenance the Spanish received from the exploited hospitality of Pueblo tribes. As Alfonso Ortiz further notes:

> Having come to find a treasure in gold and silver, expecting to live on the labor of others, the colonists proved largely unwilling to do the work required to establish a self-supporting settlement—most specifically planting and tending fields and otherwise providing for a reliable source of food. Most were of a social class that regarded agricultural pursuits beneath them, and their effort in New Mexico were characterized by lack of planning and extreme shortsightedness that would condemn not only themselves, but also the indigenous population, to extreme hardship.[36]

In this economy of textual fetish, spectacularized acts of cruel and depraved violence were continuously instrumental to the discursive force, epistemic authority, and financial functions of Spanish settlement. In 1599, Vicente de Zaldívar led a punitive mission into Acoma Pueblo to avenge the death of his younger brother, Juan de Zaldívar, at the hands of the Acoma people. Juan de Zaldívar had encountered the Acoma people the year before and was killed after forcefully attempting to take supplies and provisions from Acoma for his soldiers. The following year, his brother raided Acoma and burned the Pueblo to the ground. After a heated multiday battle, the Spanish overwhelmed the

Pueblo and usurped provisions. In the aftermath, the Spanish cut off one foot of every male over the age of twenty-five and sentenced them to twenty years of personal servitude. Likewise, males between twelve and twenty-five would be spared dismemberment yet were condemned to twenty years of servitude for the Spanish. Two Hopi men had one hand cut off and were ordered to travel to other Pueblos as a grotesque signifier designed to intimidate them into servitude. Later, Oñate would order Vicente de Zaldívar to send roughly seventy Acoma girls to the viceroy in Mexico to be distributed across different covenants.[37]

While nominally pacifying Pueblo-Spanish relations, the encomienda system formalized what Simon Ortiz calls the Spaniards' "belief system of insistent superiority" underwritten by the insatiable consumption of Pueblo land, labor, and suffering. The system forced the Pueblos to pay tithes to the church, civic leaders in the capitol, and various *alcaldes* (magistrates). In addition, it obligated the Pueblos to provide *permitías* of wheat, corn, and other crops to the Spanish religious and civil authorities. When Pueblo land was usurped to raise Spanish cattle and livestock, soil erosion and overgrazing accompanied widespread drought. Famine, destitution, disease, exploitation, displacement, and punitive religious chauvinism became hallmarks of Spanish dominance. On a number of occasions, the Pueblos filed formal complaints and grievances to the viceroy in Mexico. When, in 1621, colonial officials in Mexico City issued decrees that prohibited labor hardship on the Pueblos and sought to regulate work along gender lines, the response spurred destructive infighting between the civic and clergy branches of New Mexico's colonial authority. Each side accused the other of a number of crimes that included exploiting and abusing Pueblo servants and slaves along with illegal settlement activity.[38]

For Simon Ortiz, racism operates in this context as a crucial component of mystification because it produces "philosophical belief" about using "social and political power . . . exploitatively, manipulatively, and aggressively."[39] In 1633, Fray Estevan de Perea opened an investigation into Pueblo bigamy and witchcraft, exacerbating the reign of Spanish religious persecution and fomenting unrest and antagonism among the Pueblos. In 1650, Jemez, Isleta, Alameda, San Felipe, Taos, and Cochiti Pueblos organized with Apaches to overthrow Spanish control only to have their plans discovered by the Spanish who, in response, hanged nine leaders and sold the others into slavery. Nearly twenty years later, forty-seven Pueblo people were accused of "sorcery" by the new governor, Juan Francisco de Treviño. Treviño also accused the group of bewitching and killing

Spanish clergy and soldiers. As a result, the accused group was captured and taken to Santa Fe to be put on trial and were found guilty. Treviño ordered that four members be hanged. After one member hung himself in his cell, the others were taken to their respective pueblos at Nambe, Jemez, and San Felipe and hanged in public. The remaining forty-three were sentenced to lashings, prison, and slavery. "Among those enduring the shame of a public whipping," according to Joe Sando, "was a man from San Juan Pueblo by the name of Popé. It was he who (tradition has it) united the Pueblos in an effort to expel the hated Spaniards, resulting in the first American revolution in 1680."[40]

On August 9, 1680, as the story goes, two runners, Nicolás Catua and Pedro Omtua, set out on a twenty-seven-mile trek from Tesuque Pueblo toward the Spanish town of San Cristóbal bearing a knotted cord.[41] Days prior, a clandestine group of Pueblo war chiefs, who had been organizing the ouster of the Spanish for years, met in secret underground kivas and deliberated the final steps of their plan. The war chiefs, led by Po'pay, who had migrated to Taos Pueblo after his release, had determined that an uprising during one of the Spanish feast days would be most effective while the settlers squabbled over control of the colony and awaited supplies from central Mexico. The knotted cord was dispersed among the disparately located Pueblos involved in the plan. The number of knots served as a countdown mechanism to the day of the uprising. The last knot untied signaled August 13 as the day to commence the revolt. However, when Catua and Omtua arrived in San Cristóbal to deliver the cord, the Pueblo leader they encountered did not send the agreed-upon smoke signal to other villages but rather mounted his horse and rode off to inform the Spanish authorities. Given that the Spanish prohibited Pueblo Indians from horseback riding, Catua and Omtua embarked on their second, twenty-seven-mile trek back to Tesuque to inform the others. After making the arduous return, they were apprehended by Governor Antonio de Otermín's *maestro de campo* (chief of staff), Francisco Gómez Rebolledo, and taken to Santa Fe for interrogation. There Catua and Omtua were coerced into divulging the date of the uprising, at which point Otermín sent notification to several villages with a warning about the upcoming revolt. He ordered the execution of Catua and Omtua, who were subsequently hanged in the plaza of Santa Fe. However, by the time Otermín began to realize the extent of the planned revolt, it was already too late. Reports of a planned uprising began to file in from disparate Pueblo villages as crews of runners fanned out to Pueblo villages bearing a cord with a single knot. The following day, August 10, 1680, would be the day to rise up.

In the ensuing uprising, from the northernmost Taos pueblo to the southernmost Isleta pueblo, nearly two-thirds of Franciscan friars and roughly four hundred Spanish settlers were killed. Spanish churches, haciendas, and colonial archives were burned and destroyed. Otermín called for settlers from the villages of La Canada and Los Cerrillos to bunker with him in Santa Fe in the hope of fortifying a holdout to subdue the revolt. According to Theodore S. Jojola, "the Spanish did not expect the Pueblos to unite for a common purpose. Neither did they anticipate the defection of mixed Indian and Spanish descendants. These *coyotes* or *mestizos* were themselves inflamed with the desire to reform Spanish-Castilian discrimination. They were willing to collaborate with the natives and in a position to relay valuable military and civilian intelligence to the conspiring Pueblo war chiefs. After the melee erupted, a number of these *mestizo* citizens joined the ranks of the attacking natives. A few even commanded."[42] One Pueblo warrior, Juan El Tano from Galisteo, had worked for the Spanish prior to the revolt only to return to Santa Fe as "a leader of the native emancipators."[43] In negotiations with Otermín, El Tano demanded the release of all Apache captives, including his own wife and children, whom the Spanish had incarcerated. He presented the Spanish with two crosses—one white and one red. The white cross signified peace, while the red declared war. After intense battles, the Pueblo warriors cut off the capital's water supply. Without food or water, Otermín and his beleaguered crew surrendered and fled New Mexico on August 21, 1680, as Pueblo warriors surveyed their departure from the surrounding hillsides.

On its own terms and with those provided by *Fight Back*, the Pueblo Revolt remains remarkable as a decisive interruption of the concomitant institutionalization of religion, formalization of labor exploitation, and textual mediation of land as territorial possession that constituted the extractive industries of Spanish settlement. Or, put differently, the revolt shows the pilot logic of colonial accumulation through dispossession that harnesses the category of religion to rationalize systems of racialized and gendered exploitation and resource extraction. Andrés Reséndez notes how the geography of the revolt "maps exceedingly well onto the slaving corridors of Parral," a colonial silver-mining hub in what is now the Mexican state of Chihuahua.[44]

In this way, as a cross-tribal and multicaste uprising, the revolt also sets in relief the multiform levels of extractive violence attached to the colonial complex of text-based authority. Under these constraints, the revolt manifested through a proliferation of oral and material communicative technologies, which, however fleetingly, ultimately destroyed Spanish archival and religious materials that sanctioned colonial accumulation during nearly a century of occupation. The knotted cord, for example, stands out as a communicative material that performs the secrecy of revolt while diverging from the alphabetization of knowledge that underwrites colonial domination. Additionally, Joe Sando notes, "the lack of a written language helped to preserve their religion and culture through the years of Spanish occupation."

> The Pueblo way of life was passed to succeeding generations by the oral tradition, what they called "remembering by the eyes and ears." These remembrances could not be seized or burned like the written word. Even the closest surveillance by the Spaniards could not control this communication. In fact, the oral tradition gave the Pueblos the ability to trick the Spaniards while keeping their own faith alive inwardly. Few Spaniards realized until it was too late that conversion by the sword had been a dismal failure in seventeenth-century New Mexico.[45]

These acts of secrecy, according to Joseph H. Suina, not only enabled the Pueblos to depose the Spaniard's technomilitary advantage, but also served to "physically, psychologically and spiritually fortify each and every Pueblo community."[46] In this way, Alfonso Ortiz reframes the revolt as "a great act of restoration by the ancestors of today's Pueblo Indian people."[47] He continues that the participants in the revolt "knew they must restore fully to life the vision expressed in the ancient teaching and reminder that began and still begins so many prayers . . . This vision of the beginning, a fresh, ever renewable and vigorous beginning had to fully be restored and reaffirmed or the vitality that it had always given them as free peoples would eventually be sapped by the Spanish."[48] Likewise, for Simon Ortiz, the demystification of capitalist-colonial racialized domination is neither solely a labor of dismantling the technoeconomic relations that organize and reproduce capitalist value, nor is it merely an ideological critique of false or deceptively mediated consciousness. Rather, he locates demystification as a careful work on language grounded in "anticolonialist resistance" undertaken "with our indigenous sisters and brothers in the Americas of the Western Hemisphere."[49]

The view of the Pueblo Indian Revolt as a sacred act of ancestral restoration carries radical implications for work on language with transformative effects to conceptualizations of history, land, and their relation to the laboring process. Silko elaborates these innovations to English language and literature in her widely anthologized essay "Language and Literature from a Pueblo Indian Perspective," in which she articulates "a view of narrative particular to the Pueblo and other Native American peoples—that is, that language *is* story."[50] As story, Silko invites readers to "*hear* and to experience English in a structure that follows patterns from the oral tradition," patterns "more concerned with story and communication" over the structure of a "particular language." As story, the "Pueblo expression" of language communicates like a "spider's web—with many little threads radiating from the center, crisscrossing one another."[51] Language as story transforms the linguistic status and discursive operations of English—as well as other colonial languages—away from what Arnold Krupat terms as "linguistic/referential accuracy" and toward a "performative effectivity."[52] The former, for Krupat, mobilizes the written word out of a "concern for fixed meanings" and "appears to arise only with the shift to literacy . . . chirography, [and] typography" from orality as the "means of information storage." In this account, the textual codification of language as an instrument for definitive significations "has been the dream of Western social science and philosophy."[53]

In contrast, the "performative effectivity" of language as story opens an approach to English as an open-ended site of performative enactment through communally situated enunciation. Silko emphasizes how this shift suspends a conceptualization of language as mere *reflection* of an already ossified reality in order to activate the power of language on the plane of *creation*. As an example, Silko shares the "Pueblo Creation story, an all-inclusive story about how life began." "In this story, Tse'itsi'nako, Thought Woman, by thinking of her sisters, and together with her sisters, thought of everything that is. In this way, the world was created. Everything in this world was a part of the original Creation; the people at home understood that far away there were other human beings, also a part of this world. The Creation story even includes a prophecy that describes the origin of European and African peoples and also refers to Asians."[54] Silko's account of Thought Woman's creation here diverges from modern frameworks that would cast her story as a mythic event in the past that was once confined to the oral universe but now requires transcription into institutionalized textual forms for accuracy and longevity. Instead, as Krupat notes, Silko's "web of words" creates a network wherein "any single spoken word" connects to "other words not then spoken." This creates the "necessity of a story for each word, the words of which stories themselves necessitate further stories, with no end to storytelling."[55] Notice, in this vein, the turn toward a type of unbounded storytelling intercontinentalism, as Thought Woman's creation story frames additional prophetic stories about the "origin" of peoples in Europe, Africa, and Asia. Unbounded and yet multiply framed, story power for Silko "is the idea that one story is only the beginning of many stories and the sense that stories never truly end."[56]

Pueblo Indian Story Power is therefore an immemorial mode of contemporary enunciation that traverses and transgresses the multitextual epistemic enclosures of modern law, property, literature, and labor that sanction settler regimes of racialized labor and the occupation of Native land. Story power indexes multiple forms and functions of telling that exceed the imperatives of enclosure that constitute the regimes of settler law, history, religion, property, and literature. It is a power that surrounds settler occupation's modern fetish of textual authority and commodified value with the grounded orality and aurality of a set of tellers and listeners in alliance. It is a power that is inherently dialogic, emplaced, moving, and recurrent—an unbounded circle of tellers and listeners with neither a fixed radius nor a stable orbital trajectory.

In this infinite chain, stories live as way of coming together—an act of alliancing. In one register, alliancing manifests specific survival functions. Repetition, a key element in Pueblo storytelling, mnemonically bundles "valuable information" that Silko translates as "recipes" and "maps." At once instructive and speculative, grounded yet mobile, Pueblo "stories cannot be separated from their geographical location, from actual physical places on the land." At the same time, Silko argues that the experiences of Pueblo peoples resonate in many ways with "those of African and Caribbean peoples—one is that we have all had the conqueror's language imposed on us."[57] By activating language as story, however, what initially appears as a totalizing conceptual enclosure imposed by imperial English becomes another method of "making English speak for" the continuance and dignity of Pueblo peoples and their alliances in a global network of storytelling.

In this sense, to frame language as a story that speaks for the continuance of Pueblo Indian life is a process that entails transforming English into a verb-based language. Through this prism, Silko's invocation of the Pueblo Creation Story is not represented as an event fixed in a temporal moment. Creation is instead represented as a recurrent power activated by the alliances one makes through language with the surrounding matrix of land-based relations. Regarding Silko's vision of creation, Mary Ellen Snodgrass observes how "she connects creative energy with renewal and hope. Rather than characterize clouds, rain, gardens, edible animals, and other spiritual gifts to humanity as 'magic,' she prefers the word 'power.'"[58]

The story power of Pueblo alliancing evident in contemporary literary narratives also dwells within the transformations to Pueblo-Hispanx relations that reverberate from the 1680 Revolt. That is, instead of a temporally bounded event that concludes with Diego de Vargas's reinvasion in 1693, the revolt resonates as a power of Pueblo Indian continuance that transformed Spanish-Pueblo relations from a paternalistic mode of feudal domination to a negotiated alliance around economic production, civic rights, religious practice, and military cooperation. Over the span of the eighteenth century and into the mid-nineteenth century, the Spanish colonial order would slowly concede to a different rooting in and with the matrix of Pueblo creation.

ACCOMMODATIONS AND ALLIANCES

During the thirteen years of Pueblo-liberated New Mexico, violent conflict between and among the Spanish, Pueblo, Apache, and Navajo persisted. This period and the subsequent Spanish reinvasion would see the displacement of Pueblo tribes along the Rio Grande to the lands of the Hopi, Zuni, Navajo, and Apache. As a result, the revolt's aftermath irrevocably transformed the dynamic of Spanish colonial dominance. The historiography of this period extensively details a strategic series of alliances borne from the insurgent alchemy endeavored by Pueblo Indian Revolt.[59] While Pueblo distrust toward the Spanish civic and religious authorities remained, the Spanish drastically relaxed the fervor with which they sought to disappear Pueblo ceremonial life. Although the Spanish continued to require Pueblo peoples to upkeep the Spanish missions, the construction of their characteristically hulking mission structures was suspended. In January 1706, Governor Francisco Cuervo y Valdés convened a meeting with leaders from all of the pueblos except the Hopi in order to formalize a distinctively new era of cooperative relations as a strategic bulwark against the ascendance of the surrounding raiding economies of the Apache, Navajo, and Comanche tribes. "The sense of partnership and participation in the wars as important and prestigeful allies of the Spaniards," Edward Dozier notes, "offset the abuses that the Pueblos suffered."[60] As a result, he continues, "every major Spanish retaliatory or punitive expedition against the Apache, Navaho, and Comanche contained Pueblo Indian auxiliaries."[61]

The brisk growth of Genízarx captives notably mediated the emergent Pueblo-Spanish alliance. Not only would Genízarx subjects come to supplement the racialized scapegoating and servitude that the Spanish imposed on Pueblo tribes, but they would also come to participate in Spanish military expeditions and acquire land grants in raiding corridors that simultaneously bordered Pueblo villages. "The colonial settlements," Dozier notes, "were buffered by either Genízaro or Pueblo villages. Acoma, Laguna, and Jemez pueblos received the first attacks of Navaho raiders, while the Galisteo Basin Pueblos and Pecos were exposed to the initial thrusts of Plains Indians." As a result, "inordinate demands were made on both the Pueblos and Genizaro villages to furnish warriors for punitive expeditions."[62] Thus the entangled functions and land relations between Pueblo tribes and Genízarx communities brought about a series of fundamental transformations to the political economy of Spanish land tenure away from the feudal exploitation and religious chauvinism of the encomienda and toward a complex network of cooperative, subsistent relations. "There developed," Joe Sando notes, "a culture known as Pueblo-Hispanic culture, and the Spaniards were insidiously, slowly, and inevitably brought to embrace Pueblo ways, including the subsistence pattern of agriculture."[63]

In this context, the colonial legal architecture of the Pueblo league became formalized as a mechanism by which Pueblo tribal land tenure became articulated with rights-based frameworks. According to Malcolm Ebright, Rick Hendricks, and Richard Hughes, the "emergence of the four square league (approximately 17,350 acres), otherwise known as the Pueblo league, can be discerned from this period held in both the Spanish Archives of New Mexico and New Mexico's pueblos. By 1704, it was taken for granted that the Pueblo league was based on a law or decree issued by the king."[64] Thus Pueblo tribes maintained kinship ties to the land through a sophisticated combination of ancestral ceremonial practice and rights-based juridical claims. This combination became especially effective in warding off repeated Spanish incursions on Pueblo lands with the rationale that Pueblo Indians were not properly cultivating all of the resources within their boundaries.[65] The "Pueblo league," therefore, as Ebright, Hughes, and Hendricks continue, "was at least nominally protected from encroachment by Spanish settlers and . . . the pueblos themselves were well aware of, and vigorously asserted their rights to, this entitlement."[66]

This period of conflictive alliance was reinforced by the rapid acceleration of Apache, Navajo, Ute, and Comanche insurgency characterized by rampant raids on Pueblo, Genízarx, and Spanish communities. "Dependence," Robert

Archibald notes, "was the most effective method available to the Spanish to exert even minimal control" over the surrounding network of Pueblo and Plains tribes. As the forms of Spanish colonial control grew into dependence on the violent trade in Native life, the Catholic Church's influence over Pueblo life receded in the colony throughout the eighteenth century. The practice of Catholicism by Pueblo peoples became overwhelmingly a nominal concession that was grafted onto a resurgent continuation of Pueblo ceremonialism. This political economy of colonial-tribal dependence was supplemented through annual trade fairs at Taos, Pecos, Picuris, Santa Clara, Jemez, and Acoma Pueblos. The Taos fair in particular became a pivotal site at which the cycle of raids and counterraids between Spanish, Pueblo, Comanche, and Ute peoples would be temporarily suspended for trade in captives, tobacco, meat, guns, horses, mules, hides, blankets, and other sundry items.[67]

This form of alliancing that had been the key to Pueblo restoration, resurgence, and revitalization after the revolt became fortified and challenged by the ascendance of Mexican liberalism. As Apache and Navajo tribes became empowered through raiding expeditions on Pueblo and Genízarx communities, the Spanish elite deliberately begin to destroy relations between the Pueblos and surrounding Plains tribes with the goal of subduing rebellion and pillaging Apache and Navajo tribes for captives. In this context, the Spanish ruling class began to associate Pueblo tribes with a "civility" that contrasted with a "savagery" that sanctioned programs of destruction of Apache, Comanche, and other Plains peoples.[68] As a result, in a prelude to liberal governmentality, Spanish officials declared legal equality between Indians and Spaniards on February 9, 1811—a move that spawned a large-scale assault on the communal property protections to Pueblo land mandated by the Pueblo league. By 1813, a number of legal provisions introduced to the Spanish Parliament enabled nearly half of communal lands to be transformed for private ownership. After 1821, when New Mexico came under Mexican liberal jurisdiction and the flurry of non-Indian claims to Pueblo lands increased, many Pueblo tribes responded by asserting their rights through a variety of legal strategies. Some Pueblos, such as Taos and Okay Owingeh, mounted legal arguments on the basis that their leagues were granted on the incontestable authority of the Spanish monarch.[69] Others, such as Pecos, appealed to the Pueblos' newly ascribed citizenship as a means of arguing for the protection of their property.[70]

The emergence of liberal secularism that attended the privatized property regime in this moment coincided with the ongoing decentralization of church authority under Spanish rule in New Mexico. This ironically worked to clear a space for a widespread renaissance of Pueblo ceremonial life that coalesced into a savvy combination of spiritual, political, and economic autonomy from the Spanish and Mexican governments. This transformation altered the political economy of the Spanish-Pueblo alliance, as it at once fortified the spiritual and political economy of Pueblo agriculture while strengthening "the cooperative bonds forged between the Pueblo and rural Hispanic communities."[71] Both communities cooperated on the use of irrigation ditches, and many elite Hispanx and Genízarx families were welcome to Pueblo feast days. In addition to practicing agricultural subsistence, elite Hispanx and Genízarx communities also learned to survive from Pueblo medicinal knowledge. These cooperative bonds would nourish the 1837 revolt against the Mexican government in which a group of Pueblos, Genízarxs, and some elite Hispanxs usurped control of Santa Fe from the newly appointed governor, Albino Pérez. Pérez had planned to institute codes to increase taxes on food, irrigation ditches, and other articles, prompting the rebellious alliance to establish an independent government that lasted for roughly six months before former governor Manuel Armijo subdued the uprising for the Mexican government.[72] Ten years later, in the midst of the Mexican-American War, another coalition formed in Taos to counter the impending U.S. occupation. The coalition of Pueblo Indians and impoverished Genízarxs killed territorial governor Charles Bent before being overwhelmed, captured, and executed by U.S. forces. In both instances, wealthy Hispanxs supported the uprisings yet remained in the background for fear of death and retribution.

Pueblo-Hispanx cooperation here, in the words of Paula Gunn Allen, "meant something other than noncompetitiveness or passivity," but included a "harmony," "balance, kinship, and respect" that "did not necessarily mean the absence of conflict."[73] It rather taught genealogies of detribalized people how to become "a part of the ecological balance instead of abusing and finally destroying it" and how to accept "the terms of their existence in what may be considered today as a harsh environment," based on the instructions of those who "lived in it for thousands of years until the technological Europeans arrived, bringing in their wake the pollution and rampant misuse of the land that we see today."[74] As a result, Alfonso Ortiz notes, "much of the unique character of the New Mexican territory that would so startle the Americans upon their entry had been derived from Pueblo ways of being and living that would *not* die—ways that were inseparable from the land and survival upon it."[75]

KILLERS PURSUING KILLERS

As Alfonso Ortiz suggests, multiple scales of uncanniness mark the trajectory of Pueblo recognition under U.S. settler colonialism. While mired in a disintegrating Spanish colonial order, the Pueblo-Hispanx alliance confounded the racialized interpretive codes of tribal recognition employed in the service of U.S. colonial-capitalist expansion. Because U.S. officials encountered Pueblo peoples as emplaced in sedentary communities sustained through a vibrant ceremonial life, governing structures, and sophisticated trade and irrigation networks, they questioned whether they fit the racialized stereotypes of nomadic, wasteful, savage, and pagan Indian subjects that had been cultivated through more than a century of settler state violence. Indian racialization in the United States imputed this insufficient humanity to Native peoples as a mechanism to naturalize fee simple title as the apex of civilized land tenure and enable a paternalistic mode of federal jurisdiction over Native land to mask the destructive violence employed in settler usurpation. The predicament facing U.S. courts, according to Christine Klein, was that if the Pueblos were Indians, "then the federal trust duty would apply and any occupation of Pueblo lands without federal approval would be invalid. Conversely, if the Pueblos were not Indians, then they had the same rights as any other landowner to sell their property, including a vulnerability to the sharp-dealing of others."[76]

This indeterminacy was amplified by the role of the land grants in Pueblo claims, as the Pueblos "were the only Indians who were allowed to use the treaty [of Guadalupe Hidalgo] in their self-defense."[77] This protection preserved the status of the Pueblos as legal entities that simultaneously bypassed the 1834 Indian Intercourse Act, which would have categorized Pueblos as wards of the state and the non-Pueblo occupation of Pueblo land as a federal offense.[78] In 1863, following the directives of James C. Calhoun, the first U.S. Indian agent in New Mexico, the U.S. government initiated the removal of the Navajo from Dinétah, their homeland, to Bosque Redondo in southern New Mexico, in part from reports of ongoing raids on Pueblo communities. In 1876, years after the territorial court of New Mexico ruled Pueblo tribes ineligible for the "domestic dependent" status afforded to other Native tribes, the U.S. Supreme Court reinforced this perception in *United States v. Joseph*. As had already been happening to Hispanx and Genízarx land grants under U.S. sovereignty, this ruling sanctioned public belief in Pueblo land as freely alienable property. This decision not only clouded the titles by which Pueblo lands could be claimed, but it also aggravated the ongoing crisis of displaced Hispanx and Genízarx squatting on land either shared with or explicitly within the domain of Pueblo tribes. Over the following forty years, scores of Anglo settlers, corporations, speculators, and displaced Hispanx and Genízarx squatters facilitated the transfer of title to thousands of acres of Pueblo land away from Pueblo control. In 1912, as New Mexico acquired statehood, the United States required the newly declared state to "disclaim any interest in Pueblo land."[79] When the U.S. Supreme Court eventually reversed *Joseph* the following year with *United States v. Sandoval*, Pueblo peoples became reracialized as "wards of the state" and their lands were placed under the jurisdiction of the federal government, though they were allowed to attempt to reacquire lands that had been previously sold.

Underwriting both decisions, as Ebright, Hendricks, and Hughes note, was the presumption that "all the pueblos had at one time received written land grants from Spanish and Mexican authorities" and that all Pueblos were minimally entitled to four square leagues.[80] *Sandoval* in particular had the ironically devastating effect of unsettling the roughly twelve thousand non-Indian titles that had accumulated on Pueblo land. As a response, the United States passed the Pueblo Lands Act in 1924 with the mandate to establish a Pueblo lands board to review all non-Indian claims, execute surveys, and hold hearings to determine ownership. Despite the best efforts of its initial supporters, such as John Collier, the Pueblo Lands Board consistently favored non-Pueblo claims, completely abandoned the question of water rights, and entrenched a sizeable residence of non-Pueblo occupants on Pueblo land. As a result, the Pueblos "lost far more valuable land at the hands of the U.S. government, and especially the U.S. courts, within eighty years of the establishment of U.S. rule than they had under a quarter of a millennium of Spanish and Mexican rule."[81]

In *Fight Back*'s penultimate poem-prose piece, "Our Homeland, A National Sacrifice Area," Simon Ortiz notes how the "Aacqumeh hanoh had never seen thieves like the Mericano before. They were so shrewd, talkative, even helpful, and so friendly they didn't look like thieves."[82] Unlike the Spaniard, who "was never the outright killer and thief that he was before the revolt," the "Mericano stole unto the land, claiming it, [and] the people didn't even feel like anything was being taken away from them."[83] For Ortiz, the imposition of U.S. mercantile capital operates as the mechanism that renders stealth the violence of settler expropriation. He recalls the legacy of Solomon Bibo, the first Indian trader at Acoma, "a merchant, [who] married one of the women of Aacqu, and he opened his stores to the Pueblo. He and his brother became wealthy and powerful and the people grew indebted to them and dependent." As an interlocutor for Acoma Pueblo's land claims in the ascendant grip of the territorial period's mercantilist forces, Bibo at one time was even leased the entire Acoma grant for thirty years.[84] During this period, the Acqumeh hanoh endured repeated outbreaks of smallpox, famine, drought, and steady land loss.

Ortiz notes how "something called Manifest Destiny . . . ordained" the racialized imposition of U.S. mercantile capital upon the Aacqumeh hanoh "with a religious mission." This mission cascaded upon the Acqumeh hanoh a "stasis that could not name an enemy though surely there was one," a miasma that smothered "most of the memory of that courageous liberation struggle" of 1680.[85] The railroad would become in this context one of the most decisive expressions of the Mericano capture of Acoma labor and land. "The railroad were given grants of land by the U.S. which were Indian lands. Treaties were signed with Indian people who believed that the documents meant U.S. acceptance of their sovereign nations. To the railroads and the system of U.S. society which required capital it was a simple matter of access and right of way."[86] Rather than a mere technical modification to capitalist accumulation, the railroad for Ortiz is bound within a pervasive network of wage labor capture, resource extraction, carceral schooling, and imperial warfare. "As the Santa Fe railroad laid its rails through Aacqumeh hahtse, as well as those of its sister, Kahwaika (Laguna), to the east, it gathered up men and employed them as unskilled labor and scattered them along its route."[87] Boarding schools increased their demand on Acoma youth, timber companies increased demands on forested lands, and agri-business joined the military's and railroad's insatiable demand for water. "After Bluewater Dam was built" in the 1930s, the fields "were worked seasonally by Acoma, Laguna, Navajo, and Indo-Hispanic laborers."[88] In the compulsions of modern U.S. property-based individualism, we see the escalation of the Spanish imperative to divide and conquer taken to its most fanatical extreme, one that cast the Mericano not as a thief or a killer, but rather as "a missionary, merchant, businessman, philanthropist, educator, civil servant, and worker."[89]

For these reasons, Simon Ortiz situates the emergence of atomic warfare and nuclear militarization as a logical consequence of the racial capitalist regime of U.S. settler sovereignty. "It was not strange or out of character that [the people] would awaken that New Mexico morning with an unsettling tremor of light that was the atomic blast at White Sands" desert in Southern New Mexico.[90] The destructive power of nuclear militarization not only is tied to its astonishing capacity to instantaneously annihilate life on massive scales but also results from its economic dispersal across a variety of capitalist industries that range from mineral extraction to infrastructure development and technoscientific knowledge. In this way, U.S. sovereignty's global reign of destruction operates jointly as a regime of production and a regime of sanctioned ignorance—or what Shannon Sullivan and Nancy Tuana call the "epistemology of ignorance" that underlies "issues of race, racism, and white privilege."[91] Simon Ortiz writes that thorough "knowledge was what was always required to live by for Indian people," "but since the Mericano, knowledge has been kept in some hidden place and has been used as a controlling power."[92] For these reasons, "U.S. society" still doesn't "understand the meaning of that strange dawn in 1945" and refuses "to deal with it." In this way, the forms of confidentiality and motivated unknowing that constitute the world-destructive capacities of U.S. statecraft are based on a power that "could destroy in a way that not only had to do with savage and brute force but with the way it would face Indian people upon whose land mining and milling would take place with the question of survival."[93]

SACRIFICE, SURVIVAL, SUBVERSION

Fight Back performs the story power of Acoma survival most notably through the modalities of repetition, interlinguality, and heteroglossia. The collection recodes as sacrifice the ongoing crises of nuclear waste, the destruction of Indigenous landscapes, and the poisoning of Indigenous bodies, as well as the industries of U.S. militarization. Part I of *Fight Back* is titled "Too Many Sacrifices," while part II is defiantly called "No More Sacrifices." Thus in "Our Homeland: A National Sacrifice Area," Ortiz deplores U.S. racial capitalism's figuration of Acoma as a site of slaughter, cruelty, and indifference. "In the national interest, mine operators, oil corporations, utility companies, international energy cartels, and investors sacrificed these men and women" who performed "total and intensive work" because "the New Mexican and national economy required it." He notes how miners die "every month" in the "Grants Uranium Belt area, which is the area between Albuquerque and Gallup." And in Aacqu, there are former miners who walk around crippled, as maimed as if they had been wounded in wartime.[94] As sacrifice, the intersecting industries of U.S. nuclear proliferation become reframed as ritualized acts of consumption of Native life, land, and memory with perilous consequences for human life at the planetary scale.

In this way, by unearthing a critique of the intensified extractive devastation required by U.S. empire, *Fight Back* subsumes apocalyptic logics of racial capitalist sacrifice into a dialogic, prophetic, and creationary web of Acoma story power. In "Returning It Back, You Will Go On," Ortiz writes:

Power companies and corporations
railroads, agribusiness, electronics,
states, cities, towns,
the men and women who work in them,
all of them—all of America—
take and takes from the land and People
The land lets you.
Kudrawaa yah ahni.
The People let you.
Kudrawaa yah ahni.
But America must give back.
That is the only way the land will regenerate.
That is the only way the People will be freed.
When you plant something,
watch it grow, nourish it,
so carefully, so gently, sing, talk,
watch it grow, harvest it,
prepare it, pray, speak about it
to others, remind them, watch your children grow,
use and eat it and return it back.
With great care and planning,
with compassion and love,
you will grow, you will go on,
and you will plant again
and the plant will grow.
Returning it back, returning
it back, you will go on, life will go on.
That's what the People say.
That's what the land says.[95]

Through repetition and dialogic modes of address, *Fight Back* depicts the modern land/labor separation as a regime of unending and self-decimating extraction. In contradistinction, Pueblo Story Power figures land not as a passive object of representation and possession, but rather in a co-constituting kinship network of speech and sustenance with the people. The interconnected character of land and labor assumed in story power then reflects the fluid interdependence of forms of life and their interactions in space-time bundles that reflect incommensurably emplaced sites of memory. As such, the creation story of the Aacqumeh hanoh relayed in *Fight Back* is both an event in the past and a continual reckoning with knowledge useful for survival under apocalyptic conditions of existence. "It is certain that the people have known change for a long time," Ortiz writes, "because there is always change. . . . In the oral tradition, war, crisis, and famine are spoken about . . . The oral tradition does not ignore bad times and mistakes that people have made throughout their history. And it is told in mythic proportion in order to impress upon those hearing that there are important lessons, values, and principles to be learned."[96]

As a struggle with the forces of overlaid colonization, subversion becomes a powerful lesson learned and implemented in Pueblo Story Power. In *Almanac of the Dead*, Silko enfolds the legacy of Geronimo, the medicine man turned anticolonial insurgent from the Chiricahua Apache people in the late nineteenth century, into a framed narrative of insurgent cooperativity with the land, for "it was the land itself . . . that protected native people."[97] Considered by many to be the leader of the last Native American fighting band to formally capitulate to the U.S. military in 1886, Geronimo battled Mexican and U.S. settler forces and became nationally renowned for his persistent escape from state capture. While public knowledge narrates Geronimo as dying a prisoner of war in 1909 in the Mt. Vernon barracks in Alabama, in *Almanac* Geronimo is a subject "they never did catch," someone who got away.[98] The power of Geronimo's escape story "did not run in a line for the horizon but circled and spiraled instead like a red-tailed hawk." In its important movement, it recodes the motivated ineptitude of settler perception: "The elders used to argue that this was one of the most dangerous qualities of the Europeans: Europeans suffered a sort of blindness to the world." This blindness not only provoked a terror toward the land on behalf of settler society, but it was also seized upon by "strategists for both the Yaquis and the Apaches [who] quickly learned to make use of the Europeans' inability to perceive unique details in the landscape."[99] This inability to perceive the life of difference enabled "three different Apache warriors called Geronimo [to range] across the Sonoran desert," for "once the whites had a name for a thing, they seemed unable ever again to recognize the thing in itself."[100]

Given that the U.S. Army relies on photographs to track down Geronimo, settler blindness in this account is mediated by the modern fetish of truth sanctioned by photographic capture. Yet, as one of the Geronimos named White Ledge states, "these traces . . . preserved on paper became confused even for white people, who believed they understood these tracks so well."[101] Story power in this way installs a temporality of critique that is attuned to the technological mediation of modern violence and its paradigmatic confusion of mediated information for lived experience. It names the violence of settler modernity as confusing intimacy with technologies of mediation as knowledge of the subjects of mediation. As a result, the subversive power of Geronimo resides not as a lesson in militant strategy but as a story that performed the ways in which "the world the whites brought with them would not last [and] . . . be swept away in a giant gust of wind."[102]

CONCLUSION

On May 16, 1969, Paul Bernal of Taos Pueblo testified in a hearing before the Subcommittee on Indian Affairs over the title of the Taos Blue Lake. As the ancestral place of Taos Pueblo origination, the Blue Lake was appropriated into the Carson National Forest by the U.S. government in 1906. In what would spawn an ultimately successful struggle, the Taos Pueblo began a vigorous legal, historical, and public campaign to reclaim Blue Lake and depose Forest Service jurisdiction over the area in 1933.[103] For roughly the following thirty years, Taos Pueblo challenged numerous attempts made by the Forest Service to restrict Pueblo access to its own place of origin for its yearlong series of ceremonial practice. These restrictions worked instead to make the land available to the consumption of the timber, mining, and tourist industries fostered by the U.S. state. Paul Bernal's testimony—taken the year before President Richard Nixon would sign the bill that would grant trust title to 48,000 acres comprising Blue Lake and its access routes to the Pueblo—succinctly encapsulates the story power central to the Pueblo's victory.

> In all of its programs the Forest Service proclaims the supremacy of man over nature; we find this viewpoint contrary to the realities of the natural world and to the nature of conservation. Our tradition and our religion require our people to adapt their lives and activities to our natural surroundings so that men and

> nature mutually support the life common to both. The idea that man must subdue nature and bend its processes to his purposes is repugnant to our people . . .
>
> We are probably the only citizens of the United States who are required to practice our religion under a "permit" from the Government. This is not religious freedom as it is guaranteed by the Constitution. Moreover, the permit covers only a portion of the Rio Pueblo watershed, while our religious practices take place also in the remaining area of the watershed. Outside the permit area we are at the sufferance of the Forest Service . . . Our religion is based upon the unity of man with nature in the Rio Pueblo watershed.[104]

Bernal's testimony beats at the heart of the Pueblo's discursive strategy by which it was able to leverage such a landmark political concession. By recoding the modern category of religion and religious liberty, Bernal reclaimed religious, constitutional, and conservationist discourses to enable Taos Pueblo to continue the autonomous dignity of its kinship with its place of origin and creation. This reclamation also fostered an alliance with politicians across liberal-conservative spectrums, conservationists, and civil rights activists, one that brought the constitutional enshrinement of religious liberty to bear upon questions of labor and economic production. Carla Apachito, Bernal's niece, recalls: "Before Blue Lake, a lot of our people were not as educated and knowledgeable about the government itself and how Native people fit into that . . . We live in a spiritual world and a spiritual work in progress every day . . . it's not Sundays. It's not Mondays, Wednesdays, or Fridays, it's seven days a week, 365 days a year."[105] Pueblo Story Power in this register operates as an integrated aesthetic, activist, economic, political, and spiritual labor that stresses the situated interconnection of life itself.

In this chapter, I have pondered the power of Pueblo endurance as a storytelling practice that refuses the land/labor separation underwriting multiple modalities of settler colonial occupation. In this way, I have sought to read Pueblo Indian projects of literary and legal representation as a means of dismantling the revolutionary codes of the possessive self that undergird modern capitalist production and liberal statist domination. The yield not only clears a place for considering Spanish genealogies as a long, murderous pursuit for settler belonging in the Americas, it also prompts a consideration of the ways in which Spain was never one. The ruse of its geopolitical purity has always been sustained by a coercive, salvational quest to forcefully convert nonmodern modes of prayer, knowledge, and economy into the monarchical/modern modes of reason ritualized through Roman Catholic dogma. Pueblo Story Power remains a critique of Spain's monotheistic ocularcentrism, logocentrism, and anthropocentrism that is embedded in modern alienated capitalist individualism. Pueblo Story Power translates modern individualism as peak alienation, amnesia, cruelty, and destruction.

In addition to Allen, Silko, and Simon Ortiz, a number of contemporary Pueblo writers and artists continue to perform story power. Poetic work by Wendy Rose (Hopi and Miwok); Parsino Carlos Peynetsa (Zuni and Isleta Pueblo); Sara Marie Ortiz, daughter of Simon Ortiz (Acoma); and Nora Naranjo-Morse (Tewa, Santa Clara Pueblo) all disrupt the erasure of Native American labor in the U.S. national imaginary. In the process, they revitalize a series of critical paradigms from which to think the continuity of Indigenous land tenure through a spirituality of labor that unsettles modern politics. In the next chapter, I explore how this labor uprises escape stories by which to repoliticize the indigeneity of the Genízarx diaspora.

CHAPTER TWO

THE MEXICAN-AMERICAN WAR HAS NEVER ENDED

Escape Stories and the Genízarx Diaspora in New Mexico

As La Alianza Federal de Mercedes expanded its presence in the public culture of the radical social movements in the late 1960s, Laguna Pueblo writer Leslie Marmon Silko pursued a degree in American Indian Law at the University of New Mexico (UNM). Born in Albuquerque in 1948 of mixed Anglo, Mexican, and Laguna descent, Silko was raised on the Laguna Pueblo Reservation in eastern New Mexico. At UNM, when she realized that "we weren't going to get our land back with a lawsuit," she dropped out and began a career in creative writing.[1] Her first novel, *Ceremony*, was published in 1977, and its glowing popular and critical reception ushered Silko into a pivotal role in twentieth-century Native American literature.[2] While the long trajectory of Silko's writing and cultural production may seem incidental to La Alianza's struggle for land reclamation, it in fact bears profound relevance for rethinking paradoxes of Latinx indigeneity within the conjunctures of detribalization, resurgence, cooperativity, and storytelling that attend formations Genízarx community in Spanish and Mexican land grants.

Across her vast literary output, Silko consistently interfaces the politics of compulsory texuality and colonial territoriality with Native Story Power in order to undermine the racial logics that underwrite settler dominance in the hemisphere. "Books were and still are weapons in the ongoing struggle for the Americas," she observes more pointedly in her essay "Books: Notes on Mixtec and Maya Screenfolds, Picture Books of Preconquest Mexico." She makes this point by referencing how "the great libraries of the Americas were destroyed in 1540 because the Spaniards feared the political and spiritual powers of books authored by the indigenous people."[3] In doing so, Silko strikes a robust critique of the anti-Indian racisms that differentially animate Latin American postcolonial nationalisms and U.S. imperial sovereignty, one that centers alphabetical literacy as an insidious mechanism sanctioning settler regimes of violence and occupation. Walter Mignolo has named this mechanism as the "tyranny of the alphabet" to explain the presumed superiority of alphabetic and textual modes of writing/communication under colonial modernity.[4] In his analysis, Mignolo differentiates between "literacy" and "Literacy." The former operates as a "basic competence of reading and writing as well as the domains of ideas and values that in Western civilization have been attributed to alphabetic writing and the book."[5] The latter signifies "any kind of graphic, semio-linguistic interactions as well as to the respective conceptualization regulating the range of discursive practices of a given community or group."[6] This differentiation allows us to name the ways in which literacy under Spanish colonialism and the multiple regimes of Latin American statecraft operates, in the words of Marisol de la Cadena, "as a benevolent technology of improvement, the historical thrust of which has been to programmatically let Indians die: *Indio leido, Indio perdido* (a literate Indian is a lost Indian)."[7] De la Cadena argues further that while compulsive literacy enables Latin American states to phrase modern writing and history "as progress, protection, and cultural improvement," it also denies Indigenous peoples the right to "ontological difference" grounded in kinship relations with webs of human and more-than-human life.[8] In particular, de la Cadena identifies how modern historicism—that is, the presumption that the disciplinary prose and forms of history grants factual knowledge to counter the supposed obfuscations of myth, fantasy, and imagination in order to progress to liberation—operates as the "silent hegemony of western forms of knowledge."[9]

In a cognate though distinct manner, the colonial denial of Indigenous ontological incommensurability has led Audra Simpson to term U.S. sovereignty as a *language game*.[10] The term highlights the reliance of U.S. sovereignty on what Reid Gómez names as "a strategic manipulation of written evidence and narration, specifically tribal roll numbers; passports; and historical, governmental, and ethnographic narrative documents."[11] Yet unlike the modern Mestizo nations that sought to ground its statecraft in an *indigenismo* of a disappeared Native past, the discursive practices of state bureaucracy yield the origin story of the

U.S. state, disclosing a power manifested in permanent war, perpetual conquest, and unceasing devotion to commodified value. This has led Manu Karaka in his study of the colonial logics of the transcontinental railroad to name the U.S. state not as an organic appendage of a nation but rather as a corporate enforcer over a multiracial hierarchy of captive labor.[12] Such an entity, in Gómez's words, "feigns omnipotence and omniscience, and like the passive voice, it pretends it has no subject but exists in some state of primordial order" that is "guaranteed by colonial historicist, religious, and scientific explanations." Despite their spatial, temporal, and cultural differences, the embrace of compulsive textuality, literacy, and alphabetization that mark settler sovereignties across the Americas has produced a singular world "where language and discovery are predetermined," a world that relies on the "idea of the Indian (as a racial Other, with a single anthropological, religious, or scientific origin story)." Such a world, for Gómez, "serves as a limiting factor to narrative and analysis" not only in the study of Native and Indigenous sovereignty movements and forms but also for a wide range of indigeneities that fall from the purview of state recognition.[13]

Silko's work centers the continuance of Pueblo peoples on their homelands in New Mexico with storytelling modalities that remake the territorial and textual apparatus of Spanish and Mexican land grants into a technology of writing that halts the land grab of U.S. sovereignty. Founded as a mechanism for empire building, the Spanish land grant system existed alongside other institutions of colonial violence such as the *encomienda*, the *repartimiento*, and the *congregaciones* (missions).[14] These institutions enabled Spanish colonists to occupy arable lands and appropriate systems of irrigation from Pueblo Indians; they also provided the means by which the Spanish Christianized and coerced captive Pueblo and Plains Indians into systems of conscript and slave labor to generate tribute for the Crown. In Silko's critique of the lettered confines of settler sovereign time, she connects the labor of writing and the power of books more directly to the question of Spanish and Mexican land grant law.

> The laws were in books. The king of Spain had granted the Laguna Pueblo people their land. The Laguna Pueblo people knew their land was protected by a land grant document from the king of Spain. The Anglo-Americans who swarmed into the New Mexico Territory after 1848 carried with them no such documents. The Pueblo people fared better than other tribes simply because of these documents. The land grant documents alerted the Pueblo people to the value of the written word; the old books of international law favored the holders

> of the royal land grants. So, very early, the Pueblo people realized the power of written words and books to secure legitimate title to tribal land.[15]

Of importance, Silko's comments on the power of books points to Spanish land grant law not as a one-way imposition of colonial power, but as a textual apparatus translated *into* the means of Pueblo and detribalized Indigenous survival. In this way, land grant law is refashioned into a negotiated framework through which Indigenous life may survive and proliferate within a settler political modernity whose genocidal impulses are only compounded—and not mitigated—by U.S. sovereignty. Silko offers a "Literacy," in Mignolo's words, that transforms the terms and frameworks of domination into mechanisms of escape.

In this chapter, I turn to Silko's *Almanac of the Dead* to argue for the ways that escape stories perform a particular power by which to disarticulate Chicanx narratives of *mestizaje* from the colonial politics of literacy, a move that allows us to make visible the formative role that the Genízarx diaspora plays in La Alianza's labors of land reclamation. A focus on escape enables a naming of the ways in which patriarchal cultural nationalist narratives of mestizaje generate cartographies of containment that subjugate knowledge of Genízarx movement and presence within La Alianza's use of Indohispanx mestizaje and its multiple counternarratives of land reclamation. Through Silko's story power, we can see how uprising escape within the indigeneity of the Genízarx diaspora bears profound implications for how scholars, artists, and activists produce knowledge about what is now called the U.S.-Mexico borderlands.

Mestizaje, notable less for its uniformity than for its profound heterogeneity across and beyond the hemisphere, is premised on the idealization of racial, cultural, and social mixing between white Europeans and various Indigenous (and other nonwhite) social formations. The concept and practice emerged as a pivotal process in the formation of the Spanish colonial caste system in the Americas. Under Spanish rule, Ben Vinson notes, racial mixture "helped toss societies out of balance during the 1500s, a century of rapid and furious change."[16] In response, "Spanish bureaucrats, legal minds, governors, businessmen, and plutocrats responded" by using the "primary lexicon and instruments that they had available. They put pen to page."[17] Through text-based authority, the Spanish occupation of New Mexico and the Americas more broadly constructed a caste system to generate a racial and patriarchal hierarchy that valued whiteness and male honor as qualifications for property ownership and civic rights. At the top, those categorized as Españoles had either newly immigrated from Spain or claimed two parents of "pure" Spanish descent. "Mestizos" and "Mestizas," those legally categorized as being of Indian and Spanish descent, were positioned just below the Españoles and represented a much larger portion of Spanish colonial society. Ramón Gutiérrez indicates that many Spanish and Mexican elites were classed as Mestizx, and both the Español and Mestizx categories held *vecino* status—that is, they were landowning (and probably slave-owning) Christian men with full voting rights in town councils.[18] Underneath and always threatening Mestizx status was the precarious formation of Genízaro and Genízara detribalized Indians. The precise definition of Genízarx varies among scholars, but most affirm that it refers to Pueblo or Plains Indians captured by Spanish colonists. As Indigenous captives, Genízarx subjects were often converted to Christianity, acculturated to Spanish norms, and then put into slavery and servitude for colonial elites.[19] Below the Genízarx caste, Pueblo Indians were labeled as *indios* and categorized as "both wards of the Crown as well as property owners with acquired rights at the time of conquest."[20] This categorization worked in contradictory ways. It simultaneously enabled and nullified the colonial usurpation of Pueblo Indian lands by restricting "Pueblos' acquired rights to those lands they farmed at the time of the Spanish arrival."[21] This policy, according to Alfonso Ortiz, "unwittingly gave to all of the Pueblos except the Hopis a set of political institutions that eventually enabled them to cope successfully not only with the Spanish themselves, but with the Mexicans and, later, the Anglo-Americans as well."[22] The term *Negro* was imposed on enslaved and emancipated African peoples. Plains Indians, occupying the bottom of the Spanish caste system, were catalogued as "gentiles," or *indios bárbaros*.[23] At once upholding and undermining Spain's racial and gendered regime, the economy of Indian captivity enabled Spanish colonialism to constitute whiteness with property ownership, slaveholding, and male honor mediated through an "intercultural traffic in women."[24] The Spanish racial hierarchy was therefore beset with contradictions regarding the politics of interracial sexual intimacy. These racialized and gendered contradictions provide the conditions of possibility for Genízarx captivity to operate as "an important but overlooked source of mestizaje in the borderlands."[25]

In Spain's racial order prior to the Pueblo Revolt of 1680, Genízarx subjects were a landless servant class of Mestizx and detribalized Indians concentrated in the Barrio de Analco of Santa Fe. Spanish elites depicted Genízarx subjects as "Indians of pagan ancestry who owned no land, lacked the means to earn a subsistence, owned no horses, carried no firearms, lived like animals, spoke a twisted form of Spanish, and were characterized by their depraved habits."[26] In this setting, those cast as Genízarx were often conscripted as auxiliary soldiers in Spain's colonial army and played an important function in rampant slave raids on Pueblo and Plains Indian tribes.[27]

As discussed in the previous chapter, the 1680 Pueblo Indian Revolt radically altered the racial and territorial administration of mestizaje in New Mexico. Understood as a simultaneous insurgency of Pueblo and Genízarx Indians, with support from Apache and Navajo allies, the revolt effectively exiled the Spanish colonial elite from New Mexico for thirteen years. It is a public and scholarly commonplace to historicize this period of emancipation, which saw the destruction of Spanish colonial records and Christian iconography, as lasting until the Spanish "reconquest" of 1693. Yet its insurrectionary effects reframed New Mexico's colonial function over the following two centuries as that of a "frontier outpost to preserve the outer limits of their empire in order to protect the rich interior from competing powers."[28] The most formidable competition in this context came not from the imperialist designs of other European empires but from the long-standing resistance of Pueblo Indians and the emergent territorial dominance of the Comanche, Navajo, Ute, and Jicarilla Apache Indians and their relentless attacks on Spanish settlements. Emerging in this violent dialectic of colonial territoriality and Indigenous insurgency, Genízarx ejido settlements provided "a buffer for the colony against Indian attacks and . . . an outlet for the increasingly poor, landless class, which thereby became propertied and self-sufficient."[29]

Institutionalized in this context of colonial warfare and Indigenous territorial struggle Genízarx land grant tenure arose, in the words of Dunbar-Ortiz, "not from a change in colonial policy but from the particular situation of the colony, especially continued Indian resistance."[30] Genízarx occupation of ejido grants thus represented a complex tangle of colonial expansion and Indigenous revitalization.[31] On one hand, the land grant system expanded Spain's imperial network of territorial and racial control. Genízarx settlers' acquisition of land implied their ascendance in the Spanish racial hierarchy to vecino status; accordingly, they complied with the colonial project of Native land dispossession, which granted them land on condition that they defend the colony from Plains Indian attacks. On the other hand, the occupation of *ejido* lands by a largely derided Genízarx class required the cultivation of sophisticated and illicit trading relations with both Pueblo and Plains Indian tribes as a way of supplementing the communal and subsistence-based land tenure system of the ejidos. In these borderland contexts, "genízaros continued to play an active role with the Indians and the commerce of the Plains. Their employment as *comancheros* (traders), interpreters, and *ciboleros* (Buffalo hunters) continued until the 1870s. The frontier settlements of the genízaros also attracted some Comanche and Kiowa settlers who provided an important link with the Comanche."[32]

As Spanish rule conceded to a variety of late nineteenth- and early twentieth-century postcolonial Latin American nationalisms, mestizaje became rearticulated as a privileged icon and figure of liberal citizenship. The rise of mestizaje in the emergence of Mexican liberalism occurred in tandem with abolition of the Spanish racial caste system. With the Plan de Iguala, the newly declared Mexican republic at once legally dissolved the caste titles and granted full citizenship to Genízarxs and Pueblo Indians.[33] Rather than strengthening the multitribal network of Plains and Pueblo Indian relations that sustained Genízarx settlement, the republic's influence on Indian life "consisted largely of confusing Indian land title, ignoring the illegal taking of Pueblo land, and responding passively when Indian boundaries were violated."[34] While certain Genízarx settlers profited from the reinvigorated rationale for the usurpation of Pueblo lands, others faced the threat of disappearance into abstract liberal citizenship. Doris Avery writes that citizenship "brought up new challenges . . . over the issue of individual land ownership, particularly in Abiquiu where the genízaros' community land grant of 1754 became vulnerable to privatization."[35] However, she notes that when faced with incursion into their common lands, Abiquiú Genízarxs implemented tactics similar to those used by Genízarxs in Belén in 1750: "they asserted Abiquiu's identity as an Indian pueblo."[36] In this way, even as the abolition of the caste system enabled Genízarx subjects to achieve nominal empowerment through Mexico's burgeoning liberalism, the stigma of servitude, treachery, and illegitimacy continued to circumscribe their social mobility and to foster continued, though ambivalent, Indian identification.

The subsequent colonial imposition of U.S. law and privatization of property that followed the Mexican-American War of 1846–48 relied on nationalized historical narratives that cast the subsistence-based and Indigenous aspects of ejido land grant territorial forms as "undeveloped" and "informal" and as the ancient remnants of a decrepit colonial order.[37] This process required a dismantling of the subsistence-based political economy of ejido land grant formations and their customary practices of communal ownership of grazing, hunting, mining, and timber lands.[38] In its stead, U.S. sovereignty imposed a distinct and intensified colonial process of accumulation in which the value of land was defined by modern capitalist ownership that emphasized market exchange, resource extraction, and individual or corporate ownership rather than communal occupancy.[39] During the time in which New Mexico has been under U.S. rule, "dominant American culture (behaviors and values which operate in great part on an unconscious level) and legal system (based on juridical prescription and precedent) have viewed land and water as chattel to be bought and sold at will. So strong is this view as to erase or at least distort appreciation of subsistence farming."[40] The collective struggle for survival of Genízarx ejidos—such as Abiquiú, Tierra Amarilla, San Joaquín, Tomé, and Belén—demonstrates how the ascendance of U.S. regimes of private property in New Mexico resulted in a massive, racialized redistribution of land grant lands to Anglo settlers, corporations, and U.S. federal agencies such as the Department of Defense and the Forest Service. Among its many deleterious effects, U.S. sovereignty unevenly repositioned generations of former Mexican and Genízarx settlers under the coercion of migrant wage labor and federal and state welfare and social services.

This racialized and gendered displacement radically interrupted the land-based network of Pueblo-Genízarx relations. As a result, the successive colonization of New Mexico imposed divergent trajectories of racialization that continue to shape Pueblo and Genízarx histories of land adjudication under U.S. law. Due to what U.S. military and governmental figures saw as the sedentary nature of Pueblo communities during the late nineteenth and early twentieth centuries, Pueblo Indian status under U.S. law vacillated between citizenship and the dominant category of "domestic dependents," which remains imposed upon the majority of Native tribes in the United States in order to grant the federal government jurisdiction over all tribal land. Genízarx land grant communities, on the other hand, were immediately conferred citizenship by virtue of the Treaty of Guadalupe Hidalgo, a status that facilitated the "conception of individual, freely-alienable property rights [to be] imposed upon a land-dependent culture in which common land ownership was vitally important to community's continued survival."[41] Ironically, while steeped in modern anti-Indian racism—which presumes backwardness, paganism, intellectual deficiency, and lack of civilized maturation on behalf of tribal peoples—the status of "domestic dependent" enabled a mechanism for the "special legal protection from their new government or compensation for the wrongful taking of property."[42] This irony is compounded when we consider how the assignation of citizenship to Genízarx land grant heirs as "Spanish American" worked as a mechanism of dispossession through recognition—a mechanism, in other words, that reduced communal property rights to "individual members of Hispanic communities, rather than a collective unit to which sovereign status has been attributed."[43] The Spanish American nomenclature served as a key basis for the production of the imperial myth of the "Spanish Southwest" that managed New Mexico's overlaid regimes of white patriarchy under U.S. sovereignty. The textual inscription of this myth in academic, public, legal, and literary registers naturalized U.S. sovereignty and private property relations by framing New Mexico as a "land of enchantment" inhabited by Anglo, Spanish American, and Pueblo Indian peoples.[44] In this context, Spanish American identification was premised on a disavowal of mestizaje and relation with Mexico as a strategy of assimilative passing into whiteness for the protections of U.S. citizenship.

As the United States required the dismantling of mestizaje for the legitimacy of its imperial sovereignty, a number of differing articulations of mestizaje proliferated in the republics of Brazil, Peru, Cuba, and Mexico within a discursive field seeking to counter the social logics of U.S. imperialism and its idealization of scientific doctrines of racial purity and hypo-descent.[45] Nancy Appelbaum, Anne Macpherson, and Karin Alejandra Rosemblatt collectively point out that the varied iterations of mestizaje across Latin America, in figuring a mixed-raced subject as its ideal world historical agent, importantly reworked the hegemonic fastening of whiteness to modernity and citizenship.[46] Yet despite the articulation of anti-imperialist social imaginaries, Latin American nationalist discourses of mestizaje often reproduced many key assumptions of the Euroamerican powers they sought to counter. That is, even as discourses of mestizaje claimed to transcend conditions of racialized inequality, a number of critical race scholars routinely articulate its institutionalization and circulation in tandem with multiple strategies of colonial elimination, exclusion, assimilation, and hierarchization of Black, Indigenous, and other non-Mestizo/a difference.[47] In Mexico, one such strategy was indigenismo, which facilitated a push for nationalist unification alongside mestizaje as a solution to the social fragmentation that accompanied the revolution years (1910–20). Throughout the twentieth century, indigenismo was launched through rural educational programs, agrarian reforms, and state-sponsored projects of nationalized cultural production that sought to stylize the futurity of the Mestizo nation with appropriated Indigenous iconography. As a policy of racialized containment and appropriation that simultaneously marginalized people contemporarily marked as Indian, indigenismo also worked through strategies of antiblack and anti-Chinese racism.[48] In doing so, indigenismo recoded a hemispheric structure of colonial anti-Indian racialization that denoted "Indian" with fundamental cultural and biological inferiorities, an essential "backwardness" in progressive time, and a general incompatibility with the rationality of Western political frameworks of representative liberal democracy. Notably, this recoding was secured through "explicitly acculturationist" tactics of alphabetical literacy that "included promoting Spanish over indigenous languages."[49]

In the late 1960s, the terms "Chicano" and "Chicana" became retooled from the oral usage of working-class Mexican migrant communities across the borderlands as a nomenclature of political critique and racial identification that sought to interrupt the settler nativism of U.S. citizenship and stoke a decolonial historical consciousness of Mexican American racial, linguistic, and cultural difference in relation to peoples in Mexico and across the Americas. As the Chicanx movement proliferated across organizations, creative texts, and burgeoning academic studies, iconographies and lexicons of Mexican mestizaje and indigenismo proved to be instrumental to the movement's critical labor of fomenting a potent counterdiscourse to the colonial devaluation of Mexican and Native life and rights under the white supremacist regime of U.S. sovereignty.[50] In doing so, indigenismo and mestizaje patterned Chicanx indigeneity to invoke "the Spanish conquest of Mexico, singling out in particular the fall of the Aztec empire as the primal scene of Chicana/o identity and as a paradigm for the subsequent conquest of the territory now known as the U.S. Southwest."[51]

Indigenismo and mestizaje would also come to imbue what are now seen as the prevailing tropes and imaginaries of Chicanx mestizaje: the cultural nationalist imaginary of Aztlán and the gendered and sexualized figure of La Malinche. While Aztlán is considered a mythopoetic imaginary of the Chicanx homeland whose borders roughly correspond with the territory annexed by the United States after the Mexican-American War, the term would also inform "El Plan Espiritual de Aztlán," a geosocial platform of Chicanx cultural nationalist unification drafted in the Denver Youth Conference in 1969. Together, they would provide the nationalist framework and symbolic homeland for Chicanx historical consciousness.[52] *Yo Soy Joaquín* is the poetic counterpart to Aztlán that depicts the rise of a unified Chicanx people through the masculinized figure of Joaquín. Many critics have noted how Joaquín's hybridized identity acts as a metonym for a larger Chicanx political class through an indigenismo of Aztec and Mayan imagery.[53]

The figure of La Malinche provides a prism to the gendered politics of Chicanx cultural nationalism. La Malinche is one of many names ascribed to the Nahua woman who, while enslaved, became a translator and interlocutor for Hernán Cortés, the infamous Spanish conquistador known for leading the war that toppled Aztec dominion over Mesoamerica in the sixteenth century. She was a figure written over and about in the colonial record but who herself left no direct expression of her experience in the archive.[54] La Malinche's labor of translation between the Spanish and the Aztecs has come to be scapegoated in a number of Mexican and Chicanx nationalist narratives for mediating the fall of the Aztecs through speech that transgressed intercultural formations of patriarchal control over maternity.[55] Under Chicanx nationalism, for example, La Malinche became another way of enforcing a gendered division of radicalism under patriarchal community by identifying feminist, gay, and queer subjects as *vendidos*—that is, sellouts—to the Anglo-American order.[56] Her supposed betrayal has been repurposed by feminist critiques of both Mexican and Chicanx nationalism to explore the role that gender, sexuality, and language play in disciplining the social and discursive agency of racialized women.[57]

While La Alianza's use of Indohispanx circulated in tandem with the imaginaries and tropes of Chicanx mestizaje, it actually emerged prior to the embrace of Chicanx nomenclature as an attempt to unsettle the colonial production of New Mexico's Spanish American / Hispanx / Hispanic political class. The term Indohispano/Indo-Hispano was recovered through Reies López Tijerina's extensive foray into archival research on a number of compilations of Spanish colonial civic and territorial law such as *Las Leyes de los Reinos de Las Indias* (The Laws of the Indies) and *Las Siete Partidas* (The Seven-Part Code). Ironically, while the Spanish American political class celebrated a pure Spanish heritage, these legal codes had lived in prior obscurity during the protracted adjudication and dispossession process of New Mexican land grants during the late nineteenth and early twentieth centuries. In its retort to the historical suppression that accompanied the broken treaty governance of the United States, the recovery of Indohispanx nomenclature enabled the movement to renarrate the genealogies of Genízarx land grant heirs in terms that violated both U.S. and Mexican regimes of Mestizx and Native recognition. In open defiance of the U.S. state's public romance with Spanish heritage, Tijerina would declare the Indohispanx subject born in the Americas on October 9, 1514, as the "new breed" of mixed Spanish and Indian descent sanctioned by the authority of Spanish colonial government. "These land grants are scattered throughout South

America," Tijerina told a group of University of Colorado students in 1967. "And as our lands were taken away here in New Mexico, in Mexico [they] were taken away from the Indians . . . by blue-eyed Spaniards, rich millionaires from Mexico. In Argentina the same, in Brazil, in Chilé, Peru—all throughout South America. . . . These common lands, these lands that we are claiming belong, not to individuals, they belong to pueblos, town councils, villas and cities."[58]

The subordination of the Genízarx diaspora in Chicanx and Latinx studies often occurs in narratives attempting to parse out the difference between Chicanx and Indohispanx mestizaje. For example, while outlining La Alianza's coalitional labor of land reclamation, George Mariscal notes that La Alianza's organizing "was not so much a 'Chicano nationalism' as it was an Indo-Hispano nationalism founded on the cultural particularities of New Mexican culture and history. . . . Tijerina and the Alianza, far from the major urban centers, promoted an Indo-Hispano identity that coincided with and indirectly contributed to an emergent Chicano/a militancy in the cities."[59] Because of this shared labor, Lee Bebout adds, within various "sites of Chicano discourse" Indohispanx became "interchangeable" with Chicanx and "provided the potential for a broader citizenry in the future Chicano nation."[60] Thus while bearing distinct discursive genealogies, both Indohispanx and Chicanx mestizaje operate as political and cultural representations that sought to counter historic and contemporary forms of U.S. white supremacy with strategic rearticulations of Spanish and Mexican colonial discourses and frameworks.

Despite this interchange with Chicanx mestizaje, La Alianza's demand for land is contained by a historiographical propensity to confine Indohispanx mestizaje to a "rigid, legalistic history" that exclusively applies to New Mexican land grant heirs.[61] In this narrative, Indohispanx mestizaje becomes dissociated from the vexed indigeneity of Genízarx land grant tenure and is instead situated as an extension of a regionally distinct and idiosyncratic context of New Mexican race relations overwhelmingly known for fetishizing a "Spanish American" purity and disavowing mestizaje and other genealogies of mixed Indigenous descent. Framed in a relation of distinction from and similarity to the emergence of the "Mexican American" political class in California, Texas, Arizona, Colorado, the "Spanish American" nomenclature is traced to a diversity of causes in Chicanx historiography. In addition to negotiating the ways U.S. anti-Mexican racism coupled "Mexican prejudice with Spanish affect," New Mexico's spatial distance from Mexico is frequently cited.[62] From this, Chicanx and Latinx studies take it as a conceptual commonplace that Indohispanx mestizaje supposedly reflects an uncritical embrace of colonial law to the detriment of Native and Indigenous sovereignty. For these reasons, it is assumed that "many land grant activists could not fathom claims to Chicano and indigenous identities."[63] As Chicana/o movement scholar and activist Carlos Muñoz asserts:

> Tijerina's objectives were restricted to the land grants issue, a struggle that he did not originally place in the context of a quest for Chicano identity and political power. Although Tijerina himself was of Mexican descent, his constituency was largely from the "Hispano" rural class. Some were direct descendents of the colonizers who were given title to land by the king of Spain in the territory which became the state of New Mexico. Tijerina and his followers referred to themselves as indo-hispanos and not as Chicanos. Like New Mexicans in general, they de-emphasized their Mexican roots.[64]

Muñoz's comments set in relief a nationalist geography that frames New Mexico in general—and the emergence of La Alianza as a formation of the Genízarx diaspora, in particular—as regionalized and containable objects of knowledge in relation to other Chicanx "centers" within the annexed Mexican and Native lands of the U.S. southwest. Therefore, while La Alianza predated and also actively constructed Aztlán imaginaries, the prevalence of Chicanx mestizaje would ultimately cohere a distinctly nationalist geography that inhibits knowledge of the Genízarx diaspora. This is made possible by a historical narrative in which New Mexico is understood by its geographical isolation (both *within* the United States and *from* Mexico) as well as its inhabitation by a "Spanish American" population who had come to reject its association with all things "Mexican" and "Indian" in order to mythologize pure ties to a "Spanish" colonial past for U.S. belonging. Chicanx mestizaje, according to this script, wagered Aztlán and La Malinche as an intervention in the assimilatory politics of the broader Mexican American generation. La Alianza's deployment of Indohispanx mestizaje, while formative, is nonetheless seen as part of an overly legalistic and religious counterhistory to the assimilative discourses that sanction the Spanish American political class in New Mexico. As such, this regionalization figures New Mexico and La Alianza with the capacity to be known as either overparticular (i.e., La Alianza / New Mexico have their own sets of singularities that don't travel to the larger Chicanx movement), or as particularity in a relation of sameness in the U.S. Southwest (i.e., La Alianza is just like other Chicanx movements, but they call themselves "Indohispanxs"). This cognitive stalemate maps a uniquely ironic geography of Indigenous erasure in which the singularity of the Genízarx diaspora in the so-called U.S. Southwest disappears under the normative frames of nationalized spatialization of U.S. and Mexican state power.

Galvanized by Gloria Anzaldúa's 1987 publication of *Borderlands / La Frontera* and the 1994 Zapatista Uprising, a number of scholars have come to critically reappraise Chicanx mestizaje as a performance of an indigenismo that surreptitiously or explicitly denies the sovereign endurance of Native and Indigenous modes of life, knowledge, and governance in our contemporary moment. At the same time, many recent iterations of this critique continue to replicate the nationalist geographical strictures that diminish the heterogeneity of deployments of mestizaje in *el movimiento* solely as Chicanx aesthetic or political appropriations of postrevolutionary Mexican nationalism. For many scholars, cultural workers, and activists, *Borderlands* and Zapatismo made newly visible a prevailing critical predicament for work on indigeneity within Latinx and Chicanx studies: the extent to which the reliance on the settler colonial structures of the Spanish invasion and modern Mestizo statecraft to unsettle U.S. empire participates in the elimination of Native and Indigenous sovereign land rights and kinship relations.

Anzaldúa's text grapples with this predicament by examining the Mestiza's status as a racialized, gendered, and sexualized figure of colonial power in a way that shifted Chicanx analyses of the U.S. Southwest from a "conquered homeland" to a "borderland."[65] While deploying and subverting a number of Mestizx tropes of Mexican nationalism, the text articulates the urgency of a lesbian, feminist cultural studies and offered the touchstone term of a postnationalist Chicana feminism. In the process, it came to reframe narratives produced by women who defy linguistic and spatial strictures of white patriarchy as bearing analytical purchase for theories of Mestizx consciousness and mestizaje. Alicia Arrizón notes how Anzaldúa refigures Aztlán's "inventive assemblage" of "ancient [Aztec] mythologies" into "more complex terms as an in-between space, coinciding with the physical and metaphysical space of the U.S.-Mexican border."[66] In doing so, Arrizón acknowledges the ways in which La Alianza coincided with the imaginary of Aztlán, yet dismisses the insurgent practices of the movement by claiming that, in "practice, the goal of recovering land proved idealistic and romantic."[67]

In the same historical conjuncture, the Zapatista Uprising in Chiapas gave renewed critical attention to indigenismo as a state policy containing the "Indian" as racial difference capable of being edited away in the service of revolutionary mestizaje. Pondering the limits of Chicanx mestizaje through Zapatismo, María Josefina Saldaña-Portillo argues that the "collection of discursive practices" constituting Mexican national mestizaje "serves to reinforce a hegemonic consciousness in which indigenous identity is always in a subordinate position to the dominant mestizo identity. . . . [F]or hegemonic mestizo consciousness, this translated into a veneration of noble Indian ancestors, but a general amnesia about the living Indian peoples of Mexico."[68]

Under these discursive constraints, Saldaña-Portillo reveals how the figure of the Indian acts as the "lost racial object [that] proliferates cultural identity."[69] She notes the ways loss creates for Mexican Americans an ambivalent "melancholic structure" of attachment to their "indigenous heritage" as reflected in Aztlán, La Malinche, and a range of Chicanx literary production. This leads Saldaña-Portillo to name the limits of Chicanx indigeneity as "produced through an engagement with lost indigenous identity rather than through an engagement with contemporary indigenous struggles."[70] Sheila Contreras builds on this critique to argue that "Chicano indigenism" is an ambivalent appropriative strategy characterized by its use of myth informed by the aesthetic school of primitivism or the discipline of anthropology. She notes how "Chicana/o oppositional politics" rely on Aztlán as "an assertion of land rights based on an Indigenous myth" or the Treaty of Guadalupe Hidalgo, which "is based upon a Mexican national identity and the settler privilege bestowed by Spanish and Mexican land grants."[71] For Contreras, "Chicana/o indigenism" creates "cultural narratives of Indianness that rely most prominently on mythic accounts drawn from anthropology and archaeology."[72] The danger for Contreras is the how myth potentially "supplants history" and therefore participates in the colonial project of Native and Indigenous erasure.

These powerful reappraisals of the insidious anti-Indian racism at work in indigenismo allows us to name the trans-American circulation of mestizaje that delimits Chicanx radical imaginaries. For these reasons, Leslie Marmon Silko's *Almanac of the Dead* (1991) allows us to build out from the focus on indigenismo imaginaries to establish a different horizon for rethinking place of the Genízarx diaspora in the formation and doctrine of Chicanx and Latinx studies. In particular, *Almanac* allows us to consider how escape stories clear a different path of indigeneity by which to situate the ways the Genízarx diaspora endures the double erasure of U.S. and Mexican state violence and remains active in La Alianza's insurgency. Escape stories, according to Reid

Gómez, "reveal a universe made up of parts: parts that are not fragmented but merely and beautifully overlap, conjoin, relate in some dimension, and connect to some place or person in particular." As a narrative, escape stories refuse definitive closure in discourse, form, or genre. "There is no finished story," Gomez continues, "because like the people, it too is always in motion. It is a breathing and changing thing. Like the landscape, [escape stories] exist and continue on long after this writing and your reading—in motion, with no final words and no retractions."[73] Escape stories also surround, connect to, and proliferate other escape stories and provide a means by which to resist the diminishment of our decolonial imaginative capacities under racial capitalism and settler modernity. "For African Americans, Afro-Latinos, indigenous Latinos, and some Native Americans," Gómez continues, "the telling of getaway stories, by survivors and by the generations, is vital and relates to the strenghtening of the land and the tribes in general."[74]

As *Almanac* demonstrates, escape stories are not escapist but rather require knowledge of the architectures, infrastructures, and textualities of capture, possession, and elimination that underpin colonial regimes. Escape stories trick with the colonialist binary of textuality and orality to activate uncanny significations from the very terms and structures of containment. *Almanac of the Dead* therefore activates the power of escape stories to transform the act of reading historiography of the Genízarx diaspora into a land-based warp and wave of time-space with nonlinear entanglements to multiple Indigenous literary and activist struggles. *Almanac* narrates a transnational movement populated with Indigenous and Mestizx protagonists who communicate through dreams and visions and inhabit worlds pulsating with the agency of spirits and other-than-human beings. It is a movement demanding "nothing less than the return of all tribal lands" in the Americas.[75] Animating this demand is the novel's performance of a narrative that refuses modern analytics, textualities, and temporalities built on the presumption of Indigenous disappearance and Black captivity.

By virtue of its temporal logic, *Almanac* deposes Native American indigeneity, Latinidad, and Blackness from identity politics by abandoning revolutionary modalities premised on state recognition or capture. Refusing state recognition and legal redress as the necessary predicate to Indigenous land reclamation, the novel operates on the principle that "there never had been . . . a legal government by Europeans anywhere in the Americas. Not by any definition, not even by the Europeans' own definitions and laws. Because no legal government could be established on stolen land. Because stolen land never had clear title."[76]

Because the almanac is not a testimony for legal rights, a deed for protecting private or communal forms of property, or a treaty with or as a sovereign nation, it rejects the cultural forms that settler law demands "for Natives to be recognized as legitimately, legally, Native."[77]

This refusal of the constitutive racisms and institutional forms of modernity is vividly expressed in the "Five Hundred Year Map" that prefaces the novel's intersecting storylines. The map is immediately notable as a re-temporalization of a key site of imagination and struggle for La Alianza and Chicanx cultural politics: the U.S.-Mexico borderlands. Yet the map employs terms and spatial imaginaries for representing the borderlands that do not solely rely on U.S., Mexican, Chicanx, or revolutionary nationalist discourse. This is seen in how the term Mexico is writ the largest, while the United States is not named. There remains only our assumption that the United States is signified above. In this way, the map does not render the U.S.-Mexico borderlands as a peripheral region in relation to the geographical "centers" of the U.S. nation. But equally as important, given the explicitly foregrounded placement of "Mexico," the map neither depicts the Mexican region of *el norte* nor Aztlán. Rather, the map negotiates the constraints of Euroamerican forms of regionalization within a cartographical imaginary that constellates a field of Indigenous struggle with multiple borderland jointures between tribal lands, colonial orders, slave revolts, and national legacies. This is evident in the map's placement of Tucson as its "center." But as a "center," Tucson is not spatially anchored solely in relation to its territorial counterparts in the so-called U.S. Southwest. Instead, Tucson is figured as a conduit in a field of struggle whose relational coordinates are bundled with Haiti, Cuba, Mexico, Buenos Aires, Alaska, Albuquerque, and El Paso, to name a few locales. The interconnection of these locales thus presumes and defamiliarizes their recognizability in national frames of reference. Thus instead of reifying the U.S.-Mexico border through state and oppositional nationalist cartographies, "The Five Hundred Year map" situates the nation-form as a narrative technology of historical amnesia, one that occludes dense territorial antagonisms and hemispheric terrains of interdependence. "Foregrounding the agitated relations between and among spaces and subjects," Ann Brigham argues, "the map and the novel that follows it understand geography not as the blueprint of a presupposed fixed reality, but as the inscription of struggle. The landscape is both a moment and space of tension."[78]

This contentious terrain is further conveyed through the map's title and legends. One legend, "The Indian Connection," states: "Sixty million Native

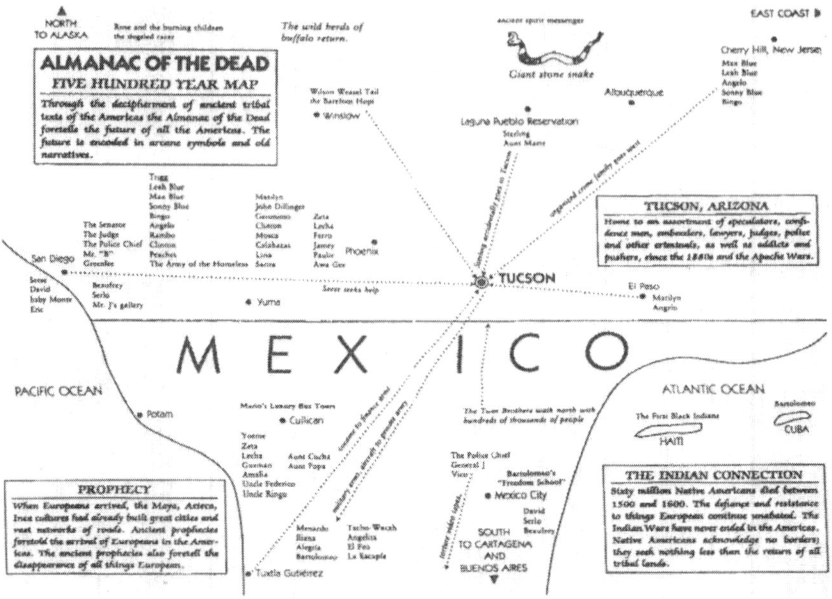

FIGURE 5 From *Almanac of the Dead*, prefatory map, by Leslie Marmon Silko. Copyright © 1991 Leslie Marmon Silko. Reprinted with the permission of Simon & Schuster, Inc. All rights reserved.

Americans died between 1500 and 1600. The defiance and resistance to things European continue unabated. The Indian Wars have never ended in the Americas. Native Americans acknowledge no borders; they seek nothing less than the return of all tribal lands."[79] Five hundred years here is not merely a chronicle, but a spatializing project securing Euroamerican political and economic borders. National borders and linear, secular time are recoded as co-constitutive genocidal structures of violence. Euroamerican regimes of geographical and historical knowledge are retermed as necropolitical strategies of representation premised on the historical eradication of Indigenous epistemologies, spiritual practices, and life forms.

Yet even as it depicts the U.S.-Mexico borderlands as a space of irrevocable Indigenous death, the map also doubles as a cartography of the "unabated" defiance to "things European" premised on "nothing less than the return of all tribal lands." *Almanac*, in other words, is prefaced by a cartography of tribal insurgency that is embedded within the devivifying constraints of Euroamerican strategies of geohistorical representation. In this regard, the "500-Year Map" suggests that the labor of land reclamation in the Americas is at once grounded in place, global in scope, and yet profoundly skeptical of the national, imperial, and revolutionary regionalisms into which place is translated. This working tension illuminates a central site of ingenuity for the novel's cast of characters charged with continuing the reclamation of tribal lands: How does one strategically marshal Euroamerican legal, cultural, and linguistic frameworks toward the simultaneous reclamation of tribal lands and abolishment of "all things European"?

Almanac's answer to this question resides in the power of storytelling as a tactic of escaping the written cloisters of Indigenous racialization that sustain colonial occupation. Central to the movement's reclamation of the Americas is an almanac-like text, variedly referred to as a "book," "notebook," and "manuscript." A collectively authored palimpsest of tribal storytelling, the almanac is understood as the crucial and secret weapon for reclaiming Indigenous land and deposing European authority in the hemisphere. As the almanac is a fugitive and mobile text that circulates in the novel's plot, its survival is maintained through a network of cross-border tribal coalitions. "Unlike the three known Mayan almanacs named after the European cities in which they are now located—Madrid, Dresden, and Paris," Channette Romero notes, "Silko imagines a fourth almanac that is protected for centuries from destruction and obsolescence by American Indians from multiple tribes located on either side of what is now the U.S.-Mexico border."[80] Simultaneously inhabiting and exceeding the discretely bounded, passive, and logocentric logic of the book, the almanac's power resides not only in its content but in the escape stories that surround and mobilize the text.

One indelible moment of many in *Almanac* occurs when Zeta and Lecha, twin Yaqui Mexican sisters who live in Tucson, acquire the almanac from their grandmother, Yoeme—whose name is also the name of the Yaqui people in their own language. Yoeme's story of "Journey of the Ancient Almanac" begins with a group of "fugitives" on a "long journey from the South . . . who carried the manuscript, suffered great hardships" and who were "last of their kind . . . those few survivors of the Butcher." The almanac "told them who they were and where they had come from in the stories." Faced with impending colonial annihilation, the fugitives divide the almanac four ways among three young girls and a small boy to be carried "North." "This way," Yoeme says, "if only one of the children reached safety far in the North, at least one part of the book would be safe. The people knew if even part of their almanac survived, they as a people would return someday." Directed to elude "the slave catchers on horseback with dogs," the four children leave at night with pages of the almanac sewn into their clothes. They "were told the 'book' they carried was the 'book' of all the days of their people. These days and years were all alive, and all these days would return again. The 'book' had to be protected at all costs."

The children journey through "barren terrains" where no large animals lived "because the aliens had slaughtered all these creatures to feed themselves and their soldiers and their slaves." Hunger drives one of the girls to consume pages of the almanac written on dried "horse gut" just before they reach an abandoned village where they encounter a "hunchbacked woman left behind by the others when they fled the invaders and their soldiers." The children stop at the village to rest and help the woman collect bulbs and roots to make a stew. The eldest, although unable to read the writing of the almanac, commits a dried horse-gut page to memory and drops it in the stew as the others sleep. Renourished, the children realize the old woman would have died were it not for their arrival. The children vow not to eat any more of the almanac and continue their journey north, knowing that their departure will bring death to the old woman. As they leave, the child who first consumed the horse-gut page separates from the group to stay longer, promising to follow right behind. Refusing the warnings from the oldest girl, we learn that the "last they ever saw of her was . . . accepting a bowl of stew from the crippled woman, who was smiling broadly and nodding her head enthusiastically." The next day the eldest girl sneaks back to the village while the others sleep. Yoeme clarifies, "she had gone for the pages, not for their companion." She encounters the woman sleeping under a cottonwood tree and searches among the abandoned houses. In one "structure that had been used by the men for ceremonial purposes," she finds her companion dead, "hanging from the crossbeams of the roof." Realizing that the hunchback woman "feasted upon the liver or the heart, known to be the preferred delicacies" and had not yet eaten the pages, the eldest girl puts her dead companion's garments over her own and escapes. Yoeme reiterates the power of the almanac. "You see, it had been the almanac that had saved them. The first night, if the eldest had not sacrificed a page from the book, that crippled woman would have murdered them all right then, while the children were weak from hunger and the long journey."[81]

In her critique of the anti-Indian violence that animates yet remains "unspoken" in the indigenismo of Chicanx mestizaje, Nicole Guidotti Hernandez turns to a probing analysis of the Yaqui genocide under the Mexican government, revealing the ways in which the "indio was invoked as Lo Azteca, the precolonial Mexican indigenous, not the contemporary one present within the context of the Yaqui Indian wars."[82] Given Chicanx mestizaje's multiple imbrications with anti-Indigenous warfare, Guidotti-Hernandez unsettles what she terms as a "chain of equivalence" that continues to animate Chicanx politics: "if Chicano, then Mexican; if Mexican, then mestizo; if mestizo, then indigenous; if indigenous, then resistant."[83] For Guidotti-Hernandez, it is this chain that constructs an "unspoken ideology or idiom of resistance that most often is articulated as 'mestizo equals indian.'"[84] This "resistive agency" is "a structure that represses and restricts what gets talked about and valued."[85] Therefore, she concludes, "the process of reconciliation begins with acknowledging national and individual participation in the forgetting and establishing an active, honest, and open engagement with history."[86]

Yoeme's story of the almanac's journey, however, is not a narrative of "resistance" that presumes an equivalence between Native and Mestizx subjects. It is, rather, an escape story predicated on the understanding that contemporary articulations of national sovereignty in the Americas inherit and reproduce structures of settler colonial power sustained by the logics of racial slavery and the erasure of tribal life worlds. The difference between escape and resistance here rests on a politics of textual authority and knowledge. As Yoeme's story indicates, escape unsettles the colonialist hierarchy of knowing that not only underwrites the narratives of resistance that Guidotti-Hernandez critiques but also challenges the sufficiency of an emphasis on the necessity of historical facticity. Rather, the epistemic politics of escape is mediated by a mode of writing that rebukes the classical characterization of Euroamerican modernity as rationalized bureaucratic disenchantment, thereby calling into question the capacity of modern secular history to deliver the terms of Indigenous liberation and survivance. As an escape story, Yoeme indeed offers a meditation on the past but eludes the prose and formalism of history. Instead, the story power of the almanac's journey enfolds modern colonial power into the narrative universe of Indigenous knowledge, recasting European invasion as the five-hundred-year "epoch of Death-Eye Dog," whose "influence has been established across this entire world." It is an epoch in which "human beings, especially alien invaders, would become obsessed with hungers and impulses commonly seen in wild dogs."[87] By encircling colonial domination with the story power of escape, Bridget O'Meara argues, the almanac restages "Christianity, modernity, and capitalism, which have been co-evolving and mutually reinforcing one another for five hundred years [into a] ritualized, sacrificial violence of sorcery [whose] destructive power . . . permeate[s] nearly every aspect of economic, social, and ecological existence in the late twentieth century."[88]

As a weapon against the sacrificial operations of colonial settlement, the almanac's fugitivity is inseparable from its living status: "Yoeme and others believed the almanac had living power within it, a power that would bring all tribal people of the Americas together to retake the land."[89] Yet as a document that joins all tribal people in the Americas and tells them who they are, the almanac is never referred to as an origin story. It is not a testimony, ethnography, autobiography, or memoir. Nor is it a manifesto, a dictionary, or an encyclopedia. Rather, because the almanac is alive, its formal and generic composition is scrupulously partial, moving, unbounded, and unfinished. It is life that nourishes life on the brink of extinction. It is life that eludes the genocidal "conceptual apparatuses" of colonial modernity, which contain Indigenous pasts, identities, and storytellers under ethnographic, literary, historicist, and legal logics that "reduce the totality of the world to its own concepts."[90]

At once a refusal of extinction and an expansion of what can be considered alive and animate under modern colonial paradigms of perception, the almanac's life is directly tied to a cooperative labor of translation and transcription. Yoeme insists that the twins "understand how carefully the old manuscripts and its notebooks must be kept. Nothing must be added that was not already there. Only repairs are allowed, and one might live as long as I have and not find a suitable code."[91] At the same time, "whole sections [of the almanac] had been stolen from other books . . . Not even the parchment pages or fragments of ancient paper could be trusted; they might have been clever forgeries, recopied, drawn, and colored painstakingly."[92] Nonetheless, the almanac requires translation because it offers prophesies to the people about the "appearance, conflict with, and eventual disappearance of things European."[93] By dwelling in the tensions between authenticity/history and forgery/prophesy, Lecha performs the "translation work" of casting Yoeme's "broken Spanish" and "corrupt Latin that no one could understand" into "narratives in English."[94] As Lecha makes the first English entry in the Almanac, she and Zeta expect Yoeme to "break into a fury," but instead "she had rocked herself from side to side, sighing with pleasure [and claimed this] was the sign the keepers of the notebooks had always prayed for."[95] The competing imperatives for textual fidelity and translation concede no transparent retrieval of a pure and idyllic precolonial past. To the contrary, the stories and knowledges of the past and future maintain life through their subversive use of and escape from the languages, mediums, technologies, and identities of a certain present and place, for "sacred time is always in the present."[96]

Put another way, the theory of escape performed by the almanac does not furnish a site where the official, definitive, or authentic history can be told. Instead, stories themselves are the agents of insurgency, and colonial subjects are refigured as the media that betray their own empires. As one fragment from the ancient almanac states: "One day a story will arrive in your town. There will always be disagreement over direction—whether the story came from the southwest or the southeast. The story may arrive with a stranger, a traveler thrown out of his home country months ago. Or the story may be brought by an old friend. . . . But after you hear the story, you and the others prepare by the new moon to rise up against the slave masters."[97] As a disassemblage of the boundaries between literary practice, ceremonies of tribal storytelling, and strategies of social movement insurgency, the almanac enables stories and storytellers to live, revolt, and proliferate under ongoing conditions of genocidal liquidation.

Such an account provides a refreshed insight into Jack Forbes's movement-driven study *Aztecas del Norte: The Chicanos of Aztlán*. As one of the first texts to disarticulate Chicanx cultural politics from mestizaje, *Aztecas* links Chicanx indigeneity directly to a long and continuous trajectory of Native and Indigenous insurgency and escape. In an essay from *Aztecas del Norte* called "Analco: The Birthplace of the Chicano," Forbes traces the emergence Chicanx consciousness to the Pueblo Indian Revolt of 1680 and returns to Analco, the colonial barrio in Santa Fe where Genízarx slaves and servants were housed prior to the revolt. Forbes writes:

> On August 15, 1680, armed Native American rebels of the Tano, Tewa, Taos, Picuris, Jemez and Apache nations entered Analco, the Mexican (Nahuan or Aztec) barrio next to Santa Fe, in New Mexico. A Tano leader met with Governor Otermín of the Spaniards and told him that the rebels carried two banners, one bearing red and the other white. The red symbolized the war which the Spaniards could choose, while the white symbolized the peace which would prevail if the European invaders agreed to abandon New Mexico.
>
> The Indian freedom fighters asked that "all classes of Indians who were in our power [says Otermín in a letter of 1680] be given up to them, both those in the service of the Spaniards and those of the Mexican nation of that suburb of Analco. He demanded also that his wife and children be given up to him, and likewise that all the Apache men and women whom the Spaniards had captured in war be turned over to them, inasmuch as some Apaches who were among them were asking for them."

> We must be very grateful that Otermín wrote that down, because it tells so much about the history of the Chicano and of the ancient unity of *la raza indígena* [the indigenous race]. Here we not only see that the Pueblo and Apache freedom-fighters were concerned about the liberation of their Mexican brothers from Spanish tyranny but we also see that the Indian town of Analco was already pan-Indian with Apache, Pueblo, and Mexican servants and slaves all living together under the common yoke of the European oppressor. Is it not from this common oppression that the Chicano has been born? An Indian with no tribe, an Indian of many tribes, or a mestizo born of the rape of his Indian mother?[98]

Through escape, Forbes's analysis is not merely historical evidence that highlights the ways Chicanx Indigeneity's horizon of possibility stems from cooperative modalities of Indigenous insurgency. Escape also sheds light ways in which Indigenous insurgency engulfs and repurposes the documents and scripts of colonial administration. Forbes specifically points out the inadequacy that Otermín's "letter of 1680" plays in staving off the revolt while simultaneously noting its instructional value that "*tells* [my emphasis] so much about the history of the Chicano." Escape stories therefore at once corroborate and violate the institutionalized narratives of Pueblo-Genízarx cultural conflict, coalition, and exchange in the historiographical and anthropological literature outlined earlier, which narrate how Pueblo and Plains Indian land, life, and culture saturate and destabilize the Spanish colonial regime and its subsequent transformation into Mexican frontier liberalism.[99] Tracy Brown, for example, discusses the "Pueblofication" of Spanish colonialism as one instance of a repertoire of tactics that the Pueblo and Hopi peoples "mounted to negotiate Spanish power and authority in their communities."[100] Likewise, Alfonso Ortiz states that after the Pueblo Revolt, "the Spaniards learned" a "humbling lesson": that "they could not remain absolutely 'Spanish' if they were to learn to live in peace in the great valley of the Rio Grande and in the province of New Mexico." Their survival was staked, in other words, on giving up "their absolute intolerance toward religious beliefs and practices other than their variant of Roman Catholicism." This meant unlearning "their arrogance toward nature and toward indigenous life forms and cultures."[101]

From this horizon, escape sheds light on the subjugated ethnography and fiction of Gilberto Benito Córdova. In work such as *Abiquiú and Don Cacahuate: A Folk History of a New Mexican Village* and his PhD dissertation for the University of New Mexico, "Missionization and Hispanicization of Santo Thomas Apostól de Abiquiú, 1750–1770," Córdova articulates the endurance of the Genízarx land grant community of Abiquiú and the ways in which its indigeneity survived through cooperative relations with surrounding Pueblo and Plains sovereignties. Through the figure of Don Cacahuate, Córdova offers a "folk history" of the ways in which the Genízarx community of Abiquiú was necessarily outfitted as a military outpost for defense yet remains a place of radical hospitality for those on the run. "*People of Abiquiú, our little village has never refused to shelter anyone, regardless of their obscure or humble origins.*"[102] As a "folk history," Córdova offers his own take on story power, arguing that "the story of Abiquiú" needs to be "approached from the two roads of history and folklore" because both merge to "form the reality of village life." For these reasons, he concludes, "any effort to separate legend and myth from the story of Abiquiú is in actuality the driving away of truth, leaving only half truths."[103] Likewise, in his novel *Big Dreams and Dark Secrets in Chimayó*, the story follows the itinerant journey of Salvador, a Genízarx trickster battling addiction, displacement, and the profound, cross-generational isolation of detribalization. In a notable scene, he encounters the Pueblo creationary deity Spider Woman, who offers invaluable escape instructions: "Hijo, hijo mio, you have misunderstood. If you tangle your yarn, your web will become a trap. . . . you are not dependent on the weaver. *You are the weaver.*"[104] As Córdova demonstrates, the story power of Pueblo and Plains tribes within and around the vexed genealogies of settlement and detribalization that mark land grant formations remains an active element in the continuous survival of Genízarx subjects.

Escape stories therefore reveal paths through which incommensurate peoples, places, languages, and trajectories may indeed converge with shared horizons of decolonization by subverting what Reid Gomez calls the temporal "boundaries of reality, authenticity, accuracy and validity," which "stay and contain Native American mobility in colonial narratives and language."[105] Storied lands enfold the institutions and archives of textual production pivotal for the maintenance of settler regimes of captivity and occupation. In this way, the cross-colonial racialization of the Genízarx diaspora opens a prism to the coloniality of Spanish law evoked by Indohispanx mestizaje as bordered and transgressed by multiple genealogies of Plains, Pueblo, and detribalized Indigenous insurgency. In the next chapter, I will explore the ways in which La Alianza's Indohispanx cultural production enacted a story power from the Genízarx diaspora that escaped the racialized traps of U.S. sovereignty and private property.

CHAPTER THREE

THE CRICKET AND THE LION

The Experimental History of Indohispanx Mestizaje

> *Right now we look like a cricket. What is a cricket? King of the Insects; a little, tiny animal. All the cricket can do is just "cricket, cricket, cricket." Just a noise, that's all. But you know, if that cricket gets in the eye and the ear of the lion and scratches the inside, there is nothing the lion can do. There is nothing; there is no way the lion can use his claws and jaws to destroy the cricket. The more the lion scratches himself the deeper the cricket goes . . . We are a cricket, but we are too deep inside of this continent, of this country.*
>
> —REIES LÓPEZ TIJERINA, QTD. IN ROBERT TICE, *RHETORIC OF LA RAZA*

In 1956, years before he would become one of the more public and controversial figures of the Chicanx movement, Reies López Tijerina was overtaken by a vision. At the time, Tijerina was a former migrant laborer and an excommunicated Pentecostal preacher from Texas who lived with his first wife, Maria Escobar, and newborn daughter, Ira de Alá, in El Valle del Paz, a religious commune he established with a group of families in rural Arizona. While visiting California with other commune members, he learned that flooding had washed away his family's subterranean residence, leaving Maria and Ira living alone under a tree. That night, filled with anguish and unable to sleep, Tijerina was struck by a "superdream" in which a group of men, "seated around something that looked like a cloud," descend from the sky.[1] They had traveled from far away and had "covered the earth" looking for Tijerina in order to take him to an "ancient realm" where he was needed as "secretary."[2] They tell Tijerina there "is no one else in the world that can do this work."[3] Immediately, Tijerina is carried away on an "unknown apparatus" to a "dark pine forest."[4] Filled with terrible dread, he runs for escape until he encounters a cemetery filled with horses that appear to be frozen. One horse rises and walks to him. Tijerina mounts the creature and it takes him, "without touching the ground, as if it were flying," to a large city with a wall around it.[5] Upon landing, Tijerina is greeted by applauding masses who carry him toward an "ancient man in long white clothes that stretched to the ground." Tijerina is lowered and walks toward the ancient man whose skin "seemed like that of a child" despite his old age. "You shall reign over all of this . . . and over you, no one else but me," he tells Tijerina. As they together explore the "ancient realm," Tijerina "opens his eyes" and realizes it is morning. Although the night air "had been very cold," his body was hot. Convinced that he had been "presented with a revelation," Tijerina awakens his travel partners to tell them about his vision.[6] "Those tall pines I saw," he would later recall, "meant New Mexico."[7] "From that day onward, I began to speak to my faithful companions of the new course we were to follow. 'Little by little,' I told them, 'the work we must carry out will be revealed.'"[8]

That work, to which Tijerina and his family dedicated their lives over the next two decades, would be carried out under the banner of La Alianza Federal de Mercedes, a movement organized to reclaim Spanish and Mexican land grant holdings dispossessed in the aftermath of the Mexican-American War. Notably, by the time Tijerina's "superdream" prompted his clandestine labor of land grant reclamation in New Mexico, a "legend" had been circulating among the state's impoverished Spanish-speaking and Mestizx land grant heirs for "generations." This legend was of a man who "was destined to come . . . of exalted spirit, indomitable courage, and dazzling legal acumen."[9] According to Nancie L. González, "their ancestors foretold a time when large numbers of persons would come 'laughing' from the east and take their land by force, thus destroying the happy life of the Hispanos. They would suffer for many years but they were urged to maintain courage and to watch for a leader who would also come out of the east to lead them against the enemy who would be forced to return 'crying' to their original homes." Locating the legend's transmission through story power, González writes that each "one who hears it feels certain he must have heard it before, and he dutifully passes it on."[10]

La Alianza scholarship within and beyond Chicanx studies focuses on the group's formative role in Chicanx movement cultural politics: its militant and "direct action" forms of protest, its connection to the complex political economy of Spanish and Mexican land grant politics in New Mexico, and Tijerina's political and religious activism.[11] Although Tijerina's "superdream" and the "legend" that foretells his arrival in New Mexico appear in the record of La Alianza scholarship, the movement's supernatural conditions of possibility pose a series of problems for modern knowledge production that restricts historical causality to human agency. As a number of scholars in South Asian and Latin American subaltern studies point out, the appearance of supernatural elements in modern knowledge unsettles what Dipesh Chakrabarty describes as the universal and "secular code of historical and humanist time—that is, a time bereft of gods and spirits."[12] For Chakrabarty and others, the presence of supernatural, spiritual, and otherworldly forces index discrete temporalities that remain incommensurate with the linear, progressive temporality institutionalized in modern text-based history. In doing so, Chakrabarty identifies how modern history operates as a mode of translation that positions the "homogenous, secular, calendrical time . . . that frames historical explanations" as a universal conceptual language that strives to subsume the temporal incommensurability of the supernatural into its own self-serving explanatory capacity.[13]

Chakrabarty's subaltern critique of historicist time illuminates the two ways in which the corpus of Alianza scholarship subsumes the supernatural catalysts of the movement into the disenchanted paradigms of modern knowledge. The first, exemplified by González, translates Tijerina's mysticism *into* the secular humanist codes of modern social scientific knowledge by narrating La Alianza as a "nativistic cult movement."[14] In this maneuver, La Alianza's mystical conditions of material emergence become reduced to an eccentric cultural artifact of New Mexico's Catholic Hispanx/Spanish-American population whose practices endured in fleeting forms despite facing systematic decimation under U.S. regimes of law and private property.[15] Subsequent studies on La Alianza have indeed departed from the colonialist presumptions about the supposed irrationality of subaltern revolt mired in González's approach. Indeed, La Alianza is currently credited for bringing the neglected histories of land grant dispossession to the attention of U.S., Mexican, and international agencies and publics.[16] However, the dominant alternative strategy—evident in the early press and journalistic scholarship on the movement—takes the form of narrating La Alianza's story power through the register of Tijerina's biography. Rather than challenging this presumption, Chicanx and Latinx studies overwhelmingly amplifies this trend by privileging autobiography, biography, and memoir as genres that translate Tijerina's vision into the personal belief of an idiosyncratically religious individual.[17] Mediated by the cultural forms of modern individualism, the category of "religion" privatizes Tijerina's vision as "an example of a singular self drawn inexorably toward divine knowledge and illumination."[18] Ostensibly distinct in their conclusions, both modes of translation posit the "godless, continuous, empty, and homogenous time" of secular history as "a higher, overarching language" into which the radical difference of La Alianza's supernatural moorings must be incorporated as "culture" or "religion."[19]

This mode of translation also buttresses a scholarly tendency in Chicanx and Latinx studies to situate the 1967 Tierra Amarilla courthouse raid as the apex of La Alianza's politics of resistance. The result entrenches a patriarchal configuration in Chicanx historiography that frames Reies López Tijerina as one of the "four horsemen" of the Chicanx movement.[20] Through these masculinist tropes, the courthouse raid and Tijerina's biography become the privileged objects of study that allow "Tijerina and the Alianza [to be] adopted wholesale as representative of the New Mexican Hispano struggle [in which] the realities of local New Mexican land grant factionalism were all ignored by Chicano Movement ideology."[21] While an important galvanizing tool for Chicanx nationalist imaginaries, the elevation of Tijerina to the status of cultural nationalist patriarch through revolutionary/*bandido* tropes also performs a complex set of erasures to the story power that animates La Alianza's struggle. In one instance, Tijerina as bandido frames La Alianza as a passive appendage of Tijerina's national leadership. This perspective works to reduce revolutionary activity and labor to a set of monumentalized direct-action tactics by brave men, thereby deactivating the insurgent power embedded within La Alianza's broader cultural and textual production and diminishing Indohispanx mestizaje to the "effective, if unintentional, naming project of Tijerina."[22] These tendencies reinforce a set of patriarchal and nationalist narratives that overwhelmingly valorize men as the revolutionary agents of the movement, subduing the heterogeneity of racialized and gendered labor that sustained La Alianza's insurgent collectivity.

In the previous chapter, I argued that escape stories provide a prism to rethink the role of the Genízarx diaspora in La Alianza's movement outside of the parameters of Chicanx mestizaje. In this, chapter, I marshal the story power of escape to read La Alianza's cultural production of Indohispanx mestizaje in a mode that deposes the temporal strictures of modern history and the patriarchal trappings of modern individualism. In particular, I examine La Alianza's public pamphlets and flyers, television and radio program scripts, and Tijerina's testimonial text, *Mi lucha por la tierra* (1978), as an unbounded archive of public culture whose story power decouples the discursive performance of Indohispanx mestizaje from individual authorship. In doing so, I argue that La Alianza's enduring insurrectionary energy resides in its experiments in collective history writing that are irreducible to Tijerina's singular protagonism. At stake is not only the imperative to broaden the scene of peoples and agents that enabled La Alianza's collectivity, but also the urgency to name and confront the thick force of state-sanctioned counterinsurgency that operates through the presumption of Tijerina's singular self. From this perspective, I demonstrate how the story power of Indohispanx mestizaje represents indigeneity in transnational and coalitional terms and affirms land as an inalienable cultural right.

Over the course of his work with La Alianza, Tijerina engaged with multiple media and devised a variety of publicity strategies with the written word. In the early days of the movement, he wrote a weekly Spanish-language column that publicized La Alianza and analyzed the Treaty of Guadalupe Hidalgo in the *News Chieftain*, an independent paper in Albuquerque.[23] In the years preceding and following the courthouse raid, he hosted a local television and radio program called *The Voice of Justice*, for which he also wrote the scripts. Shortly before a U.S. district court in Albuquerque convicted him on two counts of "aiding and abetting in the destruction of Forest Service signs and of assaulting and threatening a Forest Service agent, James Evans," he published a "Letter from Santa Fe Jail" that appears in anthologies of the Chicana/o movement.[24] In addition, the Spanish and English versions of Tijerina's life story, *Mi lucha por la tierra* and *They Called Me "King Tiger": My Struggle for the Land and Our Rights* (2001), remain touchstone movement texts.

The interdisciplinary overvaluation of (auto)biographical discourses on Tijerina has produced an ironic form of disinterest regarding Tijerina's very own autobiographical text, *Mi lucha*. That is, despite Tijerina's patriarchal valorization as one of the "four horsemen" of the Chicanx movement alongside Cesar Chavez, Corky González, and José Angel Gutiérrez, only a handful of articles since its publication offers analysis on *Mi lucha*.[25] If mentioned in the scholarship on Mexican American and Chicanx autobiography, Tijerina's text is given cursory attention and often only mentioned in footnotes. According to Rudy Busto, Tijerina as bandido constructs a "specific, useful image of Tijerina in the 1960s pantheon of movimiento leadership," one that allows "historians and social scientists" to make "spare use of Tijerina's version of events in the collective history, selectively mining it for corroborative evidence but otherwise ignoring it as a text in its own right."[26] As a result, the intersecting secular and patriarchal interpretive frameworks in Chicanx history and sociology have "not illuminated Tijerina's life so much as [they have] exposed the continuing function of traditional male leadership in cultural nationalist discourse."[27]

By virtue of the same temporal entrenchment, Chicanx and Latinx literary studies have also consigned *Mi lucha* as detritus due to its lack of "a developing subject who reaches out into the world of family, racism, labor, education, and politics (concerns prevalent in Chicano autobiographies)."[28] Indeed, the critical subjugation of *Mi lucha* stands in stark contrast to the canonized status of Gloria Anzaldúa's *Borderlands / La Frontera: The New Mestiza* (1987) and Richard Rodriguez's *Hunger of Memory* (1982), two texts that also combine religious and spiritual pursuits with hybridized autobiographical genres.[29] Despite the temporal, political, and spiritual distance between *Mi lucha* and *Borderlands / La Frontera*, Busto notes that both "originate as 'outsider' texts in Chicano literature" and share a "magical realist quality" that understands the "self in submission to the sacred."[30] In the context of *Mi lucha*, Busto notes its "secretary quality" that simultaneously discloses personal experience and "divine revelation" while replicating "other documents and genres" such as scripture, legal and historical discourse, print journalism, political critique, and cosmology.[31] He furthermore ties *Mi lucha*'s generic instability to Tijerina's distinct theory of textuality and reading that stems from his "Bible instituted education [, which] taught him that power could be unleashed from the written word. . . . For Tijerina the sense of a text is not limited to academic interest or theological speculation. [T]exts do not just mean or exist, but they *happen*."[32] However, while Anzaldúa and Rodriguez dispense with the "Roman Catholic institution and move off in directions that are of interest to critics and other readers," Busto argues, Tijerina's text "originates from and moves in different directions: from Christian fundamentalism toward embracing the ancient Church. It is this return and submission to the institution of the Church that adds to the anathema of *Mi lucha por la tierra*."[33]

Busto's antidote to the secularized sanitation of *Mi lucha* leads him to identify the text as "perhaps the premier example of the Mexican American/Chicano/a memoir." Citing the "oral quality of the writing," a "nonlinear subject," and a frequent "characterization as rambling," he argues the text figures Tijerina not as a subject forming consciousness about his social surroundings but as a figure "unhampered by the continuing struggle to know and learn about the self." As memoir, *Mi lucha* captures Tijerina as "an example of a singular self drawn inexorably toward divine knowledge and illumination."[34] Rather than confine this analysis to *Mi lucha*, Busto projects the sovereignty of Tijerina's authorship across a wide range of La Alianza cultural production, even to texts that are either anonymous or bear the signature of La Alianza Federal de Mercedes (or Alianza Federal de Pueblos Libres, the name used after 1967).[35]

Among the many things that Tijerina's "superdream" makes apparent about his prolific output, however, is that he clearly was not alone. Supernatural actors aside, empirical reports on the number of Alianza members vary wildly from six thousand at the movement's second annual convention in 1964 to roughly twenty thousand in 1966.[36] Among these members, Aliancistas such as Ida García, Felix Martínez, Maria Escobar, Santiago Anaya, Cristóbal Tijerina, Jerry Noll, Eddie Chávez, Bill Higgs, Eunice L. Myrick, and Francisco Treviño all contributed to numerous published and unpublished position papers, pamphlets, press releases, and flyers that outlined La Alianza's mission and publicized the conventions and demonstrations it organized. Housed in the Papers of La Alianza Federal de Pueblos Libres and Reies López Tijerina at the University of New Mexico's Center for Southwest Research, these flyers and pamphlets reveal a wealth of insight into La Alianza's legacy and the history of land grant tenure and loss in New Mexico. Yet because they do not conform to the model of individual authorship, they remain overwhelmingly absent from existing scholarship on the movement.[37]

In this context, to approach *Mi lucha* and La Alianza's broader cultural production as a performance of story power is to confront the enduring problem of authorship in social movement history. To impose Tijerina as the implied author of these documents not only effaces the collectivity that prompted La Alianza's textual production, but it also forecloses the multitude of meanings that texts may have as they circulate within distinct localities, temporalities, reading publics, and social struggles. The insistence on a stable and individual author for each document is tied to a demand for textual meaning to be equated with intention and therefore singular and static across time and space. From this perspective, Busto's implication of Tijerina as the author of La Alianza's cultural production—in addition to his insistence on settling the uncontainable features of *Mi lucha* as memoir—coincides with a modern conception of religion that keeps intact elementary premises of secularized reason: the individual sovereignty over words and the subordination of place to the emptiness and homogeneity of modern time.

Here, story power reveals how the terms of containment also bear the threshold for a different interpretive path. Recall Tijerina's view of the "happening" of texts. What would it mean to use this view as a lens to activate the life of La Alianza's textuality as a story power irreducible to Tijerina's singular authority?

To insist on the story power of La Alianza's textual production would acknowledge that there were indeed individuals who devoted unpaid time and labor to contemplating, debating, drafting, and circulating these flyers and pamphlets. Yet it would also generatively refuse individual authorship as the prism through which to situate and evaluate the texts. Story power instead centers the memories of the "long-ignored communal rights" of the land grants that animated the terms of La Alianza's struggle. Accordingly, the pivotal archival research undertaken by Tijerina must be situated in dialogue with stories of land from a number of impoverished and dispossessed heirs of the Tierra Amarilla, San Joaquín del Río de Chama, and Abiquiú land grants. While on the run from the Arizona police in New Mexico prior to La Alianza's incorporation, Tijerina recalls, "I could not approach or visit the centers of archival material. I could not visit libraries. So, during these first years, I had to get my information from the people. The older ones were my teachers."[38] In this way, the subjugated story power of land grant tenure and dispossession along with the material and financial support afforded by New Mexican land grant heirs provide the occluded conditions of possibility for Tijerina's archival research and La Alianza's textual production.

From this vantage point, story power allows us to name an indeterminate and dispersed collectivity signified by "La Alianza" that dispenses with the interpretive containment of modern individualism. To accept La Alianza as a collective signature in these terms is not to disavow Tijerina's influence. It is, rather, to resituate Tijerina in his own words as a secretary who acquired a type of radicalism from intersecting encounters with other-than-human actors, subjugated storytellings of land grant dispossession, and transnational engagements with archives of colonial law. From this perspective, I read *Mi lucha* as one node in La Alianza's unbounded corpus of land grant story power in order to excavate a repertoire of insurrection that nests politics of history writing, racial and gendered representation, Indigenous displacement and revitalization, and overlaid colonial political economies of Spain, Mexico, and the United States. This complex exchange therefore resituates the insurgent energy of La Alianza's movement as not merely activated with guns and dynamite, but with the material life of spirits and the power of stories, narratives, and discourses.

This horizon of insurgency draws attention to the ways in which the modern state's counterinsurgent campaign against La Alianza required an intense investment in individualizing Tijerina in biographical genres. While Tijerina's refiguration as revolutionary bandido powerfully galvanized an emergent

Chicanx political class, the presumptions of modern individualism embedded in his biographical forms also facilitated a counterinsurgent discourse of anti-communism and criminalization from the U.S. state. According to David Correia, as the "Alianza began to challenge the racial inequality underpinning the established social order," "the state responded with covert action and physical violence." Tijerina, then, "became a target in proxy for the larger Chicano movement, and therefore experienced the full measure of coercive control. Controlling Alianza required punishing Tijerina."[39] The ensuing punishment, surveillance, and scrutiny were executed alongside multiple bombings, unprovoked assaults, arrests, and detainments by the FBI, CIA, and New Mexico State Police.[40]

These deep forms of counterinsurgency also operated in tandem with a chorus of motivated misrepresentation from the media apparatus that entrenched the law enforcement of Spanish-Anglo political modernity. In local, regional, and national television stations and Albuquerque's two largest daily newspapers at the time, Tijerina was fabricated as a figure with secret communist affiliations and a dangerous disregard for the sanctity of U.S. law, one who parlayed unchecked revolutionary power to a group of misled "Hispanos."[41] In 1964, La Alianza mobilized roughly three hundred supporters on a pilgrimage from Albuquerque to Santa Fe in an effort to pressure then governor Jack Campbell to formally investigate land grant claims. After camping on the lawn of the state capitol building for a week, Tijerina and a handful of Aliancistas eventually met with and persuaded Campbell to petition President Lyndon Johnson for federal inquiry into the history of land adjudication. The following week, however, La Alianza's efforts were again challenged by Dr. Myra Ellen Jenkins, then the New Mexico state archivist, who advised Campbell against any further dealings with the organization.[42] "There is little historical validity to any of their claims," Jenkins stated. She continued to assert that many "members of the so-called Alianza were not descendants of any Spanish or Indian grantees. I feel there are outside influences which are reopening this old issue for pecuniary gain."[43]

While these setbacks and institutional evasions on behalf of the federal and local government provided the catalyst for the tactical transformation of La Alianza's mission of land grant recovery into "direct action" and "militaristic" practices, it also hardened the imperative to capture the definitive history of Tijerina in biographical forms across a range of modern ideological positions. Immediately following the courthouse raid, the radical right-wing magazine *American Opinion* published a series of articles by Alan Stang that renounced Tijerina as a Castro-like revolutionary and dismissed La Alianza as a communist conspiracy. "The point once again," Stang writes, "is that Tijerina isn't trying simply to transfer property from American to American. He is trying to use this dead issue to begin a guerrilla operation in the United States. . . . [He is] trying to destroy the United States."[44] From centrist and liberal spectrums, journalists performed settler amnesia by drawing from what Gabriel Melendez describes as "stock explanations of nuevomexicano cultural and religious mores" that "harkened back to Charles Lummis and some of the earliest travel narratives that cast New Mexico as remote, foreign, and different."[45] A paradigmatic example is *Reies Tijerina: The Most Hated Man in New Mexico*, a special report on La Alianza broadcast by NBC in May 1969. Although the report connects the multigenerational poverty affecting New Mexican land grant heirs to territorial dispossession and Anglo resource extraction, it racializes Rio Arriba County as a "rural ghetto, a cultural backwater." Throughout the half-hour segment, the land grants are deindigenized, the Spanish colonial past is overvalued, and Tijerina is cast as a migrant Mexican interloper and "foreigner" (as one Anglo rancher in the report calls him) whose image is mediated by the trope of Mexican "killability." Reporter Tom Petit intones over filtered images of New Mexican *bultos* (wood carvings of saints), "the worship of death remains one of the deepest emotions in remote mountain villages of northern New Mexico. . . . These are survivors of the 16th century Spanish dream of wealth in the new world. They exist on welfare handouts, subsistent farming, and food stamps." Later, while attempting to offer a history of land grant movements that have preceded La Alianza, Petit faces the camera to report. "Reies Tijerina arouses strong emotions in New Mexico, especially here in the mountainous north where years of isolation and inbreeding have produced a people who are intensely passionate and sometimes violent. Before Tijerina there were others who led movements to regain the land. All failed. All have left a legacy of bitterness which remains today among the dispossessed—who are clannish, suspicious, nearly hopeless, yet very proud and very poor."[46]

As the camera pans across a group of houses and fencing, La Alianza's quest is put into a balance between revolution and death. Tijerina speaks over images of a lone land grant villager riding a horse-drawn wagon over a dirt road with a three-legged dog. "The Alianza and the Alliance of Free City-States have reached the point where finally one of the pueblos will be liberated or we will go down trying." The voice of another man interviewed for the report interrupts: "He will never succeed in getting these land grants back. No matter how much he try [*sic*]. He won't succeed." The voice of Fernanda Martínez follows: "He's strong on this and he's going to fight to the end, even if somebody is trying to kill him." Slowly the camera zooms in on the text of a poster advertising Tijerina's candidacy for New Mexico's gubernatorial race and quickly cuts to the text below Tijerina's bust: "He will Champion the Constitution of New Mexico. He will Speak and Fight for the Poor. Like Robert Kennedy and Dr. King, He too will Die for the Poor." Tijerina's voice returns: "No, I'm not afraid to die. I think the danger of this pursuit is beautiful. It's exciting. I'm ready. I only hope that my death will redeem the respect and the culture of my people. For our culture comes first and the lands. This is the best choice I could make, to die for my people."[47]

The image of Tijerina as a killable Mexican resonates with Américo Paredes's account of the bandido trope in the corrido culture of Greater Mexico. Paredes identifies the border corrido's valorization of bandido violence and masculinity as a discursive contest against the anti-Mexican racism inscribed in U.S. academic, legal, and journalistic print cultures. The killable Mexican trope is woven into a "legend" that the Mexican is "cruel by nature," thieving, "treacherous," and a degenerate mixture "descended from the Spaniard, a second-rate type of European, and from the equally substandard Indian of Mexico, who must not be confused with the noble savages of North America."[48] Of importance, Paredes notes that the legend gains its prestige from "the writer of history textbooks" and the "author of scholarly works."[49] To this list we can add the television journalist, for Petit's depiction of Tijerina as a Mexican solicitor of martyrdom, despite the rest of his depiction of Tijerina, does not portend to be disparaging.[50] It, rather, illustrates how the labor of individuating Tijerina from La Alianza became a mode of historicizing land grant struggle as an inescapably nostalgic relation to a decrepit European past. As a form of counterinsurgency trafficked across ideological spectrums, the individualization of Tijerina from La Alianza became a powerful mechanism in which his actions were criminalized in order to contain the movement's critique of the racialized private property relations that underwrite U.S. sovereignty.

It would be this counterinsurgent individualization of Tijerina from the dispersed network of La Alianza activists that would paradoxically prompt him to speak autobiographically. On October 10, 1969, Tijerina was convicted in U.S. District Court in Albuquerque on two counts of aiding and abetting in the destruction of Forest Service signs and of assaulting and threatening Forest Service agent James Evans. While serving his two-year sentence in federal prison in Texas and a twenty-one-month confinement in a mental hospital in Springfield,

Missouri, Tijerina began to write his life story out of fear of state-sponsored death and harm. "While I was in prison," Tijerina recalls, "there were three attempts on my life . . . and that encouraged me to speed up. I could be killed at any time and I would write nothing. . . . Somebody else would be writing for me, or interpreting my life."[51] Although Tijerina's 1971 release from federal prison was granted on the condition that he discontinue his work with La Alianza, he traveled to Mexico in 1975 to visit Mexican intellectual Jorge Bustamante and to petition then president Luis Echeverría to intervene in the destitute state of Mexicans in the United States. In this meeting, Echeverría asked Tijerina to write his life story. *Mi lucha* was published in 1978 by the Mexican publishing house Fondo de Cultura Económica. A heavily edited transcription from four leather-bound notebooks in which Tijerina handwrote his life story at the age of fifty, *El Fondo* printed five thousand copies of the epic 573-page text.[52]

Mi lucha's first and longest section, "My fugitive life," offers a powerful representation of Tijerina as a figure the U.S. government invented to continue to legalize its "crimes and never seeing it as such."[53] He notes that while the "Anglo accuses me of violence . . . [t]hose who criticize me . . . have spilled blood of innocent people in the United States and all over the world. What for them is 'liberty, justice, and the free world' means they have crossed the lands and seas of the earth, planting hatred, racism, and war among nations."[54] By situating the U.S. occupation of New Mexico within a broader network of liberal imperialist violence, *Mi lucha* asserts that the "Anglo, without respect for authority and religion, and to get back into the colonization game, legalized piracy. They had to operate outside the law to become law."[55] Faced with such a legacy, *Mi lucha* theorizes the production of Tijerina as a punishable subject because he "had placed doubt about [the U.S. government's] right and legitimacy to govern."[56]

By reading Tijerina as a discursive effect of *Mi lucha* rather than its singular catalyst, the text morphs into a meditation on the linguistic functions of U.S. law and the power of textuality in facilitating and contesting land dispossession in New Mexico. Therefore, I do not arrest *Mi lucha*'s generic eccentricities into the protocols of a memoir in order to discover Tijerina's singular and coherent self in pursuit of sacred revelation or social justice. Rather, I read its fugitive relation to racial state violence in order to excavate a different association between Tijerina's subject position, *Mi lucha*'s politics of genre, and its performance of escape. Honoring the text's fugitivity allows for activating the runaway life embedded in the very features that confer the status of memoir to the text. From this horizon, the life of the oral quality of the writing, the text's nonlinear subject, and its so-called rambling and nondirectional prose reanimate Tijerina as a subject-effect of fragmented and stolen generic constraints. In this way, *Mi lucha* stages Tijerina's subjectivity as an entangled and contested terrain of social movement insurgency and state-sponsored violence.

In its fugitive and overlapping use of historiography, legal critique, and memoir, *Mi lucha* prompts recognition of the textual strategies that regulate territories of colonial occupation and horizons of social movement struggle for land. The text surges with recurrent exposition on "the legal tactics and maneuvers that the Anglos worked within the Supreme Court of the United States to steal the land from our people and cover their footprints." During Tijerina's transnational and fugitive archival research in Mexico, New Mexico, and Spain, he discovered how the "Anglo governors destroyed the Spanish archives holding the titles and evidence that the land belonged to our people. The first Anglo governor of New Mexico was a soldier who came to this territory with General Kearney. According to historians, he burned the Spanish archives in his chimney the first winter. . . . This was only one of many savage destructions of property that was committed in order to steal the land from our people . . . Each and every political apparatus established by the US to adjudicate the lands of our forebears was connected to the destruction of the archives."[57]

As a form of tricking with the truth, *Mi lucha's* account of U.S. land theft doesn't operate as a suppressed history that must be added to already existing historiographical accounts of Spanish and Mexican land grant dispossession. Neither is it a lament over the lack of justice land grant heirs find before an otherwise legitimate court system. It is, instead, an indictment of U.S. private property as a regime of writing built upon systemic archival destruction. Such an indictment does not merely call attention to La Alianza's land reclamation efforts as an attempt to recoup dispossessed property. Rather, it insists on an understanding of the movement as a broader reckoning with what Boaventura de Sousa Santos labels "epistemicide"—the destruction of knowledge that accompanies the genocide required by U.S. settler colonialism.[58] If epistemological destruction constitutes the inability of U.S. law and public culture to acknowledge the historical and legal basis of New Mexican land grant tenure, then *Mi lucha* stakes a complementary claim on the decolonizing power of archival research to regenerate Indigenous relations.

Given the reactivation of Indohispanx mestizaje from fugitive archival research, the nomenclature operates as a conjunctural invocation of colonial discourse for land rights that escapes the legal and historiographical codes of private property sanctioned by U.S. sovereignty. Consider, in this context, *The Spanish Land Grant Question Examined.* Published in 1966 in Albuquerque under the byline "Alianza Federal," the pocket-sized pamphlet addressed then what remains a long-standing and volatile political issue in New Mexico: the legal and cultural status of Spanish and Mexican land grants under U.S. law. Infused with biblical references and citations from international treaties and legal precedents, the pamphlet unfolds a powerful historical and legal rebuttal to U.S. sovereignty in New Mexico and argues for the ongoing rights of the state's "Spanish" and "Indo-Hispano" people to communal lands granted to their forebears by the Spanish and Mexican governments. "More than a century has passed since the United States of America invaded and occupied New Mexico," it declares. In the wake of invasion, the United States brought "their own laws and doctrines . . . into the region" in order to "terrorize the owners and heirs of these Land Grants into not exercising their rights under these grants."[59] Citing *La Recopilación de Leyes de los Reynos de las Indias*, the civil and administrative codes of Spanish colonialism known in English as the Laws of the Indies, the pamphlet transforms the land grants into "pueblo-republics" and "semi-independent city-states"—thereby making it "impossible for . . . the United States of America to give away or cancel or alienate any perpetual right held in trust by these pueblos."[60] This move clears the ground for the text's most astonishing claim: "These pueblos have all their rights intact and enforceable. And these pueblos have the right to exercise police power to support them in exercising their rights to their property, without complaint being made by any trespassers, or the criminal element in the State of New Mexico."[61]

At the time of publication, slanderous journalism and rumors swirled around Tijerina and his intentions with La Alianza.[62] Shortly after, posters appeared on the University of New Mexico campus with the following condemnation of the movement: "We true Spanish are white, and we are Catholics. We fight communists. We don't care for foreigners, Negro or White, to come and lie about our race. The only race problem is the one brought in by dirty communists who try to pass as Spanish to get our landgrants."[63]

By casting "Spanish" as a domestic figure subsumed under U.S. sovereignty, the Spanish American / Hispanx / Hispanic political class sacralizes U.S. private property relations by implying Tijerina as a deceitful and "dirty" (read: Mexican) "communist" "foreigner." It discloses a cross-colonial regime of whiteness in which "Spanish-American" subjects antagonistically differentiate from Pueblo

Indians and perform antiblackness in order to function subordinately in coalition with Anglo whiteness.

To the contrary, *Mi lucha* casts Indohispanx subjects as a "formidable people . . . born when the East and West joined together," when "Law 2, Title I of Book 6 of The Laws of the Kingdom of the Indies legalized marriage between the East and the West, between Indian tribes and Spanish citizens."[64] By unsettling the U.S. settler racial narrative of New Mexico as a land of triracial harmony amongst Anglos, Spanish Americans, and Pueblo Indians, Indohispanx discourse established an important, representational horizon that linked the erasure of Genízarx indigeneity and other hybridized tribal-Mestizx formations to the historical myopia sculpted around U.S. private property relations. "The Great Land Robbery," a public flyer published in January 1970, illustrates such movement discourse. The text is described as "An Historical Information Leaflet printed by Alianza Federal de Pueblos Libres," and its ability to condense the key discursive operations of Indohispanx is shown through the serialized nature of the narrative.[65] In September 1970, a Spanish-language version entitled "El robo del siglo" was published in *El Liberal Poblano*, a political journal based in Puebla, Mexico.[66] Two years earlier, the November 27, 1968, issue of *El Grito del Norte*, La Alianza's newspaper, had printed an anonymously written two-page story with the same title.[67] Although published in distinct domains, each version articulates Indohispanx mestizaje through a historical narrative that refuses and rearticulates the overlaid colonial logic of racialization that often posited an antagonistic relationship and rigid difference between New Mexican Indians and Spanish Americans.

The 1970 English version of "The Great Land Robbery" opens by asking, "Why are so many of the Indo-Hispano and Indian people of New Mexico so poor today? The answer is simple: They were *robbed* of their land"[68] *El Grito*'s version fronts the claim that every "member of La Raza knows in his heart that the Southwest belongs to the Indian and Indio-Hispano [*sic*] people. . . . He knows that he was robbed of his land, just as the Indian was robbed."[69] In each instance, "Indo-Hispano" displaces "Spanish American" but does not feign identification as "Indian." In this way, "Indo-Hispano" and "Indian" formations retain their discreteness yet are framed in shared conditions of poverty, disempowerment, and social abandonment that are derived from histories of U.S. imperial land theft. Escaping liberal explanations of land grant destitution that ascribed poverty to a lack of individual motivation resulting from nonwhite cultural deficiencies, the very deployment of Indohispanx prompts a consideration of the "poor" as a mode of relation to colonial extraction and indigeneity as a state of coalition.[70]

This logic of Indigenous coalition is elaborated in "An Immediate Demand from the Alianza Federal to the State Department of the United States," a document drafted during La Alianza's participation in the 1968 Poor People's Campaign and march. As the document explains, the "oppressed people of the Southwest, both Indo-Hispano and Indian, accuse the United States Government of criminal conspiracy for having stolen our land, all but eliminated our culture and defiled and violated our every-day life."[71] Another flyer, "The Alianza: What, Where, Why," pursues the issue by arguing that the "ancestry of the heavy majority of Indo-Hispanos (Mexican-Americans, Chicanos, Spanish-Americans) in the US is overwhelmingly 'indian.'"[72] While Indohispanx mestizaje is based on shared ancestry between land grant heirs and Indian formations, the flyer does not reduce its vision of Indigenous coalition to biology. Rather, it recalls through the Laws of the Indies that "the 'Indians' were rather substantially protected in their property rights . . . [because] Spanish settlements would not be established within many miles of 'Indian' ones." In contrast, the flyer claims, "the Anglo-American policy toward the 'Indian' was simple: Extermination!"[73]

"The Alianza: What, Where, Why" expands Indohispanx mestizaje's coalitional vision as a hemispheric affirmation of indigenous life, citing not only the "600,000 'Indians' alive today in the US north of the Rio Bravo" but also the "nearly 100,000,000 living south of it."[74] In this way, the text discovers the limits of national borders for regulating tribal recognition and land claims, thereby decentering the colonial apparatus of territoriality and asserting that the "argument of 'returning the land to the Indians' in fact strongly reinforces the Alianza's position."[75] The Laws of the Indies are thus mobilized not to restore a pristine Spanish past but rather to escape from the dire parameters of U.S. law and private property. For these reasons, *The Spanish Land Grant Question Examined* asserts that the "reason why the Alianza is not seeking at this time, court decisions relative to this Spanish Land Grant question . . . is due to the fact that the Supreme Council of the Federal Alliance of Land Grants, has passed a resolution of non-confidence in the Courts of the State of New Mexico. . . . The Spanish people do not want to seek to integrate with the Anglos."[76] While operating in the diasporic field of Genízarx indigeneity, La Alianza therefore mobilizes the Laws of the Indies as a tactical medium to refuse the logic of private property ownership imposed by the U.S. state and rename the land grants as inalienable and communal property with "over 95% of this land being owned in common by all the settlers."[77]

The use of "settler" here indexes a paradoxical terrain by which detribalized Indigenous survival sought to mark its visibility to the corporate empire of the U.S. state. This argument pivots on the assertion that pueblo lands, by virtue of their visibility in treaties and colonial legal precedents, are superseded yet not rescinded under U.S. law: "When the United States of America invaded and occupied New Mexico, the Royal Laws of the Indies remained in force, except as changed by legislation; but such changes apply only to newly initiated rights and do not disturb prior vested rights, such as old royal grant rights."[78] By paradoxically insisting on the enduring legal validity of the Laws of the Indies, Indohispanx jettisons the historicist explanations of Genízarx and non–federally recognized tribal disappearance that underwrite U.S. doctrines of racialization and private property. The use of the Laws of the Indies, then, is less about declaring the rights of citizenship according to the U.S. state and more about assembling a story power that revitalizes Mestizx and Native alliance in New Mexico in terms that depose the legitimacy of U.S. law, property, and sovereignty.

As a critique of U.S. sovereignty, this use of the Laws of the Indies enables La Alianza to transnationalize the Indigenous legacy of *ejido* land grants as autonomous and communal pueblos by staking a demand for inalienable land and cultural rights from the United States *and* Mexico grounded in the Treaty of Guadalupe Hidalgo. "The Great Land Robbery" argues that "U.S. representatives agreed to protect the land grants of the Indo-Hispano and Indian citizens of Nuevo Méjico and the rest of the 'southwest' . . . just as if they were still under the control of Mexico."[79] Note that the inalienable rights of culture and land apply to the "Indo-Hispano" and the "Indian" not solely because they are under the jurisdiction of the United States. Rather, as "citizens of Nuevo Méjico," the "Indo-Hispano" and the "Indian" are bearers of rights "as if they were still under the control of Mexico." The conditional tense deployed here, "*as if*," signifies in two registers. First, "*as if*" signals a speculative articulation of land rights and cultural sovereignty, pointing to a distinct horizon of Indian and Indohispanx pueblo alliance by which New Mexico may have been known. Second, "*as if*" operates as a transnational strategy of claiming rights from the United States and Mexico in terms that repoliticize the temporality of national borders and discrete racial identities posited by both state formations. Indohispanx nomenclature, in other words, is neither Mexican Mestizx, Spanish American, nor Chicanx; instead, it is coined as a transnational demand for inalienable cultural and land rights from both the United States and Mexican states in terms that disobey their respective logics of racializing citizens and discrete autochthonous subjects.[80]

As a discourse of coalitional indigeneity, Indohispanx unsettles the ironic dialectic of Pueblo-Hispanx racialization under U.S. law by repurposing Spanish law into a textual corpus that seeks to hail international recognition of land grants as sovereign entities. This logic is exemplified in La Alianza's 1966 mass occupation of the Echo Amphitheater in the Kit Carson National Forest, land that had been dispossessed from the San Joaquín del Río de Chama land grant through a variety of legal and extralegal means. Through performances that included the citizen's arrest of forest service agents, the impounding of forest service vehicles, and the establishment of a governing council composed of San Joaquín land grant heirs, La Alianza resignified the grant into the "Free City-State of San Joaquín del Río del Chama." So while *Mi lucha* traces the occupation's legal rationale and validity to "the New Recompilation of the Laws of Spain," its performance was a strategy to lure U.S. officials to charge the movement with trespassing on federal land. In doing so, La Alianza sought to frame any subsequent trial as a simultaneous demonstration of the international sovereignty of land grant formations and the fraudulent legal justification for the United States' possession of the grant and, by default, of the state of New Mexico.[81]

During the occupation, a flyer headlined "U.S.A. Is Trespassing in New Mexico" was circulated among the camp. The flyer has vertical scripts on two of its corners: "Free People Born, Oct. 19, 1514" and "Las Indias Born, April 17, 1492" (figure 6). The birthdate of "Las Indias" refers to the date Columbus acquired royal permission for the infamous voyage to the Americas, while the birthdate of the "free people" denotes the legalization of Spanish and Indian intermarriage under Spanish colonialism. Although reifying heterosexual marriage, the flyer marks the birthdate of the Indohispanx subjects not only in biological terms, but also in terms of an emancipatory legal code that repositions New Mexico outside U.S. jurisdiction. As a trespassing state, the United States is therefore without "title" to the territory it occupies and administers. It is a state that traffics in piracy. By refusing the sovereignty of "pirates," the document enacts a declaration of emancipation and sovereignty that remaps New Mexico in a hemispheric field with "Spanish and Indian pueblos" that shall be "free forever." Estranged from U.S. and Mexican national imaginaries, New Mexico is remapped onto the hemispheric temporality of "Las Indias," one that rejects

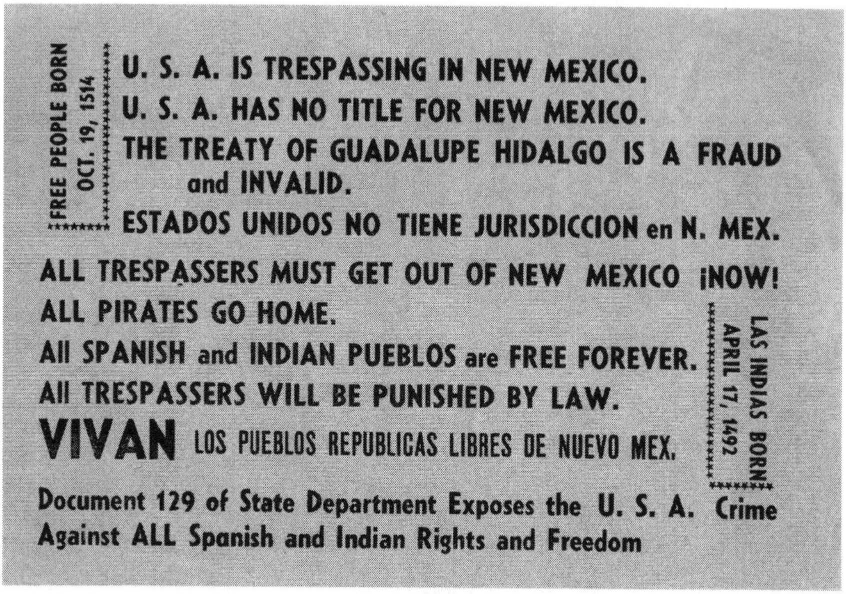

FREE PEOPLE BORN
OCT. 19, 1514

U. S. A. IS TRESPASSING IN NEW MEXICO.
U. S. A. HAS NO TITLE FOR NEW MEXICO.
THE TREATY OF GUADALUPE HIDALGO IS A FRAUD and INVALID.
ESTADOS UNIDOS NO TIENE JURISDICCION en N. MEX.
ALL TRESPASSERS MUST GET OUT OF NEW MEXICO ¡NOW!
ALL PIRATES GO HOME.
All SPANISH and INDIAN PUEBLOS are FREE FOREVER.
All TRESPASSERS WILL BE PUNISHED BY LAW.
VIVAN LOS PUEBLOS REPUBLICAS LIBRES DE NUEVO MEX.

LAS INDIAS BORN
APRIL 17, 1492

Document 129 of State Department Exposes the U. S. A. Crime Against ALL Spanish and Indian Rights and Freedom

FIGURE 6 "U.S.A. is Trespassing in NM" (1966) by La Alianza Federal de Mercedes. Box 2, folder 1, Reies Tijerina Papers, University of New Mexico Center for Southwest Research.

the linguistic order, geography, calendar, and racial imaginations of U.S. and Mexican nationalisms.[82]

This rejection is vividly articulated in *Mi lucha* where Tijerina stresses that the "mestizo does not come from Europe."[83] As he puts it, "I do not believe in importing religions or ideologies. . . . My ideology is the land, the culture, and the liberty of my people."[84] The Indohispanx, he continues, is not like the Anglos and "Europeans who left their homelands to come over to this land, to renounce their language and culture . . . The Anglo forgets that we do not abandon our homeland like they have."[85] By refusing the historiography, aesthetics, and territorialities of state-sponsored tribal, Mestizx, and citizen identities of the United States and Mexico, La Alianza invokes a temporality of mestizaje that does not align with the overvaluation of European modernity found in Mexican Mestizo nationalism. Neither is it a disinheritance of tribal presence in an attempt to comply with the assimilationist politics of U.S. white supremacy. And as an open avowal of the rights derived from "legalized marriage . . . between Indian tribes and Spanish citizens," it departs from the blood quantum politics that regulate U.S. federal tribal recognition. Indohispanx, instead, becomes a discourse of

"Indian-aligned" mestizaje estranged from its own Euroamerican discursive constraints.[86] This maneuver evokes what Gloria Anzaldúa would formulate nearly thirty years later as "*La encrucijada* / The Crossroads," a "new story to explain the world and our participation in it, a new value system with images and symbols that connect us to each other and to the planet."[87]

Given that the indigeneity of the Genízarx diaspora continues to be policed by the modes of public speech and historical empiricism sanctioned by U.S. law and private property regimes, Indohispanx discourse is not a linear, positivist retrieval. Rather, honoring La Alianza as a collective signature for the kinship terminologies evoked by Indohispanx allows it to become clear that Genízarx indigeneity is not so much the object of recovery as it is the story power that allows La Alianza to produce historical narratives that expose the limits of the racial logic of U.S. private property and the legal legitimacy of the U.S. state. Indohispanx mestizaje is therefore grounded in escape story power that leverages the discursive technologies of colonial power into vehicles of hybridized insurrection. In revealing history writing to be a lever used to both impose and contest racialized identities, legal violence, and private property relations, the racialized contingency of U.S. regimes of law, property, and history in effect are ushered toward their very demise.

From this horizon, La Alianza's famed 1967 raid on the Tierra Amarilla Courthouse refracts a different quality of insurgent light. Rather than the apex of its movement and Tijerina's land grant activism, the courthouse raid transforms into a bundle of escape narratives that wreaked broad geotemporal disequilibrium to publics and counterpublics across the Americas. After the roughly twenty Aliancistas descended upon the Rio Arriba County Courthouse to place Alfonso Sánchez under citizen's arrest, the raiding party escaped into the mountains that surround Tierra Amarilla. Tijerina found refuge in the nearby mountains and gave an interview to then Santa Fe New Mexican reporter Peter Nabokov before being arrested outside of Bernalillo five days later.[88] As other members fled to the camp in Canjilón, the National Guard deployed jeeps, convoy trucks, two tanks, flatbed tank trailers, and more than four hundred soldiers armed with about twenty thousand rounds of ammunition to an Alianza camp in nearby Canjilón, where they held roughly forty members and their families hostage in an open air cattle pen overnight.[89] Balthazar Martínez and Balthazar Apodaca, however, stayed behind and took UPI reporter Larry Calloway and Deputy Sheriff Pete Jaramillo. Under gunpoint, Calloway and Jaramillo were placed in a pickup truck and driven back and forth through Tierra Amarilla, paraded before different town folk. With Martínez at the wheel, the group made several stops at abandoned police cars. He looted firearms, cameras, and radios and unleashed rounds and rounds of ammunition into the vehicles. As state police began to follow the group, Martínez drove the car into a ditch and he and Apodaca split up with a captive into the nearby woods. Once they split up, Calloway was able to overpower and escape from Apodaca, who was shortly after apprehended by state police. Martínez, on the other hand, forced Jaramillo to run into the forest with him. On their run, Jaramillo tripped and fell in the trees, and Martínez fired a couple of shots in the air and disappeared into the mountains. Almost a month later, amid a statewide manhunt that included FBI forces, his mother, Aurelia Martínez, reported to authorities that her son was ready to surrender. Upon Martínez's surrender on July 4, Aurelia Martínez collected the announced five-hundred-dollar reward. According to Peter Nabokov, as print culture publics across the United States came to terms with a "national item . . . straight out of the gun-law Old West," their sense of linear, progressive time and enclosed national space was shattered. They were forced to "recheck the dateline to be sure they were still in the twentieth century."[90]

Precisely because escape story power renews the light given to La Alianza's movement, it also illuminates the movement's patriarchal confinements. Indeed, La Alianza's rearticulation of Genízarx indigeneity overwhelmingly kept questions of gender and sexual violence constituting the history of the land grants under erasure. Moreover, the organization's reliance on legal codes sanctioning cross-racial marriage constrained La Alianza to patriarchal investments in property in ways that naturalized and replicated the violence of the state. "The worldview of Alianza's constituency—impoverished, dispossessed small landowners—could be very conservative," writes Elizabeth "Betita" Martínez, cofounder and editor of *El Grito del Norte*. "They were not radical in the sense of consciously seeking to restructure the entire society as opposed to achieving justice in one area, recovery of land ownership. . . . At the same time, their goal could hardly be met without that restructuring, any more than the U.S. government was likely to 'give it back to the Indians.'"[91]

Indeed, *Mi lucha* and a broad array of La Alianza public pamphlets and cultural production demonstrate a persistent adherence to masculine authority and the heteronormative family as the privileged metaphor for Indohispanx collectivity. The metaphor of the heterosexual family in particular not only relies on a division of radicalism that naturalized a normative gender binarism and subordinated questions of sexuality, it also retains a colonial figuration of land as an object of possession that underlies modern logics of property. "If we save the land," Tijerina recalls telling his children during a 1966 La Alianza protest march to Santa Fe, "we can save our culture. If we save our culture, we can save the family and if we save the family we have won freedom from the Anglosaxon yoke."[92] In framing racial liberation as family coherency and land as an object in need of saving, the text traffics in state-sanctioned forms of heteropatriarchy. It is this investment in heteropatriarchal collectivity over and above La Alianza's reliance on Spanish law that reveals the movement's overvaluation of Eurocentric power.

While the heteropatriarchal logic of kinship embedded in *Mi lucha* functions as the primary vessel for Eurocentric investments in property, it also doubles as a venue to articulate the undeniable protagonism of the land as a semantic figure and an agent of justice. This appears most explicitly in the deployment of a distinct nomenclature of "El Pueblo de la Tierra / The People of the Land" to politicize land grant heirs, which offsets the usage of Indohispanx. By virtue of this interchange, the same logic that posits the family as the precondition for liberation is also permeated by a logic in which family has no coherency without the land; that the land bears and performs life in excess of property; that the land lives *as* kin. Thus, as Tijerina "began to study [the] people's laments over their stolen land, [he] noticed that land was the cause of all life. . . . The land is not an ideology but it has all that a people need to be strong and happy." Imploring people to "demand leaders that are children of the land, wise in the laws and values of the land, powerful in the knowledge of the land," *Mi lucha* declares that "ideologies and politics are superfluous." Rather, similar to "rebellious children, we must return to the land as was written by the ancient sages. And as we are already witnessing, many people are returning to their ancient inheritances."[93]

This place-centered performance of kinship unsettles the subject in the title *Mi lucha por la tierra*. The temporal and spatial imperatives of memoir prompt a literal English translation of the title as *My Struggle for the Land*, with Tijerina as the ostensible subject and land as the object of struggle. Indeed, the published English translation of the text retains this formulation in its subtitle: *My Struggle for the Land and Our Rights*. Yet as kin, the land displaces Tijerina as subject, rendering him instead as a secretary for the unfolding of land's will and agency. This translation renders the following title as both text and subtext: *My Struggle on Behalf of the Land*. Such indeterminacy marks Tijerina's absence as a discrete, autobiographical subject to double as a communal performance of place that escapes the temporalities mediating the violent force of U.S. settler sovereignty.

By refocusing La Alianza's movement through the prism of Native Story Power, I have sought to incite a rumination on the Indigenous coalition of Indohispanx mestizaje that in turn challenges how we conceptualize the movement's politics of authorship and the ways it informed divisions of radicalism that unsettled and replicated the violence of heteropatriarchal authority. From this perspective, La Alianza's subjugated institutional position in Chicanx and Latinx studies is relevant for the ways it allows us to "conceptualize multiple possibilities of creative political action rather than defining a more 'mature' political type of formation."[94] Centering Indigenous insurgency in the historiography of mestizaje and New Mexican land grants results in a power that disarticulates intellectual work on Latinx social movements from the epistemic destruction embedded in individualist agency and modern history. Deposing the politics of writing from the epistemic and material violence of whiteness, patriarchy, private property, nationalist histories, and settler colonial sovereignty permits the recognition of what José Rabasa names as the "the continuum of Indian communalism. Nothing remains the same after the invasion, and yet modes of communalism and their corresponding life forms have survived to the present."[95] Thus we can see how the unbounded corpus of La Alianza's historiography is thoroughly pervaded by the spiritual and epistemological communalism of Pueblo Story Power and by a multitude of revitalized tribal practices tied to the indigeneity of the Genízarx diaspora.

At the same time, La Alianza undeniably retained deep investments in patriarchal authority and in the normativity of heterosexual marriage that reproduced the gendered confinements that concede legitimacy to modern statecraft in the Americas. In the next chapter, I turn to Ana Castillo's 1993 novel *So Far from God* to explore how the patriarchal trappings of La Alianza's organizational structure and textual politics were challenged by the formation of the underground newspaper *El Grito del Norte*. Together, both *El Grito* and *So Far from God* express a decisive intervention in La Alianza's masculinist hierarchy of authority, an intervention that reframes New Mexico as a horizon of feminist anticapitalist story power that illuminates the insurgent designs of multiple tribes and indigeneities formed before, against, within, and beyond the overlaid colonial projects of Spain, Mexico, and the United States.

CHAPTER FOUR

REMEMBER THE WOMEN WHO DID THE BUILDING

Land Grant Cooperativity and the Folk Base of Chicana Feminism

In many respects, New Mexico has never emerged from colonial status.
—FRANCES LEON SWADESH, *LOS PRIMEROS POBLADORES*

Of the many fantastic and phantasmic scenes that occur in Ana Castillo's 1993 novel, *So Far from God*, none continue to haunt more ominously than the mysterious attack by *la malogra*. The novel follows the lives, deaths, and resurrections of Sofi and her four daughters—Fe, Esperanza, Caridad, and La Loca—as they endure the racial and gendered violence of private property in the land grant community of Tomé, located a few miles outside of Albuquerque. The night la malogra strikes, Caridad returns home "mangled like a stray cat" and covered in blood after "having been left for dead on the side of the road." Her nipples had been bitten off. She had "been scourged with something, branded like cattle" and "stabbed in the throat."[1] In the immediate months of her recovery, Caridad's "attacker or attackers were never found."[2] Because of the indifference to gendered violence held by the "sheriff's deputies and the local police department, [n]o one was even ever detained as a suspect."[3] Later, when Caridad is miraculously restored to her premutilated state and begins to apprentice as a *curandera* with her neighbor Doña Felicia, she discloses "through dreams" that it wasn't a "man with a face and a name who had attacked and left [her] mangled like a run-down rabbit. Nor two or three men. That was why she had never been able to give no information to the police." Rather, it was la malogra. "It was not a stray and desperate coyote either but a thing, both tangible and amorphous. A thing that might be described as made of sharp metal and splintered wood, of limestone, gold, and brittle parchment. It held the weight of a continent and was indelible as ink, centuries old and yet as strong as a young wolf. It had no shape and was darker than the dark night and mostly, as Caridad would never ever forget, it was pure force."[4] In his instructive catalogue of New Mexican folklore, Aurelio Espinoza identifies la malogra as "the myth about the evil one," which is also known as *la malora* ("the evil hour"). As the material incarnation and premonition of evil time, la malogra conjures "ill fate" and "bad luck." It is an "evil spirit which wanders about in the darkness of the night at the crossroads and other places . . . and has usually the form of a large lock of wool or the whole fleece of wool of a sheep (*un vellón de lana*)." Espinoza notes that because it "terrorizes the unfortunate ones who wander alone at night, . . . a person who sees la malora, like the one who sees a ghost (*un difunto*), forever remains senseless."[5]

In Castillo's depiction, la malogra incarnates as an apparatus of gendered death and harm created piecemeal from material and technology constitutive of the European colonization of the Americas.[6] As an apparatus ("a thing, both tangible and amorphous"), it converges the extracted and weaponized matter central to European settlement with the epistemic and normative imperatives of patriarchal violence, revealing both to be underwritten by "pure force." Of importance, its embodiment of patriarchal force notates disparately interconnected industries of colonial extraction with genocidal predicates and effects. The colonial hysteria of gold mining and its devastation to Indigenous bodies and lands across the hemisphere is tied to the limestone excavation required for uranium extraction and nuclear proliferation. Its "brittle parchment" at once evokes the devivifying abstraction of colonial mapmaking and the social, epistemic, and spiritual violence waged for the modern tyranny of alphabetical literacy and textual authority. To take further inventory of la malogra's material composition, its woolen garb also taps into the political economy of sheep sharecropping in New Mexico and its decisive role in facilitating the ascendance of U.S. sovereignty's private property regime through the dispossession of Spanish and Mexican land grants.[7] According to Suzanne Forrest, sheepherding not only played a key role in regulating territorial control in the Spanish colonization of New Mexico, but it also enabled the "rapid expansion of the commercial livestock business" under U.S. sovereignty, which "had the effect of imprisoning both the Hispanic and the Indian populations of New Mexico upon a land base entirely inadequate to their needs."[8]

From this perspective, the story power of la malogra's appearance in *So Far from God* resonates with what Américo Paredes terms the "folk base of Chicano literature."[9] In Paredes's corpus of influential work, the folk base does not establish a singular origin to Chicanx literature, but rather works to situate the emergence of Chicanx literary production in a heterogeneous network of oral cultures negotiating overlaid regimes of colonial domination in the U.S.-Mexico borderlands. Ramón Saldívar takes up Paredes's insight to argue that folkloric forms such as the *corrido* "can be construed as a residual cultural form that continues to underwrite contemporary Chicano narrative."[10] While drawing from the oral culture of New Mexican land grant communities, Castillo's rearticulation of la malogra also bestows to the folk "base" a distinctly political economic valence, one that signifies the conjuncture of Indigenous genocide, gendered and sexual violence, and genealogies of land grant property across successive colonial formations in New Mexico. Rather than reducing the folkloric to an aesthetic precursor and counterpart to modern Chicanx literary practice, I explore its story power in Castillo's novel to forward a materialist intervention in the historiography of capitalist ascendance in New Mexico.

In so doing, I uncover a distinct horizon of feminist anticapitalist land grant cultural production that, thirty years prior, informs Castillo's novel: the renowned underground northern New Mexico newspaper *El Grito del Norte*. *El Grito* was cofounded in 1968 after Elizabeth Martínez and Beverly Axelrod moved to New Mexico to support the New Mexican land grant struggle undertaken by La Alianza Federal de Mercedes. During its five-year press run, the newspaper provided an important community forum that pushed La Alianza's land grant struggle through a transnational feminist register and situated the organization in relation to a multitude of decolonial and civil rights' struggles throughout the hemisphere. As a formally hybrid scene of writing, *El Grito* published folkloric forms and narratives—poems, recipes, *dichos* (sayings), and children's stories—alongside historical essays on land grants, news articles on local electoral politics, reports on the Vietnam war, announcements for local agricultural and health care cooperatives, and communiqués from revolutionary movements in Mexico and Latin America. Among the expansive range of Chicanx movement print cultures, *El Grito* stood out as a publication whose emergence and daily operations were tied overwhelmingly to women's activist labor. This labor linked, in the words of Alicia Schmidt Camacho, "the local struggle [of land reclamation] to Chicana/o mobilizations in other parts of the

United States, as well as to indigenous rights, black liberation, labor campaigns, and prisoner-rights movements."[11] In its challenge to the capitalist conditions of occupation that rendered New Mexico as an overdetermined site of colonial extraction, *El Grito* also operated in tandem with a number of agricultural and sheepherding cooperatives that reimagined the gendered and sexual politics of land grant collectivity and its relations of subsistent labor.

By refracting *So Far from God* through *El Grito del Norte*, this chapter excavates a story power of feminist insurgency that draws from and informs Chicanx and U.S. Third World feminist critiques of racial capitalism and cultural nationalism. Chicanx feminisms have long critiqued the persistence of heteronormative family as the basis of racial collectivity and property ownership across the divergent yet overlapping formations of U.S., Mexican, and Chicanx nationalisms. For Norma Alarcón, the heteronormative family operates as one site where "tribal 'ethnicities' are broken down by conquest and colonizations" and thereby conjoins "male-centered cultural nationalism" and "patriarchal political economy" under differentially entangled formations of U.S. and Mexican state power.[12] Together, *So Far from God* and *El Grito del Norte* not only uncover land grant indigeneity as a submerged "folk base" to Chicanx feminist analytics, but they also shed light on the distinct power that print media and fiction bear on the collective work of dismantling the heteropatriarchal control that sustains the capitalist enshrinement of private property.

In a broad array of critical, historical, and creative work, Chicana feminist theories have unsettled what Schmidt Camacho calls Chicanx nationalism's "remasculanization of the liberation struggle," a process that naturalized "a heterosexual model of race as family, suppressing sexual difference in favor of an ideology of separate, complementary fronts of masculine and feminine social action."[13] The heteronormative family as a result remains a formation of perennial discipline and contestation not only for Chicana feminists, but for the broader articulation of U.S. Third World, women of color, and transnational feminist projects in the Americas.[14] According to Wahneema Lubiano, the articulation of patriarchal dominance under the guise of family values prescribes gender roles along a heterosexual axis of kinship that "seeks to enforce a definition of 'family' as only a household of people headed by two members of opposite sexes living with progeny produced by one of them—usually the female—and whose finances and decision making power are largely centered on the male person."[15] Chicanx nationalism's investment in heteronormative axes of kinship therefore worked not to merely "exclude women from political activity" but to replicate the operations of U.S. state power by denying the "legitimacy of Chicana militancy beyond a limited sphere of female service and domesticity."[16] In this way, while feminist critiques acknowledge Chicanx nationalism's cultivation of a critical consciousness of the U.S. state as a racial state and U.S. national culture as a farce for white culture, they also identify the centrality of the heteronormative family to oppositional nationalism's social movement cultures as a replication of state-sanctioned counterinsurgency.

In their reckoning with nationalism's gendered and sexual division of radical agency, a number of Chicana and transnational feminist theorists have found Partha Chatterjee's essay "More on Modes of Power and the Peasantry" a rich site to explore patriarchy's relation to the ongoing dispossession of Mexican and Native land under U.S. sovereignty. Chatterjee's work is an attempt to rethink the narratives that explain the ascendancy of capitalist modes of production in the social relations of India's countryside. By questioning the historical narratives that posit a linear, progressive character to the rise of capitalist dominance, he invokes a typology of three modes of power that "could exist, even coexist, in a particular state formation": the communal, the feudal, and the bourgeois.[17] Reminiscent of la malogra, the feudal mode of power Chatterjee describes is "characterized fundamentally by sheer superiority of physical force, i.e. a relationship of domination. It is founded on *conquest or some other means of physical subordination* of a subject population. It denotes not just the state formation which accompanies the feudal mode of production, but may in fact serve to describe political institutions corresponding to a whole range of forms of organization or production based on direct physical control over the life-processes of the producers."[18] The bourgeois mode of power, while drawing from feudal power, dominates its laborers and appropriates surplus value not only "by physical control over the life-processes of the producers but by complete control over the labour-process secured by rights of property in the means of production and in the product and by the impersonal operation of the market."[19] As the mode of power most readily identifiable with liberal capitalist dominance, the bourgeois mode separates the state apparatus from the workings of civil society into a "neutral institution which does not recognize the real inequalities in society." This separation institutionalizes the "individual" as a bounded "unit in political and legal transactions" and conceives of "society as the result of a contract" between abstract individuals who are "equal subjects before law."[20]

In distinction to the feudal and bourgeois modes, Chatterjee names communal power as "original property," a property that operates not as a claimed object but as a constitutive element of being and belonging in a particular place. Its originary nature furnishes the "means and materials" of the laboring process and thereby presumes community coherency on the unbounded relation between the surface of the earth and human interiority. Communal power predicates "individual or sectional rights, entitlements, and obligations . . . *on the authority of the entire social collectivity, i.e. the community*."[21] Chatterjee invokes Marx's richly suggestive language on the predicates and contexts of communal power: The "earth is the great workshop, the arsenal which furnishes both the means and material of labor, as well as the seat, the base of the community . . . The real appropriation through the labor process happens under these *presuppositions*, which are not themselves the product of labor, but appear as its natural or *divine* presuppositions."[22] Notably, Chatterjee names communal power as the "base of the community."[23] As such, communal power does not elucidate a single or "primitive" logic, but rather is differentiated by manifold social and spatial conditions. Under such logic, it is possible for communal relations of subsistence to ensure belonging and existence independent of the labor process and for "recognized offices of authoritative functionaries" to operate without "an institutionalized claim on the social surplus based on political domination, i.e. the ability to coerce."[24]

As modes of "power" instead of "production," Chatterjee questions the materiality of the economic base by turning to the question of property. Property here reckons with the "modes of power" that presuppose labor relations and decenters the question of the base of economic production that sustains capitalist dominance from "its techno-economic aspects."[25] Rather than naming merely historic stages, the idea of modes of power as predicates of labor constellates a different materialism of "institutions, and instituted processes, of power and of ideology, which intervene and give the political structures a certain relative *autonomy*" from "economic structures built around the activities of social production."[26] The signal intervention here is that rather than disappearing in conquest and settler capitalist occupation, Chatterjee notes, communal forms of power persist in "constant battle" with feudal violence and therefore signify "the *effective limits of domination* at any point of time."[27]

Under Gayatri Spivak's gloss, Chatterjee's typology of power illuminates the cohabitation of a multiplicity of "political institutions" that rely on "physical force" and on "relationships of domination" that circulate unevenly in capitalist modernity.[28] Using this insight as a point of departure, Norma Alarcón's groundbreaking essay "Chicana Feminism: in the Tracks of 'The' Native Woman" offers an incisive and provocative characterization of Chicanx cultural nationalism as a project of dismantling and replicating feudal power. Alarcón notes that Mexican nationalism and Chicano nationalism (like European bourgeois nationalisms) emerged against "feudal mode[s] of power." In "the Hispanic New World," the "feudal mode of power" in plantation and hacienda economies gave way to the construction of Mexican "mestizo nationalism." In the United States, the feudal mode of power of chattel slavery under plantation economies manifested alongside the racialized and gendered "isolation of migrant worker camps and exchange labor." For Alarcón, this explains, in part, the rise to Chicanx nationalism of the 1960s as a borderland formation of political economies rather than mere national imaginaries. Yet in the 1990s, Alarcón notes, the neoliberal explosion of unprotected and precarious forms of gendered labor led many women to find "themselves in effect separated from men who heretofore had joined forces in resistance." As a result, "'the communal mode of power' under the sign of the cultural nationalist family may be bankrupt, especially for female wageworkers."[29] Elaborating Alarcón's analysis, Grace Hong notes that if "Chicano nationalism is a mode of 'defeudalization' and the feudal modes of power over Chicano/a communities not only continue to exist but are exacerbated by global processes of hyperexploitation and concomitant state violence, then we must conclude that this process of defeudalization is still ongoing."[30]

By evoking the nonsynchronous simultaneity of communal, feudal, and liberal modes of power under Euroamerican capitalist modernity, Chicanx feminism opens a language for naming the ways in which patriarchy enables the transmission of feudal modes of power within modern regimes of race, knowledge, and territory. In these terms, an emphasis on the continuity of feudal modes of power as a force of gendering and racialization under modern nationalism counters a developmentalist narrative of modern liberalism as that which displaces both "feudal" and "tribal" modes of power with the rationality of private property, civic egalitarianism, and social scientific regimes of empirical and historical verification. In their respective and convergent reckoning with feudal modes of power under capitalist modernity, *El Grito* and *So Far from God* not only illuminate the ways that patriarchy enables and sanctions property claims predicated on gendered coercion. They also outline distinct modalities of *cooperative* power by which to rethink the dialectics of patriarchal force and Indigenous communalism in the historical narratives of capitalist production in New Mexico.

The story of *El Grito del Norte*'s founding in 1968 is one of the touchstone narratives of the emergence of Chicanx feminist cultural politics as a cooperative mode of power. Elizabeth Martínez, a graduate from Swarthmore College and former editor for Simon and Schuster in New York, was completing her time as a full-time staffer with the Student Nonviolent Coordinating Committee (SNCC) and had just finished a book on the Cuban Revolution entitled *The Youngest Revolution* before her arrival in New Mexico.[31] Axelrod, a prominent civil rights and Black Power attorney, had agreed to offer legal counsel to Tijerina for his upcoming trial stemming from the courthouse raid the previous year. As Martínez and Axelrod toured northern New Mexico, they would dialogue with numerous Alianza members and allies about starting a local newspaper. They met courthouse raid participants José Madril, Juan Valdez, Tobias Leyba, and Baltazar Martínez and began to collaborate with women such as María Varela, Enriqueta Vasquez, Valentina Valdez, Rini Templeton, Cleofas Vigil, and Fernanda Martínez.

Elizabeth Martínez recalls encountering stories of a vast underground network of folk resistance to U.S. colonialism in New Mexico. After arriving, she

> soon learned to respect names like Las Gorras Blancas (White Caps) a long-standing underground resistance group, and La Mano Negra (Black Hand), reputed to be headed by a woman at that time. . . . Examples could be found in the Penitentes (a semisecret religious organization), dances and plays performed on certain holidays reenacting key moments in the area's colonial history, the *curanderos* who cured with herbs not usually known to outsiders, along with other expressions of a long isolated, necessarily self-sufficient society—from building with adobe bricks, to cultivating a unique variety of chilies for cooking. A spirit of collectivity and interdependence ran strong in all this.[32]

With Martínez and Axelrod as coeditors, the nearly all-female staff opened *El Grito*'s office in Española and published its first issue in August 1968. "Its purpose," as stated in this issue, "is to advance the cause of justice for poor people and to help preserve the rich cultural heritage of La Raza in the area." Marking its cooperative framework, *El Grito* announces itself to its readers as "a newspaper of the people, publishing news from your communities, writing about your complaints and problems. . . . Sharing problems, knowledge, and opinions is the first step in working together against the oppressors."[33]

This cooperative mode of power enabled *El Grito* to diverge from La Alianza's predominantly masculinist form of organizing land grant families and allies. To be sure, one of La Alianza's enduring tactical innovations was its reframing of New Mexican land grant politics away from individual or familial property disputes mediated by court litigation. By organizing land grant heirs in the form of an alliance, Sylvia Rodriguez notes that La Alianza "placed the individual problem of [land loss] within a larger, collective, historically defined context and gave voice to a deep, widespread, but still largely unarticulated sense of injury and outrage."[34] Despite this innovation, La Alianza's founding president, Reies López Tijerina, retained complex and cosmic investments in the heteropatriarchal family. Martínez recalls that Tijerina's "conservatism was notable in having an almost entirely male Alianza leadership and expressing male supremacist values."[35] According to Maylei Blackwell, *El Grito*'s departure from La Alianza's gendered division of labor forged sophisticated interventions in the politics of writing. *El Grito* challenged the "realist conventions of political journalism" by embracing a "mixed-genre format [that] would form the basis of . . . a coalitional strategy among women of color" reflected in "the profusion of women of color anthologizing in the 1970s and early 1980s embodied by collaborative projects such as the 1981 publication of *This Bridge Called My Back*."[36] In Blackwell's terms, this reveals how "the early Chicana print community worked in tandem with community-based struggles, serving both as a form of community pedagogy and as a Chicana feminist politics of knowledge production, debate, and distribution."[37]

In this light, *El Grito*'s intervention in La Alianza's masculinist strictures also worked to stage a broader critique of the feudal modes of power built into the patriarchal authority of *partido* production in New Mexico, which had already enabled U.S. ranchers and livestock corporations to accumulate nearly all of the state's rangeland for cattle, sheep, and other livestock production by the mid-twentieth century.[38] The professionalized historiography of capitalist ascendance in New Mexico situates partido production as a feudal system of pastoral production with roots in fourteenth-century Spain. In sixteenth-century New Mexico, the system formalized Spanish colonial processes of land tenure and labor control by which a "large sheep owner, or *patrón*, would rent ewes to local sheepherders. The renter, or *partidario*, would acquire the flock of sheep on credit and split the flock's natural increase with the *patrón* during a negotiated time frame, often a period of five years."[39] Its colonial manifestation hovered between the two modalities of labor extraction and land occupation that regulated Spanish settlement of the Americas and beyond: the plantation and the hacienda. An offshoot of the hacienda's large-scale mode of hereditary agricultural production via enslaved and captive Indigenous American and African labor, the partido system operated through a patriarchal kinship structure in which the

> patron was responsible for the entire economic and social well-being of his peons and their families. He provided them with employment and took care of the sick, the orphaned, and the widowed. He became the godfather of the peon children at baptism. His peons were protected if they became involved with the law. He also financed church activities and supported religious and secular fiestas. The peons in return gave absolute obedience and loyalty to the patron. Loyalty was regarded as the cardinal virtue of a peon.[40]

Through a complex overlay of economic production and personal fealty, the partido system in livestock and agriculture operated in tandem with extractive silver and gold-mining economies, all of which were enmeshed in an intercultural traffic in captive Indigenous women and children. Thus, by the time it reached New Mexico at the end of the sixteenth century, the partido system had already "become a means of lending capital at interest."[41]

Unrelenting Indigenous insurgency, however, radically altered the conditions by which partido debt peonage secured Spanish colonial dominance. Approximately eighty years after the Spanish elites attempted to "build large hereditary estates using Pueblo lands and labor," the Pueblo Revolt deposed colonial rule in New Mexico.[42] While "multicausal," the revolt, Andrés Reséndez argues, stemmed from the combination of religious persecution and coercive labor extraction that attended Spanish rule, and "in fact spread far beyond New Mexico and came to involve not only Pueblos but also the Apaches, Mansos, Conchos, Sumas, Pimas, Janos, Salineros, Tobosos," and many landless Genízarx captives concentrated in the Barrio de Analco of Santa Fe.[43] When the Spanish fled New Mexico, "they left behind the largest herd of horses anywhere in northern Mexico," a factor that empowered Apache, Ute, Navajo, and Comanche tribes to at once participate in and contain the modes of colonial extraction and imperial expansion that was inaugurated by the return of the Spanish.[44]

Alvar Carlson notes that the subsequent Spanish reinvasion occurred in tandem with a revision to the "'Laws of the Indies,' Spanish laws for settlement in the western hemisphere, [with an attempt to] keep the two peoples apart and to protect Indian lands from encroachment. Specifically, the Spanish were not to reside in the Indian pueblos and no cattle ranch could be within one and one-half leagues of an Indian pueblo."[45] While delimiting Spanish territorial reach, the laws enabled large-scale sheep and cattle ranches that emerged in the pattern of other Latin American *latifundias* in which the "landowner lived in a massive fortified ranchhouse. Grouped around the ranchhouse were the church and the homes of the peons. This nucleus formed a self-sufficient socioeconomic unit isolated to a large degree from the outside world and completely dependent upon the landowner, the powerful patron."[46] Yet the dramatic expansion of Comanche, Ute, and Apache territorial networks put a brake on Spanish imperial mobility. The combination of the ongoing specter of recurrent Pueblo Indian revolt and unceasing Comanche raids remade partido production in New Mexico as a means by which Genízarx captives acquired civic rights on land grants provided they remain loyal to the Crown and defend the colony from Plains Indian attacks. In this context, partido production was "marked by the predominance of self-sufficient agricultural villages inhabited by small independent landowners owning plots of irrigated land and possessing grazing rights on the village commons."[47]

Throughout the eighteenth century and into the early nineteenth, the partido system in land grant villages such as Española, Taos, Peñasco, Abiquiú, Belén, Anton Chico, Tomé, and others at once mobilized an inheritance of Pueblo communalism through irrigated agriculture, practiced colonial forms of Indian removal and feudal bondage, and participated in complex and often illicit trading networks with the Comanche, Apache, and Ute tribes of the Plains and Rocky Mountains. According to James Brooks, the intersection of colonial territoriality, Indigenous communalism, enslaved labor, and patriarchal honor and authority in the villages exposed a number of "cultural differences in the region" and revealed the extent to which "native and colonizing peoples came to a convergence in patriarchal notions about the socially productive value and exchangeability of women and children as well as sheep, cattle, and horses."[48] In these clustered systems of communal and coercive labor and exchange, land boundaries were established through a mix of customary oral pacts and written documentation. Land and labor rights were thus at once inscribed through deeds in which the name of a *patrón* or set of *patrones* stood as a proxy for a network of families *and* "recorded in relation to prominent landmarks such as rivers, mesas, and geologic outcroppings."[49] Therefore, while land grant formations enabled private and alienable land claims, "they were not possible without various common property obligations such as digging acequias, sharing common grazing areas, and comanaging and using uplands for hunting and gathering."[50]

In many ways, the Mexican independence of 1821 and the subsequent U.S. invasion in 1846 can be seen as launching New Mexico out of the so-called feudal period by facilitating the ascendance of merchant capitalism, wage labor, secular knowledge, and liberal conceptions of mass citizenship and individual property ownership under nation-state sovereignties. At the same time, these liberal transformations intensified forms of feudal dispossession. That is, while Mexican independence disbanded the Spanish colonial caste system and recognized the legitimacy of Pueblo Indian land claims, it also broadened the scale of Pueblo and land grant commons available for private exchange and appropriation. This move toward privatization intersected with the burgeoning mode of finance, merchant, and industrial capitalist production tied to U.S. imperial expansion in ways that would devastate the livelihoods of land grant villagers. As a result, despite the ostensible protection of Pueblo and Hispanx land grant titles afforded by the Treaty of Guadalupe Hidalgo, the U.S. usurpation of northern Mexico imposed a distinct legal regime, political economy, and white heteropatriarchal imaginary that sanctioned state failure "to recognize the political and legal rights of the rural Hispanic communities [and] permitted endless varieties of chicanery, fraud, and collusion to occur."[51] The initial wave of dispossession in the 1850s–1870s prompted the introduction of the railroad system in 1879 and subsequently gave rise to a massive commercial livestock and timber industry in New Mexico. A number of land grant settlers responded by turning to the Pueblo Indians for refuge by squatting on "sizeable areas of uncleared, irrigable land within the sparsely populated Pueblo Indian grants during the late 1800s."[52] Many more, however, faced no other option but to enter into increasingly coercive partido contracts with Anglo settlers, merchants, and corporations.

If partido contracts, under Spanish and Mexican control, "amounted to a personal dependence and mutual obligation between a large landowner and the peasants living on or near his property," U.S. law and capital supplanted these relations through mercantile contracts mediated by a cash economy in which the goal of livestock production valorized profit over subsistence.[53] Mercantile credit relations therefore transferred the risks of livestock production entirely onto the *partidario* and required that they rent supplies for their labor from the merchant's store with a credit rate of at least 10 percent. To cover these risks for the Anglo merchant, contracts allowed the land grant communities to mortgage their land grant deeds as collateral. Therefore, according to David Correia, when nearly "a quarter of all *partido* contracts ended in default," it became "an event that announced the start of a debt peonage relation" that forced partidarios "to enter into new contracts with terms that now included a rental fee on lands they once owned or had free access to."[54] The combination of racialized labor exploitation, land dispossession, resource extraction, and mass commercial export tied to mercantile contracts has led Marta Weigle to describe their effects as "sharecropping with sheep."[55]

Wage labor in new Anglo monopolies on agriculture, mining, and lumber milling throughout Colorado, Utah, Wyoming, and Montana arose as the only alternative or supplement to partido entrapment by providing cash for "land taxes, grazing fees, and consumer goods." Wages were often so depressed that entire families were conscripted in cycles of seasonal agricultural labor, forcing many to move to Denver, Albuquerque, and other urban centers. In the early twentieth century, the United States undertook massive damming projects to encourage industrial farming enterprises in New Mexico that controlled the majority of grazing land.[56] A few decades later, the intensification of capitalist wage labor control and industrial livestock production in New Mexico had eroded the topsoil millions of acres of grassland in New Mexico and the plains. This ecological destruction had its counterpart in the capitalist dismantling of the "extended patriarchal family . . . of the patron-peon system" and "the slow decline in the influence of the Roman Catholic Church, the intrusion of Protestant denominations, the development of an educational system dominated by Anglo values, the draft of young men into military service during World War II and the Korean War, and the development of a massive emigration movement away from the villages."[57] By disrupting the "communal patterns of planting and harvesting," Suzanne Forrest notes, work in the fields or in livestock production "had to be recompensed with wages. Since the productivity of the Hispanic village was predicated upon its corporate nature the moment productivity became an individual rather than a group concern, it constituted the *coup de grace* to Hispanic economic independence."[58] In this way, partido production gave way to a system of mercantile credit that institutionalized capitalist systems of exchange and consumption sustained by the "capture [of] rural labor and control [of] common land."[59]

By building in the ruins of gendered and racialized displacement, *El Grito* worked in and publicized cooperative projects of health care and agricultural production undertaken by a polyglot array of activists and land grant heirs. These projects included La Cooperativa Agrícola de Tierra Amarilla and La Clínica del Pueblo de Río Arriba. By working on roughly six hundred acres of

La Cooperativa's First Harvest

The Tierra Amarilla Agricultural Cooperative is completing its first harvest. Wheat has been harvested with a combine recently acquired by the Cooperative: before that, sweet peas and pinto beans were harvested. But the main success has been the potatoes: at Tierra Amarilla, Ensenada and Placita Blanca, more than 15 tons hav been dug up and sacked.

One of the Co-op workers wrote these words about what the harvest was like:

The sun is shining, the earth is dry. Today we start the harvest of potatoes in Ensenada (near Tierra Amarilla). Last night we went around to visit some of the families and to see if they or people they know could come out to the campo today. Many said they would come.

When we get to the field, the tractor is already there and the potato digger is being attached. Others have started digging with shovels and the potatoes they are turning over are almost all good ones and large. When the potato digger starts going, everyone gets into a discussion of which is more effective--the shovels or the potato digger. Some people prefer just using a shovel but it is decided to use both--first the digger, then going over the row again with shovels. The potatoes are collected and the burlap bags swell. *(continued below)*

The 100-pound sacks are lugged across the field to the trucks where potatoes are sorted and re-sacked. Then the tops are sewn up and the sacks loaded onto trucks. It is warm as the sun reaches the middle of the sky and we all break for lunch.

Talking and laughter sounds drift all over the field, there are many people--viejos, children, young people, even pregnant women, all at work. Some are people who never knew each other before and who are now working together for a common purpose.

In the afternoon the people work with even more spirit. Together we will finish the field today!

As the sun begins to set and the afternoon grows colder, people start to leave--one by one, two by two. Everyone says goodbye and asks what time they should come the next day.

It has been a good day of work. We are tired and cold, since only a few orange streaks are left in the sky--but we feel very alive inside, and tomorrow we will all be back.

TESSA

VIVA LA PRIMERA COSECHA DE LA COOPERATIVA!

VIVA LA COOPERATIVA!

Left, the Co-op's combine

FIGURE 7 "La Cooperativa's First Harvest," *El Grito del Norte* (Española, NM), November 15, 1969. Peter Nabokov Papers, MSS 93 BC, Special Collections and Center for Southwest Research, University of New Mexico Libraries.

land grant land in Tierra Amarilla, Enseñada, and Placita Blanca, the members of the La Cooperativa engendered projects of collective farming of pinto beans, potatoes, and sweet peas alongside practices of sheep grazing. These cooperative projects of subsistent farming summoned not only the health clinic, La Clínica del Pueblo del Río Arriba, but also impelled the creation of a law office, employment center, and shoe store.[60] In a 1977 article in the *Nation* magazine, Peter Nabokov reported that La Clínica "was a most successful health facility" that served "upward of 7,000 isolated villagers, mostly Spanish-speaking, in a region where infant mortality rivals the worst in the nation and the nearest hospital is 70 miles away over treacherous mountain roads."[61]

One announcement in *El Grito*'s November 15, 1969, issue reveals cooperative power through images of subsistent labor unaligned with the heteronormative family. With photos of the fields and the workers, the announcement states: "There are many people—viejos, Children, young people, even pregnant women, all at work. Some are people who never knew each other before and who are now working together for a common purpose."[62] Under the sign of the co-op, land grant memory prompts the labor of building to lose its ability to cohere a clear division or sector of labor. As a result, cooperativity also calls for a distinct politics of study and knowledge production. Nabokov notes that La Cooperación offered "food stamps and consumer advocate counseling, as well as research into the original 17th and 18th century land grants."[63] By virtue of the co-op, *El Grito* columnist Enriqueta Vasquez speculates, these women "would be cultivating themselves and also be teaching the young ones how to relate to the earth. [They] could actually build a satisfying home life for themselves and their families. They could work and play together and they could study together and learn about nature, crops, and life in general. There would be a deep spiritual relationship and bond there." Through these teachings, co-op members could see land as original property, as life's originary matter, as "something that belongs to everyone." As the property that originates life, "Land is like air. . . . It is part of each and every one of us. It belongs to the peoples. Tribal ownership was very just and served the needs of the communities."[64]

El Grito's cooperative conditions of publication in land grant territory and its incongruent relation to Chicano nationalism's overvaluation of the heterosexual family shed a distinct light on the conditions of emergence and politics of representation that animate *So Far from God*. Roughly twenty-five years after *El Grito*'s heyday, Ana Castillo moved to Albuquerque with plans to write a novel that would take place in her hometown of Chicago.[65] Castillo had just earned her doctorate in American studies from the University of Bremen in Germany after completing her master's in Latin American and Caribbean studies at the University of Chicago. By the time she arrived in Albuquerque, she was already known for her poetic work such as *Otro Canto* (1977) and *Women Are Not Roses* (1984), as well as two novels that playfully engage with absurdist and Latin American literary forms and histories: *The Mixquiahuala Letters* (1986) and *Sapogonia: An anti-romance in 3/8 meter* (1990). While working on her novel, Castillo ran graduate workshops on creative writing with Tony Hillerman at the University of New Mexico and taught other courses as an adjunct. Yet, the novel that was supposed to be about her "own history . . . [and] travels, Chicago" was overtaken by another story because, as she recalls, "that place, New Mexico, hits you like a ton of bricks."[66] Six months later, Castillo would complete the first draft of her third novel, *So Far from God*, which she subsequently published in 1993.

El Grito's conditions of publication provide a different way of emplacing *So Far from God* in land grant horizons of cooperativity. As texts produced through encounters between formally educated feminist writers and the folk base of land grant story power localized in New Mexico, their convergent critique of the violence of the heteronormative family reveals an insistence not only on moving sex and gender out of the private realm, but also a performance of what Schmidt Camacho calls "a longer historical memory, one that predated 1848 and the nation form."[67] Their invocation of folkloric forms and tropes for his performance of memory has radical implications for embodied and emplaced theory on the patriarchal frameworks mobilized in the formation and dispossession of land grants in New Mexico. By deciphering the manifold modalities of patriarchal coercion, labor exploitation, and territorial control within capitalist dominance, *El Grito* and *So Far From God* open a distinct political horizon of cooperativity by which to exercise a "limit to bourgeois hegemony."[68]

Widely considered a landmark text in Chicana literature, *So Far from God* employs a mix of absurdist, magical realist, and realist techniques in depicting the struggles of Sofi, a Tomé land grant inhabitant, owner of the Carne Buena Carnecería, and single mother of four daughters who suffer devastating deaths and occasional miraculous resurrections. Esperanza, the eldest, obtains her bachelor's in Chicano studies and communications at the University of New Mexico and takes on a job as an anchor on a local TV station. Her success lands her an assignment in Saudi Arabia, and while covering the first Gulf War she disappears and dies. Although the cause of her death is never revealed and her body is never found, she makes occasional "ectoplasmic" visits to her family.[69] Caridad drops out of college after a year and marries Memo, her high school boyfriend. Upon discovering an ongoing affair between Memo and his ex-girlfriend, Caridad miscarries their daughter and begins "loving anyone she met at the bars who vaguely resembled Memo."[70] After her encounter with la malogra and her miraculous and spontaneous recovery to her preassaulted state, Caridad becomes a local object of saintly devotion and falls in love with a woman from Acoma Pueblo. Together, they leap off the cliffs of Acoma and are swallowed by the earth. Fe's death "is hard to talk about."[71] Believing her mother and sisters to be "self-defeating. . . . [and] unambitious," Fe works at a local bank and strives for white heteronormative marriage with her fiancé Tom. Tom devastates Fe by calling off their marriage, and she incessantly screams for months until her voice is permanently damaged.[72] She later marries a sheepherder from northern New Mexico and begins working at Acme International, a weapons and chemical manufacturing plant. After months of inhaling toxic chemical fumes, Fe's body becomes pockmarked with cancerous tumors. She is the one who dies and never returns. She's the one who remains "plain dead."[73] La Loca unexpectedly dies at the age of three only to come back to life at her funeral and levitate to the roof of the church to the amazement of the inhabitants of Tomé. Once resurrected, La Loca develops a lifelong phobia of people and devotes her time to tending to her family's farm animals and acting as a healer for her three sisters. After witnessing the demise and uneven reembodiment of her sisters, Loca develops cancer, mysteriously contracts AIDS, and dies after participating in a Good Friday procession through Tomé that protests the deaths brought to the people of New Mexico from exposure to toxic chemicals.

While signifying multiracialized and gendered land grant subjects negotiating differentiated exposure to premature death and state sanctioned harm, *So Far from God* also articulates a number of cooperative and activist organizations both within and around the land grant that counter the gendered and environmental catastrophes of late capitalism. Sofi runs for mayor of Tomé and starts "a sheep-grazing wool-weaving enterprise 'Los Ganados y Lana Cooperative,' modeled after the one started by the group of the north that had also saved its community from destitution."[74] Not without its challenges, the co-op begins to sustain the livelihood of "more than two dozen women" and allows them to use their work to attain college credit.[75] It also develops into a food co-op where families are able to raise hormone-free meat and organic produce. Prompted by the final cruelty of La Loca's death, as well as the "hundreds of petitions she received in the mail everyday," Sofi also "became the founder and first presidenta of what would later be known worldwide as . . . M.O.M.A.S., Mothers of Martyrs and Saints."[76]

The novel's treatment of cooperativity begins as Sofi decides to run for "la Mayor of Tomé" in a seemingly spontaneous act of rebellion to the deaths of her daughters and the incompetence of her estranged husband, Domingo. Notably, cooperativity in the novel emerges at the intersection of patriarchal failure, gendered labor made invisible, and feminist debate. The idea is presented as an extended dialogue with an unnamed *comadre* (friend/godmother) and fellow inhabitant of Tomé as Sofi performs housework and says "things to herself like, 'If that Domingo doesn't fix the screen door this week, *I'm* gonna have to do it myself; then I'll throw his butt out for sure; what do I want him for then anyhow?'"[77] Sofi's lament over Domingo's absence and parasitical relation to the family sheds light on the absence of competent male protagonism within the novel and refuses the gendered division of labor cohered by the (cultural) nationalist family. In the wake of patriarchal failure, it asserts dialogue and debate over familial ties as the predicate to cooperative labor. "Here's my idea," Sofi said, "I have decided to run for mayor . . . !" Her comadre, however, "really didn't get it. She especially didn't get it because Tome never had no mayor. . . . After all, Tome wasn't even an incorporated village like Los Lunas or Belen. *That* much she knew."[78]

Confronting the liminal and abandoned status of Tomé, the subsequent dialogue with Sofi's comadre reflects a critical historical account of the racialized and gendered legacies of partido production and land grant dispossession indebted to Chicanx movement counternarratives and historiographies of land loss. There is a recognition of the systematic dismantling of land grant modes of communal subsistence because of "outsiders moving in, buying up land that had belonged to original families, who were being forced to give it up because they just couldn't live off of it no more, and the taxes were too high."[79] There is consciousness of the deindigenization of land grant communities through the racialized redistribution of ejido land to Anglo settlers and corporations that works to displace land grant descendants "to Albuquerque or even farther away to work, or out of state to college, or out of the country with the Army instead of staying home to work on the rancherías."[80] And there is the ironic acknowledgment that while the "outsiders in the past had overused the land so that in some cases it was no good for raising crops or grazing livestock no more," colonial occupation has enabled a privileged class of Anglo landowners to live out pastoral fantasies on dispossessed land. "And now we have los gringos coming here and breeding peacocks," la comadre complained. "Now, I ask you, what can you do with peacocks? Do these New Yorkers eat them, like in fancy restaurants or something?" There was really only one person in the vicinity who was breeding peacocks, but the point for the comadre was that he did not have to earn his living from raising the birds, much less use them for food. He was an outsider, and there were a lot of outsiders moving in."[81]

While indebted to Chicanx historiography, the novel's folkloric voice of *la mitotera* mediates the question of land dispossession in a way that undermines the empirical investments and textual authority of modern history and print journalism. La mitotera is derived from the Nahuatl word *mitotl* or *mitotiqui* that signifies "dancer," referring to the sacred dances of a number of Native tribes across Greater Mexico.[82] While *mitote* signifies an uproar or turmoil in Spanish, a *mitoterx* is a person who traffics in gossip, secrecy, and clandestine knowledge. B. J. Manríquez notes that "a mitotera will expose people's experiences in order to ridicule and shame, feigning a sympathetic attitude while belittling the person's action and personality in private to her *comadre* who in this case is the reader. With ironic evaluation of the characters' personalities and motives, the mitotera continues to remind readers of the paradox between appearances and 'reality.'"[83] Thus while *So Far from God* explicitly sets the base of its cooperative visions in the land grant village of Tomé, the social history of Tomé's formation and dispossession by corporate capital never reaches positive enunciation in the novel.[84] In lieu of this historiographical representation, the story power of la mitotera performs a telling of Tomé's past and present as knowledge that is at once private and public, sympathetic and derisive, undependable and yet a primary source of information. La mitotera's story power disrupts the gendered division of information, memory, publicity, and secrecy under nationalism. In this way, *So Far from God* harnesses modernity's oral-textual binary into a cooperative relation that transforms the logocentrism of the novel into a vehicle for the power of story.

It is at this intersection of land grant memory, Chicanx radicalism, and situated information accrued through dialogue with multiple narrative forms and affective registers that Sofi begins to coin a language for the cooperative mode of power. Not unlike the travels of Elizabeth Martínez and Beverly Axelrod that formed *El Grito*, Sofi and her comadre "started their campaign by going around for months talking to neighbors, to fellow parishioners, people at the schools, at the local Y, and other such places to get ideas and help." Soon, "people began to respond to Sofi's 'campaign,' which they did not see as a mayoral one so much as one to rescue Tome." Sofi's campaign for "La Mayor of Tome" both appropriates liberal rituals of community empowerment and dispenses with the bourgeois mode of power that underwrites modes of public representation under liberal politics. She sees the need to change the "system" and fight for community "rights" yet eschews articulating the urgency of her struggles through a canonized history of Chicanx militancy. Cooperativity is the effect of "many community-based meetings in which debates as to what ideas would lend themselves best toward some form of economic self-sufficiency for their area before some people came up with a plan that eventually mobilized everyone into action." La mitotera continues that it "would take YEARS of diligence and determination beyond this telling to meet their goals but Sofi's vecinos finally embarked on an ambitious project, which was to start a sheep-grazing wool-weaving enterprise, 'Los Ganados y Lana Cooperative,' modeled after the one started by the group up north that had also saved its community from destitution."[85]

Born out of the need to establish some form of "economic self-sufficiency," the cooperative decenters a cash-based economy, as "neighbors who had inherited land from homesteading ancestors that was no longer farmed or used for nothing, mostly due to poverty, were persuaded to sell or barter it off for services in shares to those skilled neighbors who hadn't. By bartering, people were able to get their run-down farm equipment, homes, home appliances, cars, and trucks fixed."[86] Here we see the hauntings of La Cooperativa Agrícola de Tierra Amarilla as a model for Tomé's cooperative project coupled with a refusal or inability to name the "group up north." In line with the unreliable and partial narrative voice of la mitotera, Castillo's implicit reference to La Cooperativa's experiments in cooperative subsistence reflects a specific representational politics that at once relies on a memory and historiography of land grant struggle yet abandons an empiricist and a realist lexicon for an insurrection of that memory in the present.

By negotiating the catastrophic milieu of colonial occupation that constitutes New Mexico, *So Far from God* offers distinct-yet-coincident scenes to revisit *El Grito*'s cooperative mode of power. In particular, the novel provides a different horizon of light by which to engage the writings of Enriqueta Vasquez, a prolific *El Grito* columnist and incipient theoretician of Chicana feminism. One article, "La Chicana: Let's Build a New Life," published in the November, 15, 1969, issue, begins by addressing her "Comadres . . . on the woman thing" within the familial trappings of *Aztlán*, the mythical Chicanx homeland.[87] "The other day," she writes, "I was listening to a group of young people talking about how the Southwest is a homeland for the Chicano wherever he may be. They were saying this is an area where the Chicano can identify with the land, and how the culture is rooted here, and how it would be good to have our families move onto the land and raise our children here in OUR homeland of Aztlan." Working with a masculinist narrative of Chicanx history that positions Aztlán as the "homeland" for "Chicano" subjects, Vasquez repeats the nationalist imperatives to tie "land" and "culture" together through the metaphor of the family. Yet rather than accepting the narrative that she happens to encounter, Vasquez refuses the gendered division of radical agency that is constitutive of nationalist articulations of Aztlán. She argues that the only group with the capacity to manifest Aztlán's alternative regime of land, culture, and memory is not the Chicano at all. It is actually "The CHICANA."

Notably, Vasquez locates Chicana subjects not in some type of romantic agricultural setting, but "in housing projects in the city" because they were displaced "from small cities and farms and would love to go back to live in the country." "Many of these women," she reports, "have anywhere from 2 to 6 children, live on AID to Dependent Children, do not own homes, own very few belongings, have no jobs and truly have very little to tie them down to the city." In another column, "This Land Is Our Land," Vasquez comments on the irony of this gendered displacement under a U.S. regime of legal and social violence around "the individual owning of land."[88] As Chicana subjects endure the violence of wage labor, state welfare programs, and urban landless destitution, Vasquez notes, "the government subsidizes big land holders not to plant their land because it will upset the economy of the open market. . . . the government pays them solely to have the land in their power. There are even companies that begin to buy the land with the objective of only being paid for being the owners of the land. We have to have a 'boom' in this country while people all over the world go to bed hungry."[89]

Vasquez situates partido production within a globalized capitalist economy that values accumulation by dispossession and individual or corporate ownership over communal occupancy. By deploying a mix of speculation and memory, her work fathoms a distinct rejoinder to the disaster of U.S. private property. She proposes the formation of a "co-op of about six such families" who "would buy about ten acres of land." This cooperative would enable the people to, as she puts it in the first person, "go back to being self-sufficient, to start planting our lands, instead of just letting them lay there, and to start thinking in terms of feeding ourselves instead of feeding the grocery stores." For Vasquez, this would lead to the possibility of unalienated labor, for "in a summer they could do their home repairs and building." Moreover, this possibility of unalienated cooperative labor "for the Chicana . . . is no problem. I have talked to many Chicanos in the area and they still remember the times when it was the woman who did the building."[90]

There is a story power in the call to remember the times when the women did the building that specifically does not focus on the Spanish *patrón* as the fallen icon of land grant decimation. Rather, it invokes the endurance of Pueblo Indian communalism under the duress of racial slavery and colonial land usurpation tied to Genízarx racialization and ejido land grant formation. She writes: "The way of the Indian was to have land for the community and to work the land together for the community's use. This was our custom. Why can't we do this again?" Yet rather than trafficking in a romantic logic of Indigenous purity, the story power of the women who did the building is also an account of the destructive legacies of when "the Spaniards came along . . . and made slaves of the Indians. They forced the Indians to work in the mines and then they would send the gold to Spain. The Spaniards did live near the Indian Pueblos and intermarry. From here come the mestizo."[91] In the words of Brenda M. Romero, the story power of building "emerges as a vehicle of liminality, negotiating a wide variety of gendered cultural meanings in this metaphorical borderland."[92] It draws from the legacy of what James Brooks calls "Southwest Borderland Slavery" in which "the hapless women and children who became slaves also became the main negotiators of cultural, economic, and political exchange between groups."[93] And it is a performance of memory enunciated under a mode of gendered labor control resultant from the racialized displacement of land grant commons under U.S. sovereignty, in which the dismantling of its extended patriarchal family unit required women in land grant villages to find "jobs in the new towns as cooks, servants, seamstresses, and washerwomen. Inevitably, some also found self-employment as prostitutes."[94] In this way, to remember the women who did the building signifies a complex matrix of Indigenous communalism that endures as a relation of cooperativity between the labors of subsistence, speculation, memory, and study despite the encroachment of distinct gendered modalities and sexual control across successive waves of colonial occupation.

Cooperativity here allows us to consider the distinct ways *El Grito* and *So Far from God* name the functions and limits of patriarchal violence under U.S. sovereignty that draw from patrón authority. In Rio Arriba County in the early

1970s—where *El Grito*, La Clínica, and La Cooperativa all resided—the patrón's feudal mode of power converged political influence and police power in the figure of Emilio Naranjo. Cast by Nabokov as the "county's top political and police boss and archenemy of La Cooperación," Naranjo "wielded great power" as an "intermediary between Anglo institutions and his own people's desperate poverty."[95] Naranjo signified the ironic conversion of the Hispano patrón under U.S. sovereignty into a "*jefe politico* who could manipulate the political system" by "delivering a group of voters" to an established political party in exchange for "ethnic concessions, opportunities to further his own career, and jobs for his constituents."[96] As the subsistent economy of partido production disappeared, the patrón, according to Forrest, "was known as much for his ruthlessness, graft, and corruption as he was for a personal, and usually sincere, commitment to his constituents."[97] *El Grito*'s cooperative rearticulation of justice rooted in the communal and life-creating power of the land therefore starkly contrasted with the patrón system's enshrinement in the machine politics of U.S. representative democracy, in which residual modes of feudal coercion were sanctioned by the counterinsurgent forces of the U.S. state. While reporting on an illegal "series of predawn police attacks in November 1975 on the homes of La Cooperación supporters, and involving the ransacking of La Clínica itself," Nabokov quotes a "beer drinker in an Española bar who begged not to be named, 'Emilio has become the kind of man no one will say anything about except that he is a very kind and generous man we're afraid of.'"[98] Enriqueta Vasquez noted "near constant police surveillance" and "assumed . . . unmarked police cars following her wherever she drove."[99] Multiple firebombings targeted La Alianza's Albuquerque's headquarters. The *El Grito* reporter and Black Beret member Antonio Córdova was shot and killed alongside Rito Canales by the Albuquerque Police in January 1972. The increasing level of state-sanctioned violence surrounding the paper, in addition to the mounting costs and energy of publishing consistent monthly issues, eventually prompted the staff to relocate *El Grito* from Española to Las Vegas, New Mexico.

The sustained duress of state surveillance and terror became an important predicate in *El Grito*'s distinct analysis of capitalist property relations, one that situated the feudal violence of police brutality within an apparatus of enforcement supported by the U.S. courts and the liberal press. A special issue in September 1969 dedicated to the "Law and Order Conspiracy Against La Raza" ponders: "Why is it that in courts, the *policía*, and the newspapers all agree with each other when they move against us, the people? Why is it that the state police, Forest Service, F.B.I., the Attorney General, the U.S. Commissioner, the judges—so many separate men and so many separate men and so many separate offices and in so many different places, from Santa Fe to Washington D.C.—all move as one against La Raza?" This "conspiracy," however, does not require these "desgraciados and vendidos . . . to have a secret meeting to make plans." Instead, because "in New Mexico, the courts were originally established by the U.S. occupying forces to make legitimate the theft of the people's lands," "they already know what the other wants done—because they are all against la gente. Because they all want to keep themselves in power, fill their own panzas. *And to do this they must silence any voice that speaks out against them. They must crush any spirit that rises up to challenge them.*"[100] Notice how the "theft of the people's lands" is situated as central to the operations of representative democracy, what Chatterjee describes as the "fundamental institutional form by which the bourgeoisie [mode of power] sustains its political domination." In doing so, *El Grito* demonstrates how capitalist hegemony selectively appropriates "feudal institutions" in order to dissolve "the peasantry as a distinct social form of existence and productive labour, and hence the extinction of a communal mode of power."[101]

As a result, *El Grito* named the violence of patriarchy as a matrix for the continuity and acceleration of feudal strictures of control and possession across distinct borderland colonial modernities. This labor of naming patriarchy also articulates the urgency of excavating communal forms of power grounded in cooperative performances of memory. Particularly illustrative here is an article from *El Grito*'s very first issue, "For Machos Only," which announces "Los Comancheros," an emergent youth organization tied to La Alianza. As a mode of recruitment, the headline "For Machos Only" assumes a sardonic mode of feminist dialogue. The *machos* who seem so crucial to the coherency of Indo-hispanx and Chicanx collectivity are at once called to attention and called into question: "Listen, man, you from Bernalillo or Chama or Taos or wherever you are. . . . You think you're so macho . . . because you treat women like things, but I tell you that you're a jerk, because all those things are just what the Anglo enemy wants you to do."[102] Notably, the article opens with the discovery that the violence of masculinity replicates state violence: the "machos" who beat women and "treat women like things" are also doing what, in the author's words, "the Anglo enemy wants you to do." Disidentifying with a patriarchal narrative of Chicanx cultural nationalism that labeled feminist insurgency as divisive to movement coherency, "For Machos Only" suggests that *machismo* is itself a replication of Anglo patriarchy and therefore a state strategy of counterinsurgency.[103] For these reasons, the article does not mince words: "We don't need machos." However, as a disidentificatory expression of masculine social movement practice, there is simultaneous investment in "some kind of man . . . guys with fresh blood and ideas" who fight to "pull up" their "people." Machismo is thus recast as a type of violent ignorance sanctioned by the sovereignty of the U.S. state and decoupled from the project of gendering masculinity.

By virtue of such critical prodigiousness, *El Grito* moves against standard interpretations of ejido land grant dispossession that account for the loss of communal holdings as an effect of the incommensurability between Spanish/Mexican and Anglo legal frameworks.[104] Maria Montoya, for example, argues that "mistranslation of the Mexican/civil law system of property" enabled the U.S. court system to transfer large land holdings to individual Anglo settlers or corporations and worked to market "the land as uninhabited and immediately available for improvement and European settlement."[105] Instead, *El Grito* anticipates a recent turn in the historiography of land grant grants that demonstrates how dispossession was facilitated by the patriarchal *overlap* of these two distinct legal frameworks. Exemplified by David Correia, this approach argues that the "colonial infrastructure" of the land grants "accommodated the interests of commercial speculators" from the United States. Speculators "claimed community grants were private grants and pursued deed purchases from the heirs of these named settlers. This tactic was plausible by virtue of the practice common in grant making to name only representatives of the community in the grant documents."[106] This allows us to conceptualize the two senses of representation (as proxy and portrait) so crucial to the production of land grant dispossession and its gendered modes of subalternity. Not only does Spanish law constitute its authority through feudal modes of patriarchal representation of community (men as proxy for community), but it also inscribes a mode of textualization and legality that allows a re-presentation of men as the sole legible figures for the ownership of communal holdings as private property under U.S. law. The distinct yet overlaid feudal modes of patriarchal power constitutive of Spanish and U.S. property law therefore provide a powerful site of coalition for the ongoing colonial occupation of New Mexico.

Therefore, rather than invoking a conservative plea for family values, "For Machos Only" calls for an alternative politics of memory, gender formation, and knowledge production issuing from subjugated legacies of the Genízarx diaspora: "Los Comancheros [is] a youth organization which takes its name from the . . . original Comancheros [who] were of Indo-Hispanic blood, despised by both the pure Indians and the pure Spaniards. They were outcasts in the 18th and 19th centuries." With the "same militant spirit as that of the original Comancheros," this new youth organization has formed "to help people where the law fails to protect them."[107] According to Frances Leon Swadesh, the Comancheros of the eighteenth century were parties of traders and buffalo hunters from "detribalized Indian communities called *Genízaro*" who "traveled out on the buffalo plains to trade with Comanches and other nomadic tribes." The content of the trade ranged from horses and livestock to "dressed hides or captive women and children"; as a result, "relations of peace and trade alternated with periods of intensive raiding and counter-raiding."[108] "For Machos Only" therefore creates a window into the epistemic tension that permeates *El Grito*'s politics of writing. On one hand, the feminist critiques of historiographic realism and legal authority emerging from "For Machos Only" reflect a potent challenge to the feudal modes of power preserved within liberal regimes of race, property, and knowledge production under U.S. national sovereignty. On the other, the paper's challenge to the masculinist metaphors that regulated social movement militancy remained bound to progressive temporalities of culture and a modern will to historiographic truth that together situate Los Comancheros as the "militant vanguard of the New Breed . . . of Indo-Hispanic blood . . . [who] represented a high point in the history of the New Breed—the Indo-Hispano people of the Southwest." This uneven investment in vanguardist temporality, modern truth, and blood-based kinship culminates into a "demand [for] an educational system which gives our people a thorough knowledge of the Spanish language and which teaches the true history of the Indo-Hispano people."[109]

So Far from God's portrayal of land grant dispossession reveals an important limit to the replication of feudal power found in *El Grito*'s embrace of a "true history" in vanguardist time grounded in blood-based kinship. Sofi laments in the multiform dialogue with her comadre that her "familia once had three hundred acres to farm." "Now," she says, "all I got left of my father's hard work—and his father's and his father's is casi nada, just a measly ten acres now, nomás, comadre! Barely enough for my family to live on!" Sofi claims that she has "even less," sadly remembering "that even the tiny bit she had inherited had been sold out of Domingo's recklessness" and gambling debts. From whence Sofi and her comadre come to the subtle discovery that land grant loss is both facilitated and compounded by the patriarchal regimes of territoriality *shared* by Spanish and U.S. law. La comadre's narration of "her familia" and the patriarchal mode of descent ("and his father's and his father's") that should have prevented the gradual decimation of her land is shown to be ineffectual in preserving land grant communalism. That is, the feudal origins of land grants as territories bestowed to her "familia" as "direct grantees of a land grant from King Felipe II" loses its ability to counter the land thievery of the "gringos" and "Mexico." Instead, as Sofi realizes, it is the blood-based unit of the "familia" that has rendered her dispossessed.[110]

Thus the feudal power condensed in land grant territoriality and affirmed by U.S. private property is repeatedly depicted in the novel as the undeniable harbinger of disaster to the cooperative mode of power. As the "sheep-raising wool-weaving co-op was doing well for the unofficial village of Tome . . . and Sofia . . . experienced a brief period of economic balance for the first time in her adult life," we learn that Domingo had secretly lost her house and land to gambling debts to a local judge.[111] This event uncovers how the coalition of patriarchal ownership facilitates the dispossession of Sofi's land grant holdings; that is, U.S. law enshrines community property as bound to the heteronormative family. As the agent of dispossession, "the law," based on "'community property,' stated that the house also belonged to her legal husband who remained, even after twenty years of being la Abandonada, Domingo."[112] As a result, Sofi is "notified by the bank that her home, along with one measly acre next to her property which she had not given up to the Tome collective so as to keep Loca's horses, was being transferred over" to the judge who ruled on her case. Heightening the brutal irony of dispossession, the judge subsequently requires Sofi to pay rent in order to continue to live on her ancestral land. In this way, Sofi confronts the dissolution of all modes of original and communal property required by the patriarchal valorization of capital, for "now there was no mother to honor, no father to respect, no 'jitas to sacrifice for, no rancho to maintain, and no land left to work."[113]

Sofi's dispossession therefore returns us to la malogra, as it forces us to reckon with the overlaid trajectories of patriarchal force that mediate the political economy of U.S. settler colonialism by dispensing the will to modern historical truth. From this perspective, la malogra's impression as "pure force" takes on an uncannily prophetic apparition. It foretells patrón control as enabling the destitution and mutilation of modes of community, sustenance, and place under U.S. law and capital. Yet it also invokes folkloric tropes and memories as vital means for the transmission of such knowledge. By virtue of the same politics of representation, the novel's abandonment of the realist prose of print journalism and land grant historiography also operates as a rejection of the secular epistemes and temporalities of the settler nation form.

Such a rejection affirms that despite what its title may initially signify, *So Far from God* unfolds a narrative universe in which spirits, gods, ghosts, and the landscape itself interact with and participate in cooperative power. Although Sofi is depicted as the dominant individual protagonist for the novel's cooperative mode of power, the activation of the land as cooperative agent finds representation in the trajectory of Caridad's protagonism. As "the sister of the porcelain complexion, not meaning white, but as smooth as glazed clay," the Caridad we initially meet drops out of college after a year and marries Memo, her high school boyfriend. Upon realizing that Memo never stopped seeing his ex-girlfriend, Caridad miscarries their daughter and begins "loving anyone she met at the bars who vaguely resembled Memo."[114] After la malogra's attack and her miraculous restoration, she moves out to a local trailer park in order to become a *curandera*. During her training, she falls in love with Esmeralda, a woman from Acoma Pueblo whom she meets at the Santuario de Chimayo. Her encounter with Esmeralda prompts Caridad into self-imposed exile in a mountain cave, where she becomes an object of local saintly devotion. Upon returning from the mountain, Caridad and Esmeralda together visit Sky City, the Acoma Pueblo's ancestral homeland, which is "the oldest city in all of the Americas that has had constant habitation." It is there where, after hearing the call of the Pueblo creator deity "Tsichtinako," they jump off the mesa and fall "like broken winged moths." La mitotera interjects:

> The Acoma people heard it and knew it was the voice of the Invisible one who had nourished the first two humans, who were also both female, although no one had heard it a long time and some had never heard it before. But all still knew who It was. . . . But to all their surprise, there were no morbid remains of splintered bodies tossed to the ground. . . . There weren't even whole bodies lying peaceful. There was nothing. Just the spirit deity Tsichtinako calling loudly with a voice like wind, guiding the two women back, not out toward the sun's rays or up to the clouds, but down, deep within the soft, moist dark earth where Esmeralda and Caridad would be safe and live forever.[115]

The story power of Caridad's protagonism, then, inhabits and unsettles nearly every figuration of legible and normative femininity sanctioned by feudal patriarchy: from daughter and betrothed she becomes a "puta," suffers as a victim of patriarchal predation only to transform into a saint. Yet in her final station and as the only daughter to not "die," Caridad returns to the land. Her return offers, to use Brenda Romero's language, "a way of coming to terms with our indigenous mother."[116] Rejecting heteronormative motherhood as "simple fertility cultism," Caridad's return affirms instead Thought Woman's creative power as cooperative labor. According to Paula Gunn Allen, Tsichtinako, or "Thought Woman is not a passive personage: her potentiality is dynamic and unimaginably powerful. She brought corn and agriculture, potting, weaving, social systems, religion, ceremony, ritual, building, memory, intuition, and their expressions in language, creativity, dance, human-to-animal relations, and she gave these offerings power and authority and blessed the people with the ability to provide for themselves and their progeny."[117] This disarticulation of maternity from heterosexual reproduction unsettles the nationalist impulse to bind metaphors of the land to conceptions of heterosexual motherhood. As the "creator of thought," Thought Woman is "both Mother and Father to all people and to all creatures."[118] *So Far from God* in this sense embodies a narrative of land grant memory that does not pivot upon the disappearance of Native lives, spiritualities, epistemologies, and communalisms. Instead, it enacts a story power that weaves Pueblo communalism within land grant memory such that the politics of kinship, collectivity, and cooperativity are unbound to the human form.

On the aesthetic modalities derived from Pueblo Indian communalism, Leslie Marmon Silko writes: "Realism, as we now recognize it . . . did not catch the imaginations of Pueblo people until recently . . . Ancient Pueblos took the modest view that thing itself (the landscape) could not be improved upon. The ancients did not presume to tamper with what had already been created. . . . The land, the sky, and all that is within them—the landscape—includes human beings. For these reasons, survival depended upon harmony and cooperation not only among human beings, but also among all things—the animate and the less animate, since rocks and mountains were known on occasion to move."[119] By virtue of its cooperative deployment of Indigenous, realist, historiographical, folkloric, and speculative narrative strategies, the novel unsettles the racialized and gendered contradictions of land grant politics by avowing land as a multidimensional and pluritemporal protagonist in cooperative power. In a noted passage describing the challenges of Sofi's cooperative, la mitotera explains, "Sofia's dry and thirsty land by its very nature was a land of ingenious undertakings; and while its early Spanish transplants learned irrigation methods from the indigenous residents to sustain crops and graze animals, and how to make do with raw materials, talk with the sky, and honor mountains and streams, and despite all their relentless faith together, the sheer daily toil, the centuries going by, the world changing around them, it never got no easier."[120]

Cooperative power here is predicated by the gift of Pueblo Indian instruction for the survival of the colony, for "how to make do with raw materials," for "irrigation," for "sustaining crops," and for grazing animals, even as the work of survival "never got no easier." Building in this sense requires unbounded speech with atmospheric forces ("talk with the sky") and an economy of honor for waterways and mountains without mention of patriarchal authority. It is predicated by the endurance of Pueblo communalism as a gift of rebellious instruction for decolonizing labor relations and receiving sustenance from the land.

Despite the absence of individual discursive influence in linear time, *El Grito del Norte* and *So Far from God* represent distinct and interwoven articulations of what I have termed the "cooperative mode of power" tied to the folk base of land grant struggle in New Mexico. In the early 1970s, after Elizabeth Martínez moved *El Grito* to Las Vegas to escape police harassment, she and other staffers from the paper moved to Albuquerque and launched the Chicano Communications Center (CCC) in order to reinvigorate the tactics of the paper and the Chicanx movement. As a result, *El Grito* ceased publication in August 1973 with a closing announcement that states, "To our enemies, we say: don't celebrate. The spirit that El Grito voices will never die."[121] While there is no explicit mention of *El Grito* in the plot of *So Far from God*, Castillo extends gratitude in the acknowledgments to "the members of the Southwest Organizing Project," the publishing cooperative with whom Elizabeth Martínez worked after *El Grito* folded its operations. Aside from this acknowledgment, *El Grito* and Martínez are never represented in positive terms.

Through the two texts' juxtaposition, however, I have sought to formulate a critique of racial capitalism by situating subaltern agency, gender violence, and racialization in New Mexico within the context of a transcultural economy of patriarchy and territoriality that relied on the captivity of women, the appropriation of Pueblo lands and culture, and colonial warfare against Plains Indians. This critique reveals gendered disposability as a predicate for national coherency and a correlate of environmental destruction. As anticapitalist story power, their textual matrix connects the colonialist regimes of Spanish, Mexican, and U.S. occupation as animated by settler compulsions to reduce land to a devivified, passive, and alienable surface for individualized profit. More pointedly, *El Grito* and *So Far from God* link this cross-colonial devivication of land to an intersecting ideological and political economy of ritualizing gendered death and devaluation.

As cooperative modes of power, *El Grito* and *So Far from God* perform storytelling that uprises land as a social, historical, and political protagonist in the conditions of writing, labor, subsistence, and revolt. Its base deposes progressive, historicist, and vanguardist temporalities by articulating folkloric forms, literary genres, and historical narratives to formations of political authority inextricable from Indigenous insurgency. From this base, they instruct how cooperativity dismantles state and oppositional nationalisms by building spaces of political autonomy that transgress the actuality of social movements, the memory of folklore, and the imaginary work of literature. They instruct how cooperativity activates storytelling modalities that amplify our contemporary "organizational density and ability . . . to deal with the multiple issues, sources of oppression, and myriad experiences" under conditions of colonial land occupation and labor control.[122]

CHAPTER FIVE

BETWEEN THE WORD AND THE LAND

Zapatismo as a Quantum Theory of Indigenous Rebellion

The quality of light by which we scrutinize our lives has direct bearing upon the product which we live, and upon the changes which we hope to bring about through those lives. It is within this light that we form those ideas by which we pursue our magic and make it realized.

—AUDRE LORDE, "POETRY IS NOT A LUXURY"

THE DISAPPEARING TRICK

On the rainy, early morning of May 24, 2014, before a group of roughly a thousand companions and a few journalists, Subcomandante Insurgente Marcos ceased to exist. Prior to his departure, Marcos had been internationally recognized as a spokesperson and public figure of the Ejército Zapatista de Liberación Nacional (EZLN, the Zapatista Army of National Liberation), a multitribal movement for Indigenous autonomy in the southeastern Mexican state of Chiapas. Marcos had been "born in death" as a ski-masked figure just after midnight on January 1, 1994, when the EZLN staged an armed revolt against the Mexican government and seized a number of towns in Chiapas on the eve of the passage of the North American Free Trade Agreement (NAFTA).[1] The fulcrum of neoliberalism's entrance in Mexico, NAFTA had fulfilled an earlier announcement by the government to annul the *ejido* land redistribution and regularization inscribed in Article 27 of the Constitution as part of its broad push to privatize state functions and withdraw its role in maintaining public welfare. For the Indigenous people of Chiapas, NAFTA had signaled a blow to any attempt to working with the state to resolve long-standing inequalities and injustices through land reform. As the armed wing of the Comité Clandestino

Revolucionario Indígena-Comandancia General (CCRI-CG, Revolutionary Indigenous Clandestine Committee-General Command), the EZLN mobilized thousands of Tzeltal, Mam, Chol, Tzotzil, and Tojola'bal peoples with faces covered in ski masks and bandanas and armed with weapons ranging from wooden rifles to automatic machine guns for an uprising that fundamentally shattered the fantasies of Indigenous subordination that the Mexican elite invested in NAFTA. In his first public appearance on the balcony of the Palacio Municipal in San Cristóbal de las Casas, the capital of Chiapas, Marcos announced the EZLN's declaration of war against the Mexican armed forces with words that would be subsequently known as the "First Declaration from the Lacandón Jungle." Addressed to the "People of Mexico," the First Declaration identifies the movement as the "dispossessed," the "product of 500 years of struggle" and the "inheritors of the true builders" of the Mexican nation.[2] Counter to the ongoing plunder of Indigenous land and bodies in Chiapas, the First Declaration invokes constitutional authority and sovereign legitimacy to the Zapatista armed revolt in the context of an "undeclared genocidal war" against their people. In doing so, it calls upon the Mexican people to "join the insurgent forces of the Zapatista National Liberation Army" and participate in their "struggles for work, land, housing, food, healthcare, education, independence, freedom, democracy, justice, and peace."[3] Twelve days later, after intense battles in Chiapas and mass mobilizations in Mexican urban centers, the state agreed to begin negotiations with the rebels.

With and without Marcos's author function, the interceding twenty years would see the Zapatistas transform into a dynamic, generative, and ongoing movement for Indigenous autonomy that continues to challenge Mexican nationalism's monumentalization of *mestizaje* and invisibilization of contemporary struggles and lifeways of Indigenous peoples. Indeed, the urgency of warfare that marked January 1, 1994, also manifested a distinctly rebellious political discourse known as Zapatismo, a lexicon of struggle in which Marcos became virtually synonymous. An embodied-yet-masked discursive figure, Marcos dwelled in the unresolvable conceptual tensions that organize colonial modernity: between the local and global, individual and collective, Mestizx and Indigenous, rural and urban. "Marcos," he declared himself in a now famous quote about his identity, "is all the exploited, marginalized, oppressed minorities resisting and saying 'Enough.' He is every minority who is now beginning to speak and every majority that must shut up and listen."[4] Reflecting on his disappearance, Diana Taylor writes, "Marcos reactivated the trickster's potential of enormous trans-possibility: trans-race, trans-gender, trans-personal, trans-national, trans-historical."[5] A transcultural political discourse, Zapatismo was forged simultaneously through a series of failed peace talks and negotiations with the Mexican government *and* numerous national, planetary, and intergalactic encounters with a multitude of activists and movements fighting against the multiscalar violence of neoliberal capital. Thus, by the time Marcos utters his last words, the movement had transformed into a network of five "parallel governments" called *caracoles* (spiral shells), which serve as points of communication between thirty Zapatista Autonomous Municipalities in Rebellion.[6]

Despite these growths and transformations, the "undeclared genocidal war" that necessitated Marcos's emergence would also beckon his departure. On May 2, 2014, Subcomandante Galeano, the nom de guerre used by José Luis Solis López, a Zapatista teacher in the municipality of La Realidad, was slain in an attack by members of CIOAC-Histórica, a paramilitary organization supported and financed by the Mexican government.[7] In "killing Galeano, or any Zapatista," Marcos broadcast over Radio Zapatista during his last appearance a few weeks later, "those from above are trying to kill the EZLN. . . . Not the EZLN as an army, but as the rebellious and stubborn force that builds and raises life where those above desire the wasteland brought by the mining, oil, and tourist industries, the death of the earth and those who work and inhabit it."[8] As a result, "we think that it is necessary for one of us to die so that Galeano lives. . . . That is why we have decided that Marcos today ceases to exist."[9]

"Between Light and Shadow," the communiqué formed from this announcement, takes the occasion of Marcos's disappearance to recast his function in the "path of life" undertaken by the EZLN since that fateful first January morning in 1994. The text in this way is remarkable for the ways it at once accounts for, recurs, and therefore innovates a number of Indigenous critiques of neoliberal governmentality that have become hallmarks of Zapatismo. As in other declarations and communiques, January 1, 1994, is avowed here as a semiotic event. The enactment of violence from below is a predicate to establishing a discursive horizon through which the Zapatista struggle achieves visibility in the reduced field of life enforced by the biopolitical regime of Mexican Mestizo nationalism and its postrevolutionary state counterpart. As a biopolitical formation, the modern Mexican nation-state has long relied on corporatist techniques of managing racialized and gendered dissent through co-optation. At the national level, this occurs through a narrative of mestizaje that appropriates Aztec patrimony as the conquered predicate for the protection of Mestizo life through civic rights and public visibility. At the state level, large-scale unions, Indigenous organizations, and agrarian reform—rooted in the epistemes of liberal positivism—combined to discipline the Indigenous heterogeneity of Mexico to modern capitalism. Together they have historically administered the futurity of the Mestizo nation through the decimation of Indigenous communalisms, the effacement of the African diaspora, and the political subordination of Asian migrations.[10]

In this scene of racialized domination, the Zapatistas notice a peculiar institutional will to ignorance that summons the figure of Marcos: even after "indigenous rebels" descended "on the cities to shake the world with its step," the publics enthralled with Mexican Mestizo nationalism still could not see them. "Accustomed to looking down on the indigenous from above, they didn't lift their gaze to look at us. Accustomed to seeing us humiliated, their heart did not understand our dignified rebellion. Their gaze had stopped on the only mestizo they saw with a ski mask, that is, they didn't see."[11] For these reasons, Marcos affirms the necessity of an armed military for the emergence of Zapatista autonomy with an argument for the right of "legitimate violence" from below to know its "role" and its "moment."[12] As a semiotic event, the Zapatistas fathomed the performance of armed revolt as a pathway for the world to speak back. The speaking back from the Mexican government—in the immediate aftermath of the uprising and in the subsequent dialogue marked by lies, doublespeak, and broken accords—sheds light on the depth of motivated ignorance and social neglect to Indigenous life that buttresses Mestizo nationalism. "They can only see those who are as small as they are," the Indigenous "authorities" and "commanders" tell the Zapatistas. "Let's make someone as small as they are, so that they can see him and through him, they can see us."[13] Such an account rekindles the *sub*comandante function of Marcos within the collective organizational structure of the CCRI-CG: his hypervisibilization as the Zapatista spokesperson for globalized publics is most defiantly an effect of the communal deliberation of Indigenous *comandantes* rather than the labor of a supposedly enlightened Mestizo front man for unworldly Native peasants. Subcomandante Marcos in this account is illuminated as a "hologram," a hall of mirrors, "a complex maneuver of distraction, a terrible and marvelous trick, a malicious move from the indigenous heart that we are with indigenous wisdom challenging one of the bastions of modernity: the media."[14] Instead of a "spokesperson" for indigenous people, Marcos recasts himself as a "distraction"—a time-maker—a figure invented to make time to clear the "path to life" by finding "those who would know how to see us as we are."[15] With his diversion, the Zapatistas "launched various initiatives in order to encounter the *other* . . . to encounter the gaze and the ear that we need and that we deserve." Autonomization in this account is a process whereby the Zapatistas "failed time and again," encountering those who "either wanted to lead us or wanted us to lead them," or those who wanted to "use us . . . to gaze backward . . . with anthropological or militant nostalgia."[16]

Nonetheless, Marcos's disappearance is one step toward the vision of autonomy called forth in the Sixth Declaration in June 2005. With the Sixth Declaration of the Lacandon Jungle, "the most daring and most Zapatista of all the initiatives launched" to that point, the movement "at last encountered those who can see us face to face and greet us and embrace us. . . . With the Sixth, at last, we found you."[17] The Sixth was coined in a rejection of state failure as the sole path of politics, in particular the state's lack of political will to uphold the San Andrés Accords.[18] Addressing the predicaments raised by the Zapatista's newfound visibility in national politics is an invitation for disparately situated decolonial struggles across the planet to participate as mediating forces for Zapatista autonomy. The multitude of movements and struggles for dignified life against capitalism are positioned as mirrors by which the Zapatistas can see themselves through encounters with difference and otherness. The Sixth in this sense is an activation of autonomous organizational structures that endure and nullify the state's repertoire of counterinsurgency by decentralizing the capacity for revolutionary action. As Marcos noted early in the project, "We had to be prepared to lose our entire leadership."[19]

In "Between Light and Shadow," the Sixth manifests as an "archipelago of pain, rage, and dignified struggle" networked through "the free, alternative, and independent media." An intervention in the mediation of modern consciousness, the Sixth specifically counters what the Zapatistas call the "cult of individualism" that underwrites neoliberalism's reigning logic of dominance. In this way, the Sixth calls for modes of witnessing premised on local autonomy, anonymity, and interconnectivity. As a spatialized decolonial historical consciousness, the Sixth is situated in discrete, nonidentical-yet-convergent cartographies. The profound convergence of a range of anticapitalist struggles inaugurated by the Sixth would later impel Marcos to declare the movement at a point where the discourse of Zapatismo has overtaken the EZLN.[20] Marcos's disappearance is therefore one step in the direction of manifesting the autonomous organizational imperative to *mandar obedeciendo*, to lead by following/observing/minding. His final words draw attention to the already apparent transformation of the Zapatista structure into autonomous collectives with "purely indigenous leadership" that require "the direct participation of women." In addition, he remarks on the cultivation of a class analysis based on the "indigenous peasant" and on the "creation of power below" grounded in a politics of difference.[21]

Through these initiatives, the Zapatista struggle continues to illuminate a dignified and trickster process of autonomization from the Mestizo biopolitics of Mexican state power with profound ramifications for anticapitalist and decolonial struggles across the planet. Indeed, the global appeal of Zapatismo cannot be separated from its status as a fugitive and unbounded archive of multimedia cultural production with transnational, multilingual circulation. Its collectively drafted documents continue to rely on clandestine transnational networks of dissemination that cross multiple boundaries of race, nation, and class. By virtue of this engagement, Zapatismo has created anthologies of communiqués, declarations, testimonies, and open letters; books of short stories; detective fiction; children's stories; and a number of online videos and texts. As an Indigenous deconstruction of an astonishingly expansive network of cultural practices and tropes, legal genealogies, historical narratives, racial and gendered significations, and civic practices, Zapatismo reveals the cosmopolitical possibilities released by project of local autonomy.[22] In doing so, Alan Gómez notes that the Zapatista communities are "not simply mobilized against the neoliberal state; they are redefining the relationship to the state as well as the balance between politics, culture, and rights, between economic policies and environmental concerns, and most notably, between meanings of citizenship and indigenous identity."[23]

The response it provoked from Chicanx and Latinx activists, artists, and scholars in particular has been decisive in reinvigorating critiques of mestizaje and capitalism. Groups such as Estación Libre, El Kilombo Intergaláctico, Acción Zapatista, and the ARMA Collective and others across North America have activated Zapatismo to build a "politics of *encuentro* [encounter]," which includes "local assemblies, local knowledge, creative intergenerational projects, and local forms of justice (restorative/community) that are as much an experiment as they are a project, a work in progress."[24] Roberto González Flores and the Chican@-Zapatista Artist Connection in 1997 built upon a multiyear engagement with the Zapatista movement to create educational and artistic collectives that facilitate "the initiation of a transformational paradigmatic shift within the Chican@ movement."[25] Through these networks, Zapatismo has been powerfully mobilized to rethink the politics of urban space, as "Zapatismo Urbano" has come to signify a sophisticated activist network that connects autonomous struggles in Los Angeles, Mexico City, San Cristóbal, and other urban sites.[26] The Zapatismo-Chicanx encounter not only tapped into a legacy of Chicanx–Central American solidarity politics, but it also opened up a discursive horizon by which to rethink the transnational politics of mestizaje and indigeneity in Chicanx and Latinx racial formations. Work by María Josefina Saldaña-Portillo, Maylei Blackwell, Alan Eladio Gómez, Marisa Belausteguigoitia, and others have engaged Zapatismo to produce pivot points for a different transnational framework for situating the colonial residues of Chicanx mestizaje that continue to haunt its decolonial horizons. In this context, what would it mean to face the Zapatistas from the "calendar" and "geography" invoked by New Mexican land grant struggle? What would it mean to situate the Sixth in a time-space horizon such that New Mexican land grant struggles come to face the innovations to ejido land reflected in Zapatismo? What story power is sufficient for such a task?

In what follows, I argue that the terms of Zapatismo furnish a story power for naming a continuum of insurgency between New Mexico and Chiapas, what are currently the northernmost and southernmost borderlands of Greater Mexico. In particular, I explore how the terms of Marcos's disappearance in "Between Light and Shadow" offer a vocabulary for a quantum horizon of Indigenous rebellion by which to interface Zapatismo with the Genízarx-Pueblo Indian matrix that animates the Indohispanx story power of La Alianza's land grant struggle. Quantum mechanics is notable for its study of the ways in which the smallest scales of matter and energy—that is, *quanta*—disobey the object-based theories of motion in Newtonian physics and general relativity.[27] The study of light in particular has proven to be simultaneously elusive and generative for quantum theory because its "duality" as particle (matter) and wave (energy) has forced scientists to confront a series of limits to the politics of scientific representation rooted in the epistemes of secular positivism. To explain the horizons of quantum theory, I turn to the set of dialogues between groups of quantum physicists, linguists, and Indigenous scholars, elders, and intellectuals initiated by Dr. Leroy Little Bear (Blackfoot) in 1992 in Kalamazoo, Michigan.[28] Through the power of these dialogues, quantum theory does not become the means through which to legitimate Zapatismo in the language of science. Zapatismo's legitimacy is already activated by the autonomous dignity with which its discursive network lives and moves with the Indigenous people of Chiapas. Rather, these dialogues reveal the ways that the reason and consciousness called forth by quantum mechanics pulsate as an already active element within Indigenous languages and story power. In the process, these dialogues translate quantum mechanics as a speculative labor of constructing verb-based analytics and conceptual frameworks of movement through language and story. "If our western science is to move beyond that sterility that views the world as object," participant F. David Peat subsequently writes, "then it too must be willing to enter into new logical forms and new orders, orders that will tolerate ambiguity, paradox, and metaphor." By tolerating and embracing the paradoxical nature of reality "more than a mathematical form of logic," Native Story Power expresses a "multileveled and multi-purposed nature of the telling itself." As a result, "the figure of the clown or joker occupies a privileged position within these stories," as these figures calibrate "order and transformation, logic and paradox, the establishment of harmony and its subversion."[29]

From this perspective, the holographic function of Marcos invokes Zapatismo's trickster work on the politics and epistemology of virtuality. "Between Light and Shadow": the title alone insinuates a horizon of virtual presence, a trick with light, matter, obscurity, and silence. Virtuality in this instance is not merely an effect of digital mediation but rather an activation of the trickster's long-standing play with the multidimensionality of Indigenous knowledge. "Between Light and Shadow" in this instance becomes notable as an extended meditation on the unbounded materiality of light and the attendant paradoxes it raises for a decolonial politics of movement and vision. As such, it allows us to consider pluriversal political practice—a mode of brokering transmissions between radically distinct worlds, life-beings, and states of animacy enlivened by the struggle for land. The pluriversality of such struggles, according to Marisol de la Cadena, "allows assertions of indigenous and nonindigenous conditions outside of state taxonomies that, based on the evolutionary or multicultural practice of plurality (i.e., the idea that the alternative to one is many), demand the purity of a unit or deny existence."[30]

Quantum theory in this regard offers the term *entanglement* as a particularly relevant concept-metaphor for the labor of pluriversal comparison. Entanglement refers to the phenomenon in which clusters of particles emerge or interrelate at the quantum level across vast distances in such a way that the materiality of one particle cannot be studied without consideration of the entire network.[31] Mobilizing the term for the study of Indigenous land struggle across Australia and Canada, Francoise Dussart and Sylvie Poirier argue that "each thread-entity-agent-world involved in the entanglement keeps its identity, relative autonomy, and potentiality, while the spatial and temporal interactions with the other components do bring transformations to each one of them; it is an ongoing and somehow embodied process."[32] From this vantage, entangling the borderlands of New Mexico and Chiapas is not the pursuit of similarity, but rather the illumination of recurrence across disparate space and time regulated by the noncontiguous horizons of ejido frameworks and racial formation.[33] To entangle here is an act of nonidentical doubling that sheds light on "the kaleidoscopic simultaneity of similarity and difference" in distinct movements for Indigenous insurgency.[34] By entangling disparate geotemporal formations of anticapitalist insurgency against each other, Zapatismo and Indohispanx mestizaje refract unexpected paths of Indigenous endurance and escape while highlighting, in the words of Roberto D. Hernández, the "simultaneously 'national' and global colonial episteme that underpins violence" on the U.S.-Mexico *and* Mexican-Guatemalan border.[35] I explore how the entanglements between Zapatismo and Indohispanx mestizaje bear relevance for a horizon of comparative insurgency that disorganizes the chronological staging of neoliberal capitalist accumulation. Rather than a mere historic stage of capitalism, the dispossession of New Mexican land grant commons harbors, foretells, and necessarily diverges from the logic of neoliberal evisceration imposed upon Chiapas. What is termed *neoliberalism* becomes reframed as a totalitarian logic of accumulation with multiple temporal iterations and limitations. At stake is the unhousing of narratives of revolutionary struggles from nationalized attachments to linear time and spatial homogeneity that have thus far patterned our critical paradigms of capitalist accumulation and Indigenous insurgency.

EJIDO STATE FORMATION AND THE BIOPOLITICS OF MEXICAN MESTIZO NATIONALISM

When pondering the divergent trajectories of ejido land grants under the respective formations of modern U.S. and Mexican state power, one is struck by a distinct historical irony. If the communal property rights of ejido land grants in New Mexico were the targets of colonial dispossession for the ascendance of privatized, individual property rights under U.S. sovereignty, then ejido land grants would also come to provide the institutional lynchpin for the formation of the modern Mexican state. Indeed, the historiography of postrevolutionary state formation reveals the ways that the ejido came to be the privileged institutional form for countering the unregulated growth of hacienda land holdings that marked the dictatorship of Porfirio Diaz from 1876 to 1910.[36] The ejidos served an important function in consolidating the social and political fragmentation that marked the Mexican revolution of 1910–1920 by mandating the redistribution of land to peasants from the large landholders of the hacendado. Prior to the Porfirian dictatorship, Indigenous land tenure since the arrival of the Spanish in 1519 was regulated by a tenuous combination of the Spanish encomienda and the Aztec *calpulli* tribute system in which familial and individual land rights were bound up with inalienable communal relations and obligations.[37] While the dictates of the encomienda canceled any communal Indigenous rights within its territory, the Spanish monarchy also worked to limit its application in determining land usage in the aftermath of the genocidal carnage it heaved upon Caribbean tribal peoples. The ejido thus became embedded in a series of royal colonial decrees and legislative acts that generated legal protections for the Indigenous organization of communal lands. "Underlying these policies," Emilio Kourí points out, was "an Indian settlement policy designed to both congregate native people and . . . keep their residential spaces separate from those of Spaniards." It was a policy "predicated (and justified) on the belief that Indians as a class of people were supposedly akin to minors . . . all of whom—as immature, uncivilized, or inferior beings—required special protection and tutelage from the Crown."[38]

As a result, the ejido provided a shared horizon for the proliferation of Indigenous autonomy and the ascendance of liberal forms of statist domination. In the aftermath of Mexico's war for independence from Spain in 1810, a number of liberal legal reforms incentivized and coerced the privatization and alienation of lands held by the church and by Indigenous villages. While subsequent legislation prohibited the alienation of ejido lands, the Constitution of 1857 ended the exemptions and catalyzed a massive move to privatize lands upon which many Indian villages lived and worked under tenuously formal recognition from the Spanish Crown. These years that led to the election of Porfirio Díaz in 1876, James J. Kelly Jr. notes, "had witnessed the virtual obliteration of communal ownership of rural land. Indigenous villages lost their land to speculators in transfers made possible by several laws designed to promote the use of agricultural land."[39] The Porfiriato would seize upon these already established liberal imperatives to empower the growth of large-scale haciendas built upon dispossessed Indigenous land.

The Porfiriato's encouragement of unrestrained hacienda landholdings fomented among rural Indigenous villages a profound disaffection from the national project that would culminate in Diaz's expulsion from office in 1910. At the same time, it also laid the epistemic groundwork for the coordination of liberal citizenship, individual private property, and racialized social improvement that would characterize the biopolitics of the modern, postrevolutionary Mexican state. The emergent discourses of Darwinism and positivism would be of particular importance to this transformation, as the Porfiriato fostered an intellectual circle known as the *científicos*, who transferred the presumed racialized inferiority of Mexican Indians from the plane of Catholic salvation to that of liberal assimilation, public hygiene, and education administered through the disciplines of biology, medicine, and anthropology. By establishing scientific rationality as the predicate for legitimate political practice, the científicos galvanized the liberal state as the site where, according to Charles A. Hale, "society should be administered and not governed."[40]

The ten years that followed the overthrow of Díaz known as the Mexican Revolution unfolded as a series of battles between warring political coalitions over the conditions and recipients of land redistribution. The agrarian and land reforms articulated by Emilano Zapata became a pivotal revolutionary force in countering the hacendado's monopoly of land and control of Indigenous labor. Before his assassination in 1919, Zapata proposed the repatriation of lands usurped by the *hacendado* to the communities from which they were taken, with the imperative that these communities be guaranteed the autonomy to determine the forms of production and governance according to their respective resources and lifeways. For early-twentieth-century Zapatismo, according to Arturo Warman, "popular sovereignty" was not mediated through the rule of expert-based electoral politics but, rather, stemmed from "direct democracy, permanently located in the social units that controlled the land" with the "autonomy to organize production [and] political-military functions."[41] Although the postrevolutionary state would be forged in the containment of rural social movements such as Zapata's, the ruling elite would subsequently appropriate his image to enshrine ejido structures as the basis of agrarian reform in Article 27 of the Mexican Constitution.[42]

Although the broader project of revolutionary agrarian reform enabled the market-based transfer of small farms and private lots, Article 27 prohibited the alienation of ejido lands as part of its effort to redistribute the hacendados to Indigenous and peasant farmers. Ineligible for sale, rent, or mortgage, ejido lands came to supplant the Aztec land system that emphasized communal ownership property and limited monetized land speculation. Unlike the científicos under the Porfiriato, who undertook intensive measures to whiten the republic through policies that encouraged European immigration, the institutionalization of ejido land protections reflected a governmental embrace of mestizaje as the political practice for revolutionary citizenship. In this way, ejido land reforms became a key site for the proliferation of what Alexandra Minna Stern has called "the cult of the mestizo"—that is, the juridical, scientific, medical, and agrarian convergence on the Mestizo as the idealized figure for racial assimilation and social resolution. Central to the cult of mestizaje was a biopolitics of property that targeted the modernization of Mexican Indians as the key to national homogenization. According to Stern, the philosophical architects of ejido reform, such as Manuel Gamio, "idolized the valiant Indian and pre-Colombian past; at the same time he looked toward the future, insisting upon large-scale anthropological surveys of the country's many indigenous groups."[43] Thus while the liberal turn in Mexican politics waged a fiercely antisectarian battle against Christian religious imperialism, its embrace of the "supremacy of the secular state" would replant an already established racialized hierarchy into scientific explanations that recast Mestizx "civility" as the sacred endpoint of modern Mexican progress.[44]

As a negotiated framework for Indigenous life and liberal state formation, the biopolitics of ejido reform perpetuated what Allen Knight calls an "instrumental Indianness" that sought to racially recode Mexico's Indigenous peoples as *campesinos* (or peasants) and channel their land claims through class-based rationalities.[45] Over the course of roughly 50 years, ejido reforms would facilitate the transfer of more than 70 million hectares to roughly 3 million campesino recipients.[46] At the same time, the conversion of Mexico's Indigenous peoples to campesino identities mediated by ejido frameworks firmly rooted land tenure in the reduced field of life sanctioned by liberal politics and state corporatism. "Agrarian reform," according to María Josefina Saldaña-Portillo, "extended political citizenship to indigenous people *not* on the basis of their Indian identity, but on the basis of their peasant identity. Peasant identity, in the developmentalist logic of modernization, represents an advance in consciousness from indigenous identity because such an identity formation is contingent on the concepts of individual or family-based land ownership. Agrarianism, as the grounds for political incorporation, privileges economic consciousness over other cultural or religious forms of consciousness."[47]

Under the roughly seventy-year dictatorship of the Partido Revolucionario Institucional (Institutional Revolutionary Party, PRI), the ejido system became a powerful mechanism for regulating the state's role in peasant politics.[48] At the same time, it coalesced a broad range of Indigenous and Mestizx peasant movements that centered land rights as indispensable to political emancipation. The ejido, in the words of Jonathan Fox and Gustavo Gordillo, operated as a "state apparatus of political control and an organ of peasant representation."[49] Thus, by compacting questions of Indigenous land tenure to a class framework, ejido politics simultaneously expanded an institutional structure, legal apparatus, and economic rationality that allowed the state to manage and subdue these movements to the diminished partitions of human life sanctioned by capitalist development. In these decades, the economic and social contradictions that would eventually lead to the neoliberal disentailment of the ejido were already manifest. While the Mexican state opened up pathways for incentivizing foreign investment in agricultural exports and resource extraction, student and peasant movements, radical anthropologists, and liberation theologians began to push for the political recognition of the cultural differences between and among Indigenous and Mestizx peoples. As this contradiction intensified in the Mexican state's embrace of neoliberal policy in the 1980s, it worked to sever the corporatist ties and social welfare contracts organizing state-peasant relations in the name of enabling individuals to rationally broker market-based relations. In this way, if ejido politics were instrumental in the formation of the cult of mestizaje that rationalized the modern Mexican state, then the same structures would also permit the emergence of what the Zapatistas call neoliberalism's "cult of individualism"—that is, a rationality that sanctions the privatization of capitalist accumulation and the mass dissemination of exploitation and peril.[50]

The ascent of neoliberalism in Mexico therefore became a critique of the legitimacy of the liberal nation-state to arbitrate capitalist economy, a critique that indexes a broad range of social, political, economic, and cultural transformations, continuities, and revivals. In Mexico, as in other locales, neoliberalism is marked by the tension between a fanatical embrace of market-based freedoms and the imperative to recognize and value multicultural difference. The elimination of the ejido system's protection signaled by NAFTA's deletion of Article 27 of the Mexican Constitution in 1994 remains perhaps the most visible symbol of the neoliberal evisceration of the Mexican state. However, as Courtney Jung points out, during the same year, "the government amended Article 4 of the Constitution to recognize, for the first time, the multicultural character of the nation, described explicitly as the coexistence of different languages and cultures." In some instances, Jung notes, the rearticulation of peasant struggles through an expanded juridical terrain of Indigenous rights represented evidence of a "political trade-off between redistribution and recognition, class and culture."[51]

After the Zapatista revolt, however, demands for land "were increasingly interwoven with, and justified by, Indigenous identity."[52] Zapatismo's revolutionary innovations to constitutional discourse notably rejected the anti-Indigenous biopolitics of mestizaje while at the same time positioning the movement as the defender of Mexican sovereignty.[53] As the "Sixth Declaration of the Lacandon Jungle" states,

> we wanted democracy, liberty, and justice for all Mexicans, although we were concentrated on the Indian peoples. Because it so happened that we, the EZLN, were almost all indigenous from here in Chiapas, but we did not want to struggle just for our own good, or just for the good of the indigenous of Chiapas, or just for the good of the Indian peoples of Mexico. We wanted to fight along with everyone who was humble and simple like ourselves and who was in great need and who suffered from exploitation and thievery by the rich and their bad governments here, in our Mexico, and in other countries in the world.[54]

In this way, the Zapatistas wage a defense of Mexican sovereignty that counters the neoliberal assault on the legal and political architecture of the ejido and disorganizes how mestizaje's biopolitical regime reduces Indian life and valorizes Mestizo citizenship. The "Second Declaration of the Lacandon Jungle" (1995) states, "In December 1993, we said *Enough!* The 1st of January 1994 we called upon the legislative and judicial powers to assume their constitutional responsibilities in order to stop the genocidal policy that the federal executive imposes on our people, and we founded our right on the application of Article 39 of the Political Constitution of the United States of Mexico: 'National sovereignty resides, essentially and originally, in the people.'"[55] Zapatismo's indigeneity refuses the (post)modern impulse to contain Indigenous cultural forms through static notions of tradition or multicultural authenticity that posit "Indian" culture as exotic, timeless, and antithetical to the secular, progressive temporalities of Euroamerican colonial modernity.

In 1995, the Mexican state identified the figure of Marcos as Rafael Sebastián Guillén Vicente, a former professor of philosophy at the Universidad Autónoma Metropolitana's Xochimilco campus.[56] Born to a poet and furniture salesman in Tampico, Tamaulipas, in 1957, Guillén was identified as a Jesuit-educated middle-class Mestizo who obtained his doctorate in the early 1980s with a thesis on the political theory of Louis Althusser.[57] This revelation provided the catalyst for a renewed assault on Zapatista formations by the Mexican Army and revealed the extent to which the compulsion to individualize social movement protagonism through realism coincides with state counterinsurgency. In trademark trickster fashion, the Zapatistas acknowledge the existence of Guillén but deny that he is Marcos's "true" identity. In this context, Marcos's disappearance adds a virtual component to Zapatismo's insurgency that dismantles the logic by which Indian subordination and exploitation sustain the life of a cloistered, singular world contained by the "realism of power politics."[58] Marcos's invocation of the cult of individualism recurs in this context as a way of naming the racialized and gendered regimes of social control and mediated docility that underwrite the fundamentalism of state-enforced liberty. In assessing modernity's predication of Indigenous extinction and subordination as an effect of mediation, Marcos was and continues to be a play on the matter of modern mass media that makes time for the continuance of Indigenous knowledge while simultaneously dematerializing the racialized fortress of state authority. In the words of Paul Virilio, his holographic function reveals the "space of sight" not as "absolute space" but "relative space" whose light "also comes to us from out of the distant past, out of the mists of time. The weak light that allows us to apprehend the real, to see and understand our present environment, itself comes from a distant visual memory without which there would be no act of looking."[59] The holographic light of Marcos reveals a quantum logic that indigenizes the labor of "breaking reality" and establishing "our own time" and "our own place."[60] To explore these dimensions further, we must return to the "birth" of Marcos in the mountains of Chiapas.

CHIAPAS AND THE INSURGENT HORIZONS OF THE MEXICAN SOUTHEAST

When the person who would become Marcos and a handful of members from a newly formed movement called the National Liberation Forces went underground in the Chiapas jungle, they had aspirations to educate Indigenous peasants with Marxist-Leninist theory and organize a guerrilla force. Marcos was initially tasked with teaching literacy but instead of elevating the consciousness of supposedly isolated and provincial Indigenous peasants, Marcos is the one who was schooled. One immediate lesson was the inadequacy of Marxist political economy to explain the social, political, and epistemic contradictions of Indigenous life in Chiapas. "They would tell you that they had understood nothing, that your words were not understandable, that you had to look for other words," he recalls.[61] The Indigenous people of Chiapas would offer more lessons over the course of Marcos's birth, for it was "the Indians who taught him how to negotiate the jungle, how to walk so as not to exhaust himself, how to hunt, and how to prepare and cook what he caught—how to make himself, as they put it, 'part of the mountain.'"[62] Marcos recalls: "It's very difficult when you have a theoretical scheme that explains the whole of a society and then you arrive in that society and you realize that your scheme explains nothing." The people of Chiapas requested instead a "political word-history. The history of [Mexico] and of the struggle."[63]

What is now the state of Chiapas has been and remains the ancestral land of a number of Mayan tribes—such as the Tzotzil, Tzeltal, Ch'ol, and Tojola'bal—for at least the past five thousand years.[64] At the same time, over the course of its contact with colonial domination since the 1530s, the land has also hosted a transborder complex of Indigenous diasporas from Guatemala and other regions in Mexico. Since the establishment of Ciudad Real by the Spanish conquistadors, the state has remained a horizon that fosters deep tensions between racialized forms of control over Indian labor and land and tenaciously inventive genealogies of Indigenous insurgency. Prior to the 1890s, this tension was marked by the presence of large estates that exported sugar, grain, and cattle produced and raised by captive and coerced Indian labor to the Spanish Crown. As the Catholic and civic authorities of the Spanish regime erected a mix of plantation and hacienda settlements and planned expeditions to resettle a number of tribes to serve their labor needs, the Indigenous people were ravaged by disease and exploitation. In 1712, after the Spanish had established a number of Indian *municipios* (townships) around Ciudad Real based on the specialized production of certain commodities, Indigenous workers turned to spaces conceded by the Dominican clergy to organize a confederation of more than twenty communities for revolt. Motivated in part by appearances made by the Virgin Mary in the villages of Zinacantán, Santa Marta, and Cancuc, the revolt also spawned from the hyperexploitation and famine imposed by Spanish settlement. Although the colonial authorities violently suppressed the uprising the following year with practices that included physically dismembering rebel natives, the extractive conditions that conjured the uprising would continue to foment over the following two centuries.[65]

In 1823, just over twenty years before the U.S.-Mexico border would shift south through the violence of U.S. settler colonial accumulation, the regional elite separated Chiapas from Guatemala, annexing the state to Mexico without consultation of the majority of the Indigenous inhabitants.[66] Buoyed by the emergent liberal ideology sweeping across the crumbling colonial order, this violent border imposition translated into an intensified juridical and political push toward stripping previously established protections over Native landholdings to facilitate privatized appropriation. While increasing the tax burden and labor demands on Indigenous communities, the reforms stimulated a number of clashes in 1848 that culminated into the 1867 rebellion that lasted three years. "As in 1712," Neil Harvey notes, "resistance was made possible by the affirmation of religious-cultural identities that were clearly not reducible to the political ideologies of either conservatism of liberalism. It was this space for resistance that allowed Indians to contest ladino rule and affirm a distinctive ethnic consciousness."[67] However, by the 1870s, the empowerment of the local plantation-hacienda complex under the Porfiriato enabled the ascendance of a globally integrated export economy in Chiapas. During the following decades, according to Jan Rus, Shannan L. Mattiace, and Aida Hernández Castillo, "booming world markets for tropical agricultural commodities" would ensure that "approximately one-third of Chiapas's surface area—the third most appropriate for tropical agriculture—was sold by the government in tracts of thousands of hectares at almost giveaway prices. The purchasers were overwhelmingly foreign—Germans, Americans, Spaniards, English, and French—and they quickly began to establish plantations."[68]

As the conditions for the biopolitical control of Mestizo nationalism coalesced across Mexico through ejido reform, in Chiapas the expansion of the area's plantation economy calibrated the expropriation of Indigenous land and the discipline of Indigenous labor. The result would be a remarkably durable regime of plantation control that, for roughly a century, maintained prerevolutionary levels of poverty for Indigenous villages while displacing tens of thousands of Indigenous workers to newly established circuits of seasonal migrant wage labor around the region.[69] "Thereafter, the better part of the region's Tzeltal, Tzotzil, and Ch'ol people had been forced to become *acasillados*, in effect serfs, on their own ancestral property."[70] From the 1940s to the 1970s, the Mexican economy underwent high growth rates in income and employment, while a "massive migration by largely indigenous semiproletarianized peasants from the highlands and other parts of the area" began to pour into the Lacandon jungle encouraged by the agribusiness and cattle ranching sanctioned by state patronage.[71] In this context, the Mexican state faced an overlaid crisis to its legitimacy to govern and its ability to maintain economic stability. The aftermath of the Tlatelolco Massacre of 1968 and a systemic effort to replace domestically produced agriculture with cheaper exports obtained on the world market were just two events in a larger series of social and economic transformations that began to decay the corporatist ties maintained between the state and the Indigenous people of Chiapas.

As a result, a resurgence of Indigenous organizing began to unfold that dispensed with the established corporatist channels that funneled Indigenous struggle into campesino politics. Instead, confederations of cross-tribal ejidos began to take shape. The 1974 Indigenous Congress sponsored by the Catholic bishop Samuel Ruiz García provided a crucial forum for the subsequent proliferation of newly independent peasant organizations such as the Confederation of Agricultural Workers and Peasants, the Organización Campesina Emiliano Zapata, the Central Independiente de Obreros Agrícolas y Campesinos (Independent Confederation of Agricultural Workers and Peasants), and the Union of Ejido Unions and Peasant Solidary Groups of Chiapas. According to Thomas Benjamin, the object of these organizations "was to come together in the bureaucratic and political struggle to reactivate land reform."[72] Thus by the time Marcos planted his first step in the mountains of the Mexican Southeast, there was already "an explosion of peoples' organizations."[73]

THE COMPLEMENTARITY OF ZAPATISTA AUTONOMY

The singularity of Chiapas and the rebellious endurance of Mayan Story Power that underwrite the virtuality of Marcos require that he invoke the testimonial "I." In "Between Light and Shadow" he notes that it is "one thing to say, 'We are All Marcos' or 'We Are Not All Marcos,' depending on the situation, and quite another to endure persecution with all the machinery of war."[74] Later, he recounts his transformational experience in the mountains of southeastern Mexico ten years prior to the uprising:

> Before the dawn of 1994, I spent 10 years in these mountains. I met and personally interacted with some whose death we all died in part. . . . In many of the smallest hours of the morning I found myself trying to digest the stories

> that they told me, the words that they sketched with their silences, hands, and gazes, their insistence in pointing to something else, something further. Was it a dream, that world so other, so distant, so foreign? Sometimes I thought that they had gone ahead of us all, that the words that guided and guide us came from times that didn't have a calendar, that were lost in imprecise geographies.[75]

This seemingly normative embrace of testimonial transformation of a middle-class literate Mestizo subject is undermined through what B. V. Olguín terms "the Zapatista testimonial corpus" that "consists of a variety of genres . . . such as the communiqué, allegorical fiction, and Mayan folktales that individually appear to be nontestimonial in nature." Olguín continues, "the interplay among all of them creates a paradoxical new permutation of the now commodified and co-opted testimonial precursor," performing a "literary sleight of hand" that "disperses the Zapatista hero throughout the world's oppressed."[76] As testimonial trick, Marcos learned that his Indigenous hosts "weren't telling me about an inexact, and therefore, improbable world." Rather, it was a "world . . . already unfolding." To which he asks his audience: "And you? Did you not see it? Do you not see it?"[77] Marcos in this instance acts as a multimedia performance of anti-Mestizo transformation that stages an unending invocation and dispersion of the testimonial subject within a field of entangled Indigenous insurgency.

In this corpus, the figure of El Viejo Antonio, a Mayan elder who prophesized the EZLN and permitted Marcos and his beleaguered unit to stay in the mountains in the 1980s, became a key interlocutor into the Indigenous Story Power of Chiapas. Out of this contact, Emiliano Zapata recurs as Votán-Zapata, a discursive figure that interfaces the lettered history of Mexican Revolution and the unevenly textualized genealogies of Mayan storytelling. A Tzeltal word, Votán entangles a number of functions and stories. Votán signals the third day in the Tzeltal agricultural calendar. In English, it translates to "the heart of the people." According to Elizabeth Greenwood, Votán complements what is "discussed in the *Popol Vuh*" as the "heart of the sky" and "heart of the earth."[78] Juana Ponce de León describes Votán as "the first man sent by God to distribute land among the indigenous."[79]

While rooted in Mayan storytelling, the series of communiqués and stories invoking Votán demonstrate a heightened play with the paradox of quantum complementarity. According to Dan Moonhawk Alford, the principle of complementarity came from the study of light, wherein scientist "asked incoming light, 'Are you a particle?' and it answered Yes; 'Are you a wave?' and it answered

Yes."[80] For Alford, this is "equivalent to asking whether something is a noun or a verb and getting a yes answer for both," which reflects a "higher level of formal operations . . . beyond normal Western Indo-European development."[81] In "The Story of the Questions" (December 13, 1994) we see this complementarity at work as El Viejo Antonio encounters Marcos for the first time in the mountains "ten years before the dawn of January."[82] "I've heard of you," El Viejo Antonio tells Marcos. "In the canyons they say you are bandits. In my village, they're upset because you are here." El Viejo Antonio asks Marcos to account for his presence in the mountains. Marcos responds by talking "about the times of Zapata and Villa, and the revolution, and the land, and the injustice and the hunger, and sickness, and repression and everything." He finishes by telling El Viejo Antonio that they are "the Zapatista Army of National Liberation."[83] El Viejo Antonio asks for more information about Zapata. Marcos starts with "Anenecuilco," Zapata's birthplace and pivotal location for the organization of his "Army of the South." From there, Marcos recounts the "Plan de Ayala," drafted in 1911, that called for the "fields, timber, and water" usurped by the "landlords, científicos, and bosses" to be repatriated to "pueblos and citizens."[84] He continues by discussing "the military campaign" that prompted an alliance with Pancho Villa in the North and concludes with the "betrayal of Chinameca," where Zapata was assassinated in an ambush while attempting to persuade a rival colonel to join his army.

"It wasn't like that," El Viejo Antonio says to Marcos. "No, I'm going to tell you the real story of Zapata." As El Viejo Antonio begins his story, "which merges and confuses modern times with old times," Marcos "is surprised and can only 'babble.'" In his story, El Viejo Antonio invokes Zapata through the doubled deities of "Ik'al" and "Votán," who together move in an unending and entangled duality. Ik'al and Votán were "opposites" and therefore "when one turned, the other could be seen. . . . One was like the light. . . . the other was dark." They "were the same. One was two, because one made the other." However, they were "stationary, these two gods who were one." They learn to walk by asking questions. They learn to ask "'How do we move?' and that it brought the answer of 'Together but separately and in agreement.'" El Viejo Antonio states that "since then, the gods walk with questions, and they never stop. They never arrive and never leave . . . They are never still."[85] According to Frédérique Apffel-Marglin, Niels Bohr's concept of complementarity addresses the paradox of light as a function of the observational process itself. "The paradox," she notes "consists of the following: under certain experimental arrangements, light or matter display particle-like properties. Under different experimental arrangements, incompatible with the former, they display wave-like properties."[86] As a result, "Bohr argues that theoretical concepts are defined by the circumstances required for their measurements. Therefore, there is no unambiguous way to differentiate between the 'object' and the 'agencies of observation' since there is no preexisting cut between them. The cut is *enacted* or *performed* through the use of a particular experimental apparatus." As a result, the "conceptual and physical dimensions of the measurement process" are in a perpetually transformative state of interconnection and separation from the objects of study.[87]

Fearing that he "will disrupt something very serious," Marcos asks: ". . . and Zapata?" Smiling, El Viejo points to a multilevel set of entanglements between his story and Marcos's own actions: "You've learned now that in order to know and walk, you have to ask questions." Zapata himself is subsequently manifested through this cross-dimensional act of inquiry. "Zapata appeared here in the mountains. He wasn't born, they say. He appeared just like that. They say he is Ik'al and Votán." As proof, El Viejo Antonio pulls out a "very old picture of Emilio Zapata . . . from 1910" taken by Agustín Casasola. However, through Mayan Story Power, the analogue representation of Zapata is reframed though a theory of light that activates unstoppable play of complementarity. El Viejo Antonio continues:

> In his left hand, Zapata has his sword raised to his waist. In his right hand, he has a pistol, Two bandoliers cross his chest, one from left to right, the other from right to left. His feet are placed as if he's standing still, or as if he's walking. And in his gaze there is something that says, "here I am," or "There I go." There are two staircases. One emerges from darkness, with dark-skinned Zapatistas, as though they were coming from the depths of something. The other staircase which is lighted, is empty, and one cannot tell from where it comes and where it goes.[88]

El Viejo Antonio's gloss of Zapata's analogue photograph illuminates Votán-Zapata as an astonishingly virtualized presence in the analogue object, one whose material existence in *only* this world is no longer securely assumed because this world now appears as an effect of its mediation in contrast to presupposing it. Votán-Zapata in this instance is now and has always been simultaneously beyond and within the reality the state deems representable in the analogue or digital object. This subversion of the observational process

FIGURE 8 "Emiliano Zapata con rifle y sable," 1911, Colección Gustavo Casasola.

summons a significant epistemological shift within the visual mediation of colonial modernity. Under Mestizo nationalism, the actuality of Zapata's analogue image in historical time served as the appropriated predicate for the state-enforced biopolitical reality. For Votán-Zapata, duality becomes a predicate for an autonomy that dematerializes the temporal principle of the state itself.[89]

El Viejo Antonio's story of Votán-Zapata signifies the "mutual exclusivity" between the storyteller, Zapata's analogue image, Marcos, Votán, and Ik'al while at the same time enfolding these connections within the power of Mayan storytelling. According to Thomas Benjamin, the lettered and oral cohabitation that marks the apparatus of Mayan Story Power "telescoped" the "remote past" into the "present," "while events were related in a distorted temporal fashion or presented outside of time altogether. Stories were populated by supernatural beings, anthropomorphic animals, and human actors. Such tales of the past were believed to be true but were not concerned with realistic representation of the past."[90] As a result, El Viejo Antonio's imperative to move by asking questions is a long-standing acknowledgment of the peoples, movements, suspensions, and interdimensional transits inaugurated by the storytelling process itself. "I would be lying if I told you that I noticed all those details" in the photograph, Marcos confesses to his reader, acknowledging that it was El Viejo Antonio "who pointed them out."[91] Questions, in other words, provide the quality of light by which to see and name the autonomous dignity of the objects and agents created by observation.

Votán-Zapata's play on light manifests, according to Elizabeth Greenwood, in "a very physical and precise sense . . . through the formation of the five Zapatista communities, or *caracoles* [spiral shells]. . . . The *caracol*, meaning 'entrance and exit of the community,' is the very frame for Votán-Zapata, whose spirit occupies the center."[92] Formally created on August 9, 2003, the five caracoles are the homes of the Juntas del Buen Gobierno (Councils of Good Governance). They are predicated on the idea that power is manifested by its very exercise rather than an object of possession that requires taking or administration from above. Shannon Speed and Alvaro Reyes note how the caracoles offer a "distinct conceptualization of . . . rights which functionally eliminates the legal regimes of the State as the external referent for the existence of rights." In doing so, the "Zapatista interpretation also eliminates the notion of a Supreme Being as the source of those rights. The source of rights in this conceptualization is the actors themselves, who are collectively exercising them."[93] Zapatismo in this sense reveals the logic of taking power from the state to resonate with a conception of neoliberal governmentality as a historic stage of capitalism. According to this logic, the state must be taken and dismantled so that alternative modes of production can subsequently appear. The duality of the caracol, however, is a marker of communally performed authority grounded in the legitimate right to self-defense without the compulsion to manifest state authority or defer the limits of the state to a pending historical transformation. Votán-Zapata here translates the duality of light into a practice of governance that is at once immanent to the activities of the people in Chiapas within state enclosure yet dispersed across vast distances, actors, and states of material flux and anticapitalist struggle. "Votán-Zapata," states the communiqué from the CCRI-CG on the anniversary of Zapata's assassination in 1994, "light that came from afar and was born here from our land. . . . Without a name he is named, the faceless face, all and no one, one and all, alive in death."[94] One insight materialized by Votán-Zapata's unstoppable paradoxical play is that story power illuminates the conditions for the enaction of different places and registers of autonomy that detour the state as a legitimate entity worthy of speech. The result is a different transformational velocity in the global struggle against neoliberal evisceration, as "the EZLN achieved in ten years of ideological and political struggle what no other Marxist-oriented political or guerrilla organization had managed to achieve in decades."[95] Through the register of duality, Zapatismo comes into focus as a paradox of singularity via virtual forms to address and signify an unceasing multiplicity of Indigenous life and struggle that surrounds the modern "cult of individualism." In this way, the Zapatistas are reframed as insurgent theorists of light who subvert the ways mass media coheres publics supine to nationalist, statist, and capitalist forms of racialized and gendered domination. The rebellious light of the Zapatistas illuminates a distinct horizon of dignified struggle against the biopolitics of Mexican Mestizo nationalism with the capacity to interface a pluriversal network of insurgent change and decolonial transformation.

NEW MEXICO–CHIAPAS CONTINUUM

Suppose one day in the recent past or future you take a drive up north to Tierra Amarilla, New Mexico, from Albuquerque. About a mile south of town on U.S. 84, you encounter a large, white billboard with a hand-painted monochrome visage of Emiliano Zapata next to the phrase "Tierra o Muerte" (Land or Death). Below, the phrase "¡Zapata Vive!" is spray-painted in black and red. A play on "Tierra y Libertad" (Land and Freedom), the Mexican revolutionary slogan popularized by Emiliano Zapata's Army of the South, the phrase "Tierra o Muerte" emerged in a poster that circulated around northern New Mexico in 1967, with an animation of the Casasola image, in the aftermath of the courthouse raid. The borrowed image would also mark the masthead of *El Grito del Norte* throughout its print run. In 1970, The Radical Education Project out of Detroit, Michigan, published a pamphlet of selected articles by *El Grito* with the same image under title: "Tierra o Muerte: The Land Belongs to the People."

Erected in 1988, the billboard restages Zapata's visage and the "Tierra o Muerte" slogan in the context of the land grant struggle of Amador Flores against Vista del Brazos, an Arizona development company that planned on subdividing the land for the construction of vacation homes for the nearby ski area. Flores had been working the parcel since 1966, when he and his family built an enclosure around five hundred acres of land to plant a garden and graze livestock. In 1985, however, Flores encountered a surveyor for an insurance company

FIGURE 9 *Tierra o Muerte* (1967) by Emanuel Martínez. Smithsonian American Art Museum, Gift of the artist. © 1967, Emanuel Martínez.

FIGURE 10 “Tierra o Muerte” sign on U.S. 84 to Tierra Amarilla, erected in 1988 during the standoff between El Consejo and Vista del Brazos.

who was working for Vista del Brazos after the company had filed a quiet lawsuit for a plot that encompassed Flores’s land. The sign is placed on the site of a fourteen-month standoff between Vista del Brazos and El Consejo del Tierra Amarilla, El Comité en Defensa del Pueblo Mexicano, and the Movimiento de Liberación Nacional Mexicano (Mexican National Liberation Movement; MNLM), organizations who began to council Flores and organize on his behalf. Over the course of the standoff, El Consejo dug a number of fortified bunkers, initiated armed patrols of the land, and set a series of booby traps around the encampment. After multiple court hearings that even resulted in a month-long imprisonment for Flores, he and Vista del Brazos reached a settlement that granted Flores $117,205 and two hundred acres of land.

At the end of the clearing on the west side of the road—right before it is overtaken with piñon, spruce, and juniper trees—you notice a white structure with a tin pitched roof. Across the wall that faces the road, you see the letters “EZLN” painted in red. In the initial discussions that led to the support of Flores’s case by El Consejo, El Comité, and the MNLM, all parties came to an agreement with Flores about the title of the land. According to Daniel Salcido, if "the action the *gente* were about to engage in to free the land resulted in any type of victory, the land would be placed in a community trust so that it would belong to the Mexican@ people as a whole."[96]

After his settlement, Flores transferred the two hundred acres to El Consejo and El Comité, who would subsequently come into contact with a group of Latinx and Mexican parents in Denver who had been organizing around issues of youth empowerment in the city. Out of this encounter, the Tierra Amarilla Youth Leadership Institute was born. Salcido notes, "the acquisition of land for the Mexican people created the possibility for Mexican youth from the inner cities of the Occupied Territories to re-establish their lost connections to their land, history, and cultural roots."[97]

The white structure with "EZLN" you see is a classroom for the institute, which runs a variety of camps, workshops, and cultural programs to teach youth how to work "centered around cooperation as opposed to competition" and how to "hold positions of leadership and also share all responsibilities."[98] A local project of land grant autonomy, the Tierra Amarilla Youth Leadership Institute entangles divergent genealogies of ejido struggle while also remaining distinct in its conditions of emergence and its network of actors.

On the other side of the billboard, you see a painting of a black and white skeleton figure walking through a tryptic of green, white, and red—the color scheme of the Mexican flag. It is as if the figure's traversal of the line between the green and the white panes transforms the quality of light by which it is seen. In the green pane, its right black hand sways behind its gait, pointing back as

FIGURE 11 Amarilla Youth Leadership classroom, 2009.

FIGURE 12 The south-facing side of the Tierra o Muerte sign, a walk between light and shadow.

if to say, "there I was." In its crossing, skeletal features are illuminated, as if to say, "I once was alive and now in death I continue walking." The green paint cascades from above, following the contour of his arm yet never crosses the line he establishes with his hand. As its black left foot pivots forward, it leaves behind a mark that could either be a shadow from a light ahead or a cut in the ground below. The skeleton's right leg steps into the next pane and is subsumed into the white. In its left white hand, the skeleton clutches the lapel of a jacket that is fitted around an exposed ribcage. In its resolute gaze, between light and shadow, there is something that says, "here I come" or "there I go," though one cannot tell from where it comes or where it goes.

In this light, the dignified rebellion enacted by Zapatismo is not only a project of autonomization from the Mexican state. The dignity that constellates the New Mexico–Chiapas continuum also uprises a submerged astrological horizon to the term *dignity*, as "a situation of a planet in which its influence is heightened, either by its position in the zodiac, or by its aspects with other planets."[99] Dignity in this sense signifies a condition of heightened cosmological influence in which discrete localities come to bear upon one another, revealing conjunctural horizons and entanglements of decolonial struggle. One may think of it as a shared yet discontinuous wave of light mirrored between the mountain ranges of the northern and southern borderlands of Mexico that allows us to conceptualize overlaid and interpenetrating colonialisms and the insurgent limits to multiple national formations. Mirror doubles as a noun and a verb, to reflect and refract light in various and specific ways. As technology and medium, a mirror is mix of heat and sand, but it is also activated by the surrounding landscape, as water can mirror. According to the *Oxford English Dictionary*, a mirror can be a model or an example, or a person or thing embodying a pattern—mirroring not as a task of identifying homologies or similitude, but of naming the connective particles and paths of light that illuminate convergences and differences while obscuring and bypassing others.[100] In the words of John Holloway, this mirrored entanglement "does not deflect people from the question of organization. What it does rather is to open up perspectives in a world that seems so terribly closed. More than that, it suggests forms of action that break with the logic of capital and are more difficult for capital to integrate into the texture of domination."[101]

The disparate genealogies of land grant struggle in Chiapas and New Mexico converge in this regard through a shared conjuring of an Indigenous discourse for ejido rights in Greater Mexico that diverges from the biopolitics of Indian racialization codified under Mexican Mestizo nationalism. What becomes illuminated, then, is an entangled network of insurrection that deposes the dictatorship of private property by strategically translating colonial structures and discourses into localized horizons of Indigenous Story Power. Marcos in this play of light and shadow becomes illuminated as a secretary—a term that Tijerina elucidates as both a scribe and a keeper of secrets. Together and in separation, they expose the space between light and shadow to be not only the space of life, but also, as Eduardo Cadava notes, the space of writing.[102] Like Tijerina, Marcos is not Indigenous to the lands he writes about in order to reclaim. However, while La Alianza operated through the openly patriarchal status of Tijerina as its president and predominant spokesperson, the anonymity of Marcos and the collectivity of the CCRI-CG point to a distinctly communitarian organizational politics attempting to eschew paternalistic and patriarchal hierarchies. Marcos writes, "We use ski-masks and other methods of hiding our faces as an elementary security precaution and as a vaccine against *caudillismo*."[103] B. V. Olguín argues that the use of masks allows the Zapatistas to "decenter both the revolutionist and the primacy of the revolution itself. . . .

the CCRI-CG resists various internal and external attempts to construct the EZLN as a vanguard army while simultaneously explicating the strategic and ideological efficacy of rejecting the caudillo politics that have plagued Latin America (and especially Mexico) since the independence movement of the early nineteenth century."[104] Thus after pronouncing his disappearance and walking off stage in the announcement that would become "In Between Light and Shadow" ("Great, now that the mask has come off, I can walk around here naked, right?"), Marcos is reborn under the moniker Subcomandante Galeano, the name of his slain comrade. From offstage a voice proclaims, "Good morning compañeras and compañeros. My name is Galeano, Subcomandante Insurgente Galeano. Anyone else here named Galeano?" The crowd responds, "We are all Galeano!"

"Ah," Subcomandante Galeano replies, "that's why they told me that when I was reborn, it would be as a collective."[105]

"If to theorize," Lydia French argues, "is to make concepts visible . . . then theory visualizes through refraction."[106] By following the path of light back to New Mexico, the task here would not be to dismiss La Alianza for the retention of patriarchal structures. The task would, rather, be the naming of the patriarchal logic that facilitated Tijerina's entrance and ascendance in New Mexican land grant politics. In this frame, Tijerina came to embody and unsettle patrón authority embedded in land grant forms. His secretarial labor at once replicated patriarchal control, yet decoupled social justice from legal redress and recognition. This disjunct between Zapatismo and Indohispanx mestizaje reveals an overlap in the ways Marcos and Tijerina became targets of counterinsurgent individualization from collective struggle. The entanglement of their incommensurate public functions allows us to name the "cult of individualism" as counterinsurgent rhetoric that naturalizes the violence of private property across a variety of state forms and modalities of capital accumulation. David Correia notes how this counterinsurgent violence waged at El Consejo and the broader struggle for land grant reclamation in the twentieth century relies on the "claim that land grant activists are domestic terrorists."[107] In doing so, he reveals how the Domestic Terrorism Operations Unit of the FBI actually used the connections land grant activists were making with the Zapatistas as a definitive factor in the state's amplification of police violence against them. Correia quotes an FBI memo stating that Tierra Amarilla land grant activists "are believed to have identified with the Ejército Zapatista de Liberation National [*sic*] and the Mexican National Liberation Movement. These are known rebel movements within

Mexico that believe in reclaiming the lands originally ceded to the United States from Mexico in 1848."[108] By refracting the borderlands of Chiapas and Mexico, the cult of individualism becomes reframed as a historically and territorially mobile complex of counterinsurgent state violence, property ownership, and racialized patriarchy.

The New Mexico–Chiapas continuum here works against the instrumental "realism of power politics" in order to vitalize an anticapitalist materialism through a verb-based time-space horizon of Indigenous feminism.[109] Out of this entanglement, quantum theory is translated into a displaced quest for a verb-based language—or, rather, a story power—for the study of the insuperable paradoxes immanent to movement and light. According to Alford, "physics in the western world has been essentially the quest for the smallest noun (which used to be a-tom, 'that which cannot be further divided')." However, "as they went inside the atom things weren't acting like nouns anymore. The physicists were intrigued with the possibilities inherent in a language that didn't depend on nouns but could move right to verbs when the circumstances were appropriate."[110] Zapatismo's activation of verb-based analytics and organizational structures reveals the already-present feminist sleight of hand tied to Marcos's emergence and disappearance, as his "birth" on January 1, 1994, also worked as a productive distraction from the coincident announcement of the "Women's Revolutionary Law." A document circulated simultaneously with the "First Declaration from the Lacandón Jungle," the "Women's Revolutionary Law" calls for women's rights to work, reproductive authority, education, and protection from rape and assault as fundamental to Zapatista autonomy.[111] In an early linguistic study of Native American languages, Nathan Altshuler argues that "American Indian languages taken as a whole are decidedly verb-based as compared to other languages of the world." He notes how this verb-based structure materializes important "matricentered cultures" that cluster the "linguistic elements" of social structure "about the verb and/or greater verb complexity and enhancement."[112] This tendency, he continues, operates in distinction from societies organized around "patrilineal descent [and] patrilocal residence" that tend to cohere around "noun complexity and enhancement."[113] As a result, in the social "freeing of the elements from the verb we should expect some indication of patri-centeredness" in the collective conception of the people.

This horizon allows us to think the shifting U.S.-Mexico and Mexican-Guatemalan borderlands in an asynchronous simultaneity that radiates a conceptual vocabulary for Indigenous insurgency that curtails the appropriation of its findings by dominant classes.[114] As a transaction of critical paradigms derived from partially connected anticapitalist land grant struggle, this continuum includes the practice of solidarity but is not only bound to that horizon. "Indigenous women activists," Maylei Blackwell notes, "move in and between scales of power in order to use existing arenas of participation and create new ones." This multiscalar movement, she argues, "gives a more complex and mobile mapping of transnational social movements and their internalities of power' because indigenous women are social actors who have been marginalized even within their own oppositional national, local, and transnational movement."[115]

The New Mexico–Chiapas continuum in this sense also reflects an entanglement of cooperative modes and mediations of power predicated on the ongoing vitality of memories of Indigenous and feminist insurrection within institutional and constitutional frameworks that ossify the noun-based fulcrum of patriarchy. This continuum, rather, manifests as a comparative borderlands analytic that counterpoises discrete historical conjunctures and visions of Indigenous insurrection and racial capitalist political economy through each other as an ongoing project of dematerializing the state. As such, the imperative here is not about keeping constitutional or institutional authority as the sole horizon for Indigenous movement but rather about activating pluritemporal iterations of Indigenous insurgency that disclose how constitutional authority becomes overtaken by illegitimate political authority. Such insurgency reveals the political illegitimacy of colonial and national domination paradoxically through the performance of constitutional authority. By enacting what Roberto D. Hernández calls "epistemic and cartographic disobedience" as a "decolonial imperative," the New Mexico–Chiapas continuum recenters the people as predicate for constitutional authority while deposing the racialized and gendered channels of power that sanction the constitution of modern politics.[116]

CODA

Secrets, Scribes, and Secretaries

On the cold, rainy morning of December 14, 2012, my family and I took a road trip from Albuquerque, New Mexico, to El Paso, Texas, to pay a visit to Reies López Tijerina. At the time, El Viejo was months deep in dementia's terrible delirium, and though we repeatedly told him whom we were going to visit, it was clear that conveying his understanding of the significance of such a journey was already beyond his reach. My Nana, however, understood fully what such a visit entailed. For her own reasons, she declined my invitation to join in our excursion, yet she encouraged our journey and told us to deliver her salutations and regards to Tijerina and his family—people she and El Viejo hadn't seen in decades. I was accompanied by my mom, Gail; my sister, Michelle; my stepfather, Robert; and my partner, Pacharee. That morning, we sat in a McDonald's parking lot on Albuquerque's Westside as I called Tijerina's residence and spoke with his wife, Esperanza, to relay our departure and likely time of arrival. I had spent most of the fall season arranging the visit and corresponding with Mary Gladys Mendoza, Tijerina's niece. "Does he remember my grandparents?" I asked Mary in one of our initial conversations. "Oh, yes," she said. "Your grandfather's name is on a list." Reies, Esperanza, and Mary welcomed the opportunity for us to visit and become acquainted. While I had already spent considerable time researching Tijerina's archive at the University of New Mexico and recorded dozens of hours of conversations with El Viejo, I knew that there was no amount of reading *about* Tijerina that could substitute for a face-to-face visit.

And yet such an encounter was daunting for a number of reasons. Not only was there the complex history of La Alianza shared between him and my grandparents that I was slowly uncovering, but there was an even larger set of more quotidian interactions, intimacies, and antagonisms between them that remain unspoken. In my conversations with El Viejo before he got sick, I had inquired about his relationship with Tijerina. El Viejo spoke with reverence of the work Tijerina enabled with La Alianza and yet was also critical of what he and others saw as the eclipse of the land grant movement under the prerogative of Tijerina's own intensely controlling style of personal leadership and his activist and spiritual pursuits. Tijerina had also long been sought after for interviews, documentaries, speeches, and feature films, but I had also heard of his skepticism of outsiders who sought to capture his narratives for academic and cinematic production. There was also the unfortunate fact that since the late 1970s, Tijerina had taken to narrating a cosmopolitical worldview of "Spanish-American" birthright with anti-Semitic tropes and narratives.[1] And then there was his old age. Born on September 21, 1926, he was about a month older than El Viejo. Although his memory was still intact, it was already well known at the time that his physical health was in decline. It was an encounter that I knew and felt necessary for the work I was undertaking, yet it was also one that surfaced an uneasy confrontation with the accelerating vanishing of El Viejo's memory that was unfolding before my eyes. It was an encounter, in other words, that insisted on a meeting with my own limitations as a scholar, thinker, social agent, and witness to intergenerational memory.

The drive down was filled with dark rain clouds that hung over the vast desert plains and jutting mountain ranges of southern New Mexico. It was windy and sleeting as we drove into El Paso, and clouds engulfed the Franklin Mountains. The gray of the sky and the gray of the sprawling border cityscapes of El Paso and Ciudad Juárez blended together and contrasted with the reddish browns and tans of the surrounding hills, steep valleys, and jagged mountains. It was a beautiful and unsettling sight. As we checked into our hotel, the sense of unsettlement became grotesquely amplified by breaking news of a gunman who had invaded the Sandy Hook Elementary school in Newtown, Connecticut, and murdered twenty children and six adults before killing himself. Dazed from such horrific news and tired from the drive, we unloaded our luggage into our rooms and rested before heading to Tijerina's residence. When we arrived, Esperanza warmly greeted each of us and led us into their humble one-bedroom apartment. Reies was waiting for us in their bedroom, which doubled as a living room and library. He was a remarkable sight. A beard of bright white hair framed his deeply wrinkled face. His stare was piercing and resolute. His stature and demeanor and voice retained the unbounded charismatic energy that marked the singularity of his activist labor. And yet it also uncannily evoked El Viejo's repertoire of storytelling performance—a feeling that was shared by my family later as we drove back to Albuquerque.

Over the course of that evening and the next day, my family and I had the opportunity to share meals and converse about La Alianza, the land grants, my grandparents, and the contemporary political climate. Although he was eighty-six years old at the time, Tijerina astonished me with how sharp his memory remained. He was able to quote from biblical scripture and legal codes from the Laws of the Indies, as well as recite complete passages from a number of different historical studies of land grants and philosophical treaties on law. During our conversations he pulled out a number of books from shelves around the room that he had collected during his research and activism. As I flipped through the texts, I noticed that each one was marked by meticulous annotation. Scrupulous, dense, and copious notes on the margins of his books competed with the words typeset on each page. The abundance of notes not only disclosed the urgency of study for Tijerina but also unveiled the texts comprising his library as a surface of living entities that catalyzed palimpsestic forms of memory. Books, in other words, are anything but static repositories of knowledge. This became clear when I asked him where he got the idea for performing citizen's arrests. He quickly cited *The Law of Arrest in Civil and Criminal Actions* by Harvey Cortland Voorhees, a foundational liberal legal treatise outlining the parameters and procedures of arrest for police and attorneys.[2] After he told me the title I anticipated a detailed recitation of the specific legal codes that inspired his actions, but instead he shifted:

The citizen is like the joker
en las cartas
in a deck of playing cards.
Do you know what the joker is for?
Well it can become any card that you want!

I immediately thought of Gabriel García Márquez's observation that the production of literature is nothing but an elaborate form of carpentry. "With both you are working with reality, a material just as hard as wood. Both are full of tricks and techniques."[3]

At the same time, it was evident that he was skilled in the delicate art of evasion. He spoke fondly of my grandparents and the dedication they put toward La Alianza, yet was either unable or unwilling to recall the specificity of their relationship or any tensions that arose between them. Similarly, it became clear that the clarity of his memory was tied to a tightly crafted script that he had cultivated over decades about La Alianza, the land grants, and the sanctity of his own patriarchal status. In this he repeated his anti-Semitic narratives, conservative arguments against abortion, and familiar patriarchal refrains about the need for women to reproduce progeny for the movement—a mandate he specifically intoned toward Pacharee during our conversation. In the same breath, he turned to me and repeated the imperative of secretarial labor.

Do you know the sacred work?
It was revealed to me by the three Angels.
Every day that passes for me that revelation gets stronger and stronger
This is what you are obligated to do.
You are a secretary.

The charge of secretarial labor, although shrouded in Tijerina's patriarchal language, continues to haunt me and indeed has taken on a life that has escaped the racialized and patriarchal strictures that governed its enunciation. Secretaries function as both scribes and keepers of secrets. Secretaries are those whose vocation is to write for and on behalf of an "other" entity. A secretary can be someone who is entrusted with the secrets of a deity as well as someone who is aware of the secrets of the natural world.[4] While stereotypically associated with a specific type of feminized clerical work, unhousing the labor from its corporate and bureaucratic functions opens up a different orientation toward the politics of writing, interlocution, authorship, collectivity, subversion, and knowledge that I've attempted to outline in the previous pages. The secretarial mandate recurred not only as I transcribed El Viejo's journals, but it also reappeared as a dimension to the insurgent labor that constitutes what I've called the Native Story Power that animates the writings of Subcomandante Marcos, Ana Castillo, Elizabeth Martínez, Simon Ortiz, and Leslie Marmon Silko.

Silko, in particular, is well known for framing the process of writing *Almanac of the Dead* as a type of secretarial labor, one that relinquishes the modern notion of authorship as individual protagonism. She recalls the early years of the 1980s as a period that marked the onset of compulsions to "spontaneously write down things" from "transmissions" she received. In "Listening to the Spirits," her interview with Ellen Arnold, she states: "I look now and I see thats and whiches that shouldn't be there in *Almanac*, but it was like those little spirits who rode me, they said: your vanity? Your vanity about how your prose looks on the page, your vanity about wanting to satisfy the Ph.D. students and readers, your vanity? Your vanity! When I tried to get it finished and published within two or three years like the publishers wanted, the old spirits said, your vanity? You want to do something on a schedule like that? No, it's our book."[5]

Rather than verifying a stable authorial intention, Silko highlights secretarial labor as a pursuit that undermines the unidirectional causality between stories and storytellers. Such an undermining not only resonates with Tijerina's activism, but can also be seen in the cooperative mode of power fathomed by Ana Castillo and Elizabeth "Betita" Martínez, both of whom came to see their literary and activist work as inextricably tied to a labor of interlocution with the memory and diasporic movement of Genízarx indigeneity. Silko's recollection of the period of *Almanac*'s secretarial emergence would also be the same period in which the figure who would eventually become reborn as Subcomandante Galeano departed for the mountains of southeastern Mexico in the hopes of organizing a clandestine guerilla force of Indigenous Mayan rebels in Chiapas. The figure of Subcomandante Galeano in particular highlights the secretary's convergence of secrecy and scribe that lies at the heart of the Zapatista's insurgent labor. Indeed, the Zapatista's performance of autonomy straddles a delicate balance between publicity and secrecy, what Graham M. Jones calls "the concealment of revelation—dissimulating that something has been disclosed."[6]

The valences of secrecy that dwell within secretarial labor are thus woven into the insurrectionary energy that animates the 1680 Pueblo Revolt, the 1967 courthouse raid, and the 1994 Zapatista uprising. Each scene of insurrection is fundamentally distinct, yet each also required elaborate veils from the gaze of authority, a fluency in knowledge of the surrounding landscape, and a metalanguage of escape. Secrecy from this vantage is not merely insider knowledge of a bounded set of agents but also "a multimedia, multisensory phenomenon, manifested simultaneously across a plurality of domains."[7] From this we can see how La Alianza, the Zapatistas, Silko, Simon Ortiz, Martínez, and Castillo differentially enact secretarial vocations by installing storytelling networks for land reclamation within legal, historical, and literary discourses in a way that disobeys the logocentric theories of writing through which modern law, history, and literature administer and enforce settler colonial violence. They reveal how secretarial labor indeed engages with historiographical content and modern literacy yet also dialogues with the unboundedness of Native storytelling in a way that contravenes the secular, empiricist, and visual codes of modern knowledge. Secretarial labor thus reveals how the network of Indigenous insurgency that surrounds land grant formations at once operates on a chronological plane yet exceeds historicist assignations of primary and secondary relations. These networks disband stringently individualized, empirical, and linear conceptions of temporal causality and discursive influence. They reveal horizons that are *local* in a way that disfigures the colonial politics of nationalized regional space and *planetary* in a way that underlies yet eludes the literalism of the local. Horizons of secretarial labor reconfigure colonial regionalisms by allowing us to consider a longer trajectory of Indigenous movement within formations and peoples designated as detribalized by settler regimes of Native recognition.

As I have argued in this book, such a conception of working on behalf of an "other" does not necessarily devolve into exploitation and appropriation, nor does it cascade into a relinquishment of autonomy. Rather, the secrecy required by secretarial labor opens up a distinct epistemic humility in work with the intellectual sovereignty of Native and Indigenous peoples. Secrecy has long been an important tactic employed by the Pueblo Indian peoples to evade elimination and capture under the regimes of modern knowledge imposed through successive colonial occupations.[8] In this, the Pueblo Indians are not alone, as secrecy is also an important component to the ceremonial vitality of many Native peoples who negotiate intense forms of ethnographic and bureaucratic capture. Thus the charge of the secretary is not one of mastery or total knowledge or the reassertion of an imperialist right to know. It is, instead, a certain way of approaching the sovereignty of Native and Indigenous modes of creation, story, perception, and governance as a predicate to decolonial enunciation while simultaneously respecting the limited and incomplete access that one may have to such knowledge. "The continuity and endurance of native cultures up to our present," José Rabasa reminds us, "is bound to the refusal to seek the recognition of their capacity to reproduce European forms."[9] The exigence of secretarial labor is a broader dismantling of settler colonial epistemicide rather than a presumption that modern forms are sufficiently capable of transmitting Native knowledge systems.

What I've termed throughout this book as Native Story Power thus conjures secretarial labor as one model for the ways in which the Mestizx trappings that underwrite Latinx indigeneities may speak and cooperate with movements for the Indigenous reclamation of the Americas. Its specific work opens up unforeseen cooperative, insurgent, and creative horizons to the activity of reading, listening, transcription, and translation—horizons that halt the binaristic oppositions that commonly organize dominant conceptions of originality, authenticity, and artifice. Such a cooperative horizon for critical enunciation diverges simultaneously from the impulses of ethnographic capture *and* from analytics presumed on the passive boundedness of the literary object. Secretaries thus outline a specific practice that repoliticizes the paradoxes of Latinx indigeneity by avowing land as a living narrative force, dislodging English and Spanish as European languages, and dismantling the lettered margins of literature and history from their colonialist and nation-building functions. Native Story Power allows secretaries to interweave texts with performances of literature and orature, history and prophesy, and dwells in secular and sacred temporalities. Secretarial labor transform texts that perform the logic of the law into ungovernable life. Secretaries subvert texts that perform the containment of property into uprising the land.[10] From this outlook, the possibility of Indigenous land reclamation resides in the power of intense study and "the power of intense dreaming, of the felt intensification when boundaries shift and other views become available."[11] Secretaries reframe the question of land reclamation beyond legal redress in order to fathom a distinct method of translation that detours the totalizing, monolinear logic of secular time. Therefore, rather than coordinating relations between and across texts and movements in historicist time or reducing reclamation to a legal procedure, this book has staged the vitality of Native Story Power within land grant cultural politics in order to unleash a bundled set of ruminations on land, language, and insurgency that unsettles the dialectic of Indigenous-settler identities within racialized and gendered regimes of property and sovereignty in the Americas. At stake is the cultivation of a nested theory of language, land, writing, and translation that enlivens Indigenous land reclamation as an unending possibility immanent to the temporalities that organize the present moment.

NOTES

NOTE ON TERMS, OR X MARKS A SUTURE

1. Alan Pelaez López, "The X in Latinx is a Wound, Not a Trend."

PROLOGUE

1. This prologue is based on a eulogy I delivered at my grandfather's memorial service in Albuquerque, New Mexico, on March 17, 2013.
2. "eulogy, n."
3. Williams, *Marxism and Literature*, 129.
4. Her name was Dolores Lucero. As a detribalized Indigenous servant for the Lucero family, Dolores would have been racialized as a *genízara*. For an extended account of La Alianza's relationship to the vexed genealogies of genízara/o racialization in New Mexico, see chapter 3.
5. Du Bois, *Darkwater*, 29.
6. Robinson, *Black Marxism*, 45.
7. Moten and Harney, *Undercommons*, 28.
8. Davis et al., *If They Come in the Morning*, 96.
9. Davis et al., *If They Come in the Morning*, 96–97.

INTRODUCTION

1. Shannon Speed (Chickasaw Nation) uses the term *multicriminal* to name the ways in which the captivity of migrant women sustains the economic and disciplinary operations of modern statecraft in the Americas. See Speed, "States of Violence."

2. “Constitución Nacional de La Alianza Federal de Mercedes,” box 1, folder 1, Reies Tijerina Papers, University of New Mexico Center for Southwest Research, 1963.
3. See “The Spanish Background: Problems Concerning Ownership, Usurpations, and Defense of Common Lands in 16th Century Castile,” 12–23.
4. See Malcolm Ebright and Rick Hendricks, *The Witches of Abiquiú: The Governor, the Priest, the Genízaro Indians, and the Devil* (Albuquerque: University of New Mexico Press, 2006), ch. 2: “The Genízaros.”
5. See Tyler, “Ejido Lands in New Mexico,” 24–35.
6. See Stoller, “Grants of Desperation,” 22–39.
7. Gene Barak writes: “To many Americans, at the time it was an unjust war of conquest launched conspiratorially by Southern Democrats against an unoffending neighbor for the evil purpose of extending the inhuman institution of slavery.” See Barak, *Mexico Views Manifest Destiny*, 3.
8. This is a conservative estimate. John Van Ness and Christine M. Van Ness note that the U.S. Court of Private Land Claims established in 1891 adjudicated “approximately 300 claims embracing about 35,000,000 acres.” See “Introduction” to *Spanish and Mexican Land Grants in New Mexico and Colorado*, 10.
9. See Knowlton, “Violence in New Mexico,” 1054–84.
10. See Rosenbaum, *Mexicano Resistance in the Southwest*, ch. 6.
11. Torrez, “Tierra Amarilla Grant and Thomas B. Catron.”
12. Gonzalez, “Struggle for Survival,” 314.
13. Tijerina, *They Called Me “King Tiger,”* 7.
14. Tijerina, *They Called Me “King Tiger,”* 37.
15. “Constitución Nacional de La Alianza Federal.” 1963, Reies López Tijerina Papers, University of New Mexico Center for Southwest Research.
16. Spain, *Recopilación de Leyes de Los Reynos de las Indias.*
17. La Alianza defined the concept of the “free city-state” as “also known as a ‘pueblo’ . . . the approximate English description of the status of the community land grants under the Laws of the Indies. In general, each pueblo had its own flag, municipal government, administration building, police force, judge, mayor, seal, and other such independence attributes.” “Absentee ownership was not permitted. . . . In many ways, the pueblo is like the ‘Indian’ pueblo in New Mexico today.” “The Alianza: What Where and Why,” box 1, folder 1, Reies Tijerina Papers, University of New Mexico Center for Southwest Research, 1968.
18. Valdez and Steiner, *Aztlan*, 241.
19. The Tierra Amarilla Courthouse raid, as it is also called, is credited as the lynchpin of Alianza’s entrance into national and international consciousness and Tijerina’s elevation to a national Chicanx and civil rights leader. In addition to catalyzing the largest manhunt in New Mexico’s history, the raid’s militant radicalism and break from traditional politics is also said to have stoked the imaginations of Chicanx Movement participants against U.S. systems of governance and the visions of assimilation offered by previous generations of Mexican American and Spanish American leadership. Yet Tijerina’s elevation into a symbol of resistance

and spokesman for an emergent Chicanx political class across the United States occurred in tension with his entanglement with a number of court cases stemming from the courthouse raid and the Echo Amphitheatre takeover. All of Tijerina's biographers, as well as numerous Chicanx historiographers, note the state responded to Tijerina's ascendancy with an excessive campaign of surveillance and criminal and civil charges against him and other Alianza members. See Blawis, *Tijerina and the Land Grants*; Gardner, *¡Grito!*; and Nabokov, *Tijerina and the Courthouse Raid.*

20. For La Alianza's coalitional ties with Black Power movements, see Mariscal, *Brown-Eyed Children of the Sun*. For Tijerina's relationship with American Indian movements, especially Hopi elder Thomas Banyaca, see Nabokov, *A Forest of Time*. See also Mantler, *Power to the Poor*.
21. Gómez-Quiñones and Vásquez, *Making Aztlán*, 106.
22. For useful work that grapples with this distinction, see Jackson, *Creole Indigeneity*; N'Gweno, "This Land That Diaspora."
23. Hernandez Castillo, "Indigeneity as a Field of Power," 379–402.
24. As Mary Louise Pratt observes, "The idea of 'prior-ness' or 'ab-originality' is produced at the moment of encounter. It cannot preexist it." Pratt, "Indigeneity Today," 401.
25. Cotera and Saldaña-Portillo, "Indigenous but Not Indian?," 562.
26. Cotera and Saldaña-Portillo, "Indigenous but Not Indian?," 562.
27. Eng and Kazanjian, "Introduction: Mourning Remains" in *Loss*, 4.
28. Cotera and Saldaña-Portillo, "Indigenous but Not Indian?," 563.
29. Cotera and Saldaña-Portillo, "Indigenous but Not Indian?," 563.
30. Blackwell, Boj Lopez, and Urrieta Jr., "Introduction: Critical Latinx Indigeneities," 126.
31. Blackwell, Boj Lopez, and Urrieta Jr., "Introduction: Critical Latinx Indigeneities," 131.
32. See Alberto, "Nations, Nationalisms, and *Indígenas*," 107–27; Alarcón, "Chicana Feminism," 248–56; Rodriguez y Gibson, "Imagining a Poetics of Loss," 23–50; Beltrán, "Patrolling Borders," 595–607.
33. Blackwell, Boj Lopez, and Urrieta Jr., "Critical Latinx Indigeneities," 131.
34. Blackwell, Boj Lopez, and Urrieta Jr., "Critical Latinx Indigeneities," 126–27.
35. Blackwell, Boj Lopez, and Urrieta Jr., "Critical Latinx Indigeneities," 130.
36. Johnson, "Theorizing the Loss of Land," 293.
37. Johnson, "Theorizing the Loss of Land," 294.
38. See Peña, *Chicano Culture, Ecology, Politics*; Rodriguez, *The Matachines Dance*; Gandert et al., *Nuevo México Profundo*.
39. Atencio, "The Human Dimensions in Land Use and Land Displacement in Northern New Mexico Villages," 47.
40. Coulthard and Simpson, "Grounded Normativity," 254.
41. Article 25 of the United Nations Declaration of the Rights of Indigenous Peoples states that Indigenous peoples "have the right to maintain and strengthen their

distinctive spiritual relationship with their traditionally owned or otherwise occupied and used lands, territories, waters and coastal seas and other resources and to uphold their responsibilities to future generations in this regard." See UN General Assembly, "United Nations Declaration on the Rights of Indigenous Peoples."

42. Blackwell, Boj Lopez, and Urrieta Jr., "Critical Latinx Indigeneities," 128, 133.
43. Goldstein, "Toward a Genealogy of the U.S. Colonial Present," 15.
44. Brady, "Territoriality," 225.
45. Kuokkanen, *Reshaping the University*, 23, 24. The concept of the gift, of course, has voluminous studies devoted to it. In addition to Kuokkanen's work, I find Anna Tsing's theorization of the gift relevant for my argument here. Tsing outlines how the logic of the gift "is a useful tool because it urges us to look for difference. Rather than relax into economic common sense, we stay alert for contrasts across value regimes." Tsing, *The Mushroom at the End of the World*, 122. See also Maldonado-Torres, "Césaire's Gift and the Decolonial Turn," 435–62.
46. Kuokkanen, *Reshaping the University*, 23.
47. Pratt, "Afterword: Indigeneity Today," 402.
48. See Vizenor, *Fugitive Poses*; Basso, *Wisdom Sits in Places*; Womack, *Art as Performance*; Deloria Jr., *Sacred Lands and Religious Freedom*; Momaday, "Native American Attitudes to the Environment," 79–85.
49. See Warrior, *Tribal Secrets*; Barker, *Sovereignty Matters*; Simpson, *Mohawk Interruptus*; Barker, *Critically Sovereign*.
50. Deloria, *God Is Red*, 66.
51. Coulthard, *Red Skin, White Masks*, 60.
52. Goeman, "Land as Life," 73.
53. See Swann and Krupat, *Recovering the Word*; Gerald Vizenor, *Narrative Chance*; Goeman, *Mark My Words*; Silva, *The Power of the Steel Tipped Pen*; Byrd, *The Transit of Empire*.
54. Simon Ortiz, "Towards a National Indian Literature," 244.
55. The concept of Indigenous land rematriation in relation to the politics of study is discussed in la paperson's *A Third University is Possible*. This text in particular strives to imagine a politics of study within the entrapments of modern academia that expose horizons of Native and Black futurity.
56. Tuck and Yang, "Decolonization Is Not a Metaphor," 5.
57. See Kauani, "Tracing Historical Specificity," 257–65; Day, "Being or Nothingness," 102–21; Simpson, Walcott, and Coulthard, "Panel Discussion," 75–89.
58. For Tuck and Yang, "Settler nativism, or what Vine Deloria Jr. calls the Indian-grandmother complex, is a settler move to innocence because it is an attempt to deflect a settler identity, while continuing to enjoy settler privilege and occupying stolen land" ("Decolonization Is Not a Metaphor," 11).
59. Tuck and Yang's article is groundbreaking yet relies on a material vs. metaphor binary that overlooks the decolonizing work that their own use of metaphorical language performs—a binary, in other words, that belies the decolonial energy of their decisive critical phraseology of "settler move to innocence" and "incom-

mensurability is unsettling." Tuck and Yang are not alone here. In a similar vein, Pablo Villa performs the same confusion of metaphor as substitution rather than transformation and dismisses the metaphoricity of border theory as installing "the Chicano border crosser or hybrid as the new essential, privileged subject" who "not only silences the experience of other border inhabitants but also claims for itself the monopoly of virtue" (328). See "The Limits of American Border Theory."

60. Stuart Hall, "For Allon White," 286.
61. Leanne Simpson, *As We have Always Done*, 43.
62. "horizon, n." This entry is notable because it indexes the ways in which the term is used name transformation, movement, and embodiment across a variety of disciplines. For the discipline of astronomy, horizons indicate a "great circle of the celestial sphere, the plane of which passes through the centre of the earth and is parallel to that of the sensible horizon of a given place." For geology, horizons index "a stratum or set of strata characterized by a particular fossil or group of fossils," while for archaeology, horizons mark a "level at which a particular group of remains is found, or which is taken as representing a particular culture or cultural period." Anatomy and zoology employ horizons to name the paralleled calibration of the eyes, throat, and teeth of mammalian creatures, while embryology has used the term to indicate the stages of embryonic growth.
63. Goeman, "Land as Life," 72.
64. Crapazano, *Imaginative Horizons*, 14.
65. See Gadamer, *Truth and Method*. See also Ricoeur, *The Rule of Metaphor*.
66. Laclau, "Horizon, Ground, and Lived Experience," 100–111.
67. Laclau, "Horizon, Ground, and Lived Experience," 109.
68. Satz, *Ultimate Horizons: Probing the Limits of the Universe*, 4.
69. Nichols, "Disaggregating Primitive Accumulation," 26.
70. Nichols, "Disaggregating Primitive Accumulation," 26.
71. Goeman, "Land as Life," 74.
72. Adajania and Hoskote, "The Nth Field," 31–32.
73. Sando, *Pueblo Nations*, 17.
74. Alfonso Ortiz, "The Dynamics of Pueblo Indian Survival," 302.
75. This is a play on Hernández-Avila's reading of Chrystos's poem, "Dear Indian Abbey" in "Relocations Upon Relocations," 181.
76. Goeman, "Land as Life," 79.
77. Subcomandante Marcos, *Professionals of Hope*, 211.

CHAPTER 1

1. Dunbar-Ortiz, "Preface," vii.
2. Dunbar-Ortiz, "Preface," vii.
3. Saldaña-Portillo, "Critical Latinx Indigeneities," 142.
4. Dunbar-Ortiz, "Preface."
5. Dyck, "Indigenous Ways of Knowing in Simon Ortiz's *Fight Back*," 97.

6. Alfonso Ortiz, "The Dynamics of Pueblo Indian Survival," 297.
7. Nichols, "Disaggregating Primitive Accumulation," 18.
8. Silko, *Almanac of the Dead*, 315.
9. Allen, *The Sacred Hoop*, 3–4.
10. Lugones, "The Coloniality of Gender," 383.
11. Lugones, "The Coloniality of Gender," 27.
12. Cheyfitz, "Balancing the Earth," 157.
13. See Wolf, "Settler Colonialism and the Elimination of the Native," 387–409; Tuck and Yang, "Decolonization Is Not a Metaphor"; Goldstein, *Formations of United States Colonialism.*
14. Castellanos, "Introduction: Settler Colonialism in Latin America," 778.
15. Castellanos, "Introduction," 778.
16. Balibar, "Racism and Nationalism," 39–40.
17. Speed, "Structures of Settler Capitalism in Abya Yala," 789.
18. Molina and Shorter, "Geographies Yoeme," 115.
19. Roppolo, "Vision, Voice, and Intertribal Metanarrative," 543.
20. Roppolo, "Vision, Voice, and Intertribal Metanarrative," 545.
21. Silko, *Almanac of the Dead*, 408.
22. Silko, *Almanac of the Dead*, 414–15.
23. Silko, *Almanac of the Dead*, 416.
24. Maldonado-Torres, "Secularism and Religion in the Modern/Colonial World System," 367.
25. Maldonado-Torres, "Secularism and Religion in the Modern/Colonial World System," 369.
26. Silko, *Almanac of the Dead*, 428.
27. Simon Ortiz, *Fight Back* (1980), Copyright page.
28. Simon Ortiz, *Woven Stone*, 30–31.
29. Simon Ortiz, *Woven Stone*, 31.
30. Simon Ortiz, *Woven Stone*, 3.
31. Simon Ortiz, *Woven Stone*, 29.
32. Seed, *Ceremonies of Possession in Europe's Conquest of the New World*, 69.
33. Seed, *Ceremonies of Possession in Europe's Conquest of the New World*, 83.
34. Ebright, *Four Square Leagues*, 3.
35. Simon Ortiz, *Woven Stone*, 29.
36. Alfonso Ortiz, *The Pueblo*, 38.
37. See Sando, *Pueblo Nations*, 248; Minge, *Ácoma*, 12–15.
38. Kessell, *Pueblos, Spaniards, and the Kingdom of New Mexico*, 66.
39. Simon Ortiz, *Woven Stone*, 28.
40. Sando, *Pueblo Nations*, 63.
41. Folsom, *Indian Uprising on the Rio Grande*, 21–33.
42. Jojola, "The Legacy of the Pueblo Revolt and the Tiquex Province," 63.
43. Sando, "The Pueblo Revolt," 34.
44. Reséndez, *The Other Slavery*, 169.

45. Sando, "The Pueblo Revolt," 19.
46. Suina, "Underestimation of Pueblo Power," 78.
47. Alfonso Ortiz, "The Pueblo Restoration of 1680," 2.
48. Alfonso Ortiz, "The Pueblo Restoration of 1680," 4.
49. Simon Ortiz, *Woven Stone*, 27.
50. Silko, "Language and Literature from a Pueblo Indian Perspective," 48–50.
51. Silko, "Language and Literature from a Pueblo Indian Perspective," 48–49.
52. Krupat, "Post-Structuralism and Oral Literature," 118.
53. Krupat, "Post-Structuralism and Oral Literature," 117.
54. Silko, "Language and Literature from a Pueblo Indian Perspective," 49.
55. Krupat, "Post Structuralism and Oral Literature," 117.
56. Silko, "Language and Literature from a Pueblo Indian Perspective," 50.
57. Silko, "Language and Literature from a Pueblo Indian Perspective," 57.
58. Snodgrass, *Leslie Marmon Silko*, 90.
59. See Knaut, *The Pueblo Revolt of 1680*, 185; Brown, *Pueblo Indians and Spanish Colonial Authority in Eighteenth-Century New Mexico*, 169. See also Weber, "Pueblos, Spaniards, and History"; Ebright and Hendricks, *Pueblo Sovereignty.*
60. Dozier, *The Pueblo Indians of North America*, 78.
61. Dozier, *The Pueblo Indians of North America*, 79.
62. Dozier, *The Pueblo Indians of North America*, 85.
63. Sando, *Pueblo Nations*, 43.
64. Ebright, Hendricks, and Hughes, *Four Square Leagues*, 7.
65. G. Emlem Hall writes, "As early as 1731 in New Mexico, and probably earlier in the Valley of Mexico, officials began using the term *sobrantes* ('surpluses,' 'extras') to describe unused Pueblo Indian lands. The term implied that the lands so described had owners and that the owners did not need them. . . . As applied, the idea became a critical vehicle for attempting to take unused Pueblo land and give it to non-Indians." *Four Leagues of Pecos*, 11.
66. Ebright, Hughes, and Hendricks, *Four Square Leagues*, 11.
67. Alfonso Ortiz, *The Pueblo*, 72–73.
68. Alfonso Ortiz, *The Pueblo*, 79. Edward Spicer notes that a feature of the Spanish policy of Apache extermination "proposed the bribing and corruption of Apaches into accepting" Spanish dominance. It "was a frankly cynical policy" with the goal of "moral destruction" that "relied as much on the creation of a taste for liquor as on any other feature." *Cycles of Conquest*, 332, 333.
69. Ebright, Hughes, and Hendricks, *Four Square Leagues*, 32, 33.
70. Ebright, Hughes, and Hendricks, *Four Square Leagues*, 42.
71. Alfonso Ortiz, *The Pueblo*, 83.
72. Dozier, *Pueblo Indians of New Mexico*, 97–99.
73. Allen, *Sacred Hoop*, 206.
74. Sando, *Pueblo Nations*, 24.
75. Alfonso Ortiz, *The Pueblo*, 85.
76. Klein, "Treaties of Conquest," 213.

77. Menchaca, *Recovering History, Constructing Race*, 274.
78. Minge, *Ácoma*, 58.
79. G. Emlen Hall, *Four Leagues of Pecos*, 53.
80. Ebright, Hughes, and Hendricks, *Four Square Leagues*, 245.
81. Ebright, Hughes, and Hendricks, *Four Square Leagues*, 238.
82. Simon Ortiz, *Woven Stone*, 347.
83. Simon Ortiz, *Woven Stone*, 347.
84. Minge, *Acoma*, 68.
85. Simon Ortiz, *Woven Stone*, 348.
86. Simon Ortiz, *Woven Stone*, 350.
87. Simon Ortiz, *Woven Stone*, 351.
88. Simon Ortiz, *Woven Stone*, 344.
89. Simon Ortiz, *Woven Stone*, 350.
90. Simon Ortiz, *Woven Stone*, 353.
91. Sullivan and Tuana, *Race and Epistemologies of Ignorance*, 1.
92. Simon Ortiz, *Woven Stone*, 353.
93. Simon Ortiz, *Woven Stone*, 355.
94. Simon Ortiz, *Woven Stone*, 358.
95. Simon Ortiz, *Woven Stone*, 330–31.
96. Simon Ortiz, *Woven Stone*, 345.
97. Silko, *Almanac of the Dead*, 222.
98. Silko, *Almanac of the Dead*, 224.
99. Silko, *Almanac of the Dead*, 224.
100. Silko, *Almanac of the Dead*, 227.
101. Silko, *Almanac of the Dead*, 227.
102. Silko, *Almanac of the Dead*, 235.
103. See Gordon-McCutchan, *The Taos Indians and the Battle for Blue Lake.*
104. *Taos Pueblo—Blue Lake, Hearings before the Subcommittee on Indian Affairs of the Committee on Interior and Insular Affairs*, Ninety-First Congress First Session on H.R. 471, May 15–16, 1969, 65–69.
105. Qtd. in Logan "Blue Lake."

CHAPTER 2

1. Leslie Marmon Silko, interview by Donna Perry, 322.
2. Silko, *Ceremony.*
3. Silko, "Books," 165.
4. Mignolo, "Literacy and Colonization," 60.
5. Mignolo, "Literacy and Colonization," 60.
6. Mignolo, "Literacy and Colonization," 60.
7. De la Cadena, "Indigenous Cosmopolitics in the Andes," 346.
8. De la Cadena, "Indigenous Cosmopolitics in the Andes," 347.
9. De la Cadena, "The Production of Other Knowledges and Its Tensions," 14.

10. Simpson, *Mohawk Interruptus*, 105.
11. Gómez, "The Storyteller's Escape," 146.
12. Karaka, *Empire's Tracks*.
13. Gómez, "The Storyteller's Escape," 150, 151.
14. Dunbar-Ortiz, *Roots of Resistance*, 36.
15. Silko, "Books," 160.
16. Vinson, *Before Mestizaje*, 15.
17. Vinson, *Before Mestizaje*, 15.
18. Gutiérrez, *When Jesus Came, the Corn Mothers Went Away*, 190.
19. Cobos defines *genízaro* (*jenízaro*) as "a person of mixed blood; an Indian captive ransomed by the Spanish authorities from his Apache, Comanche, Navajo, or Ute masters and used by his rescuers as a domestic or soldier; also, a descendant of these ransomed Indians; *adj.*, dark-skinned" (*A Dictionary of New Mexico and Southern Colorado Spanish*, 129). See also Ebright and Hendricks, *The Witches of Abiquiu*; Laura Gómez, *Manifest Destinies*, 56, 119; Blackhawk, *Violence over the Land*, 57–58, 67–68; Thomas Hall, "Genizaros," 356.
20. G. Emlen Hall, "The Pueblo Grant Labyrinth," 75. See also Ebright and Hendricks, *Four Square Leagues*.
21. G. Emlen Hall, "Pueblo Grant Labyrinth," 74.
22. Alfonso Ortiz, "Dynamics of Pueblo Indian Survival," 301.
23. Marez, "Signifying Spain, Becoming Comanche, Making Mexicans," 273.
24. Marez, "Signifying Spain, Becoming Comanche, Making Mexicans," 273.
25. Marez, "Signifying Spain, Becoming Comanche, Making Mexicans," 269.
26. Gutiérrez, *When Jesus Came, The Corn Mothers Went Away*, 189.
27. Dunbar-Ortiz, *Roots of Resistance*, 35. See also Brooks, *Captives and Cousins*; Swadesh, *Los Primeros Pobladores*.
28. Dunbar-Ortiz, *Roots of Resistance*, 46. See also Reséndez, *The Other Slavery*.
29. Dunbar-Ortiz, *Roots of Resistance*, 53. See also Gonzales, "The Genizaro Land Grant Settlements of New Mexico," 583–602; Gonzales, "Si eres Genízaro."
30. Dunbar-Ortiz, *Roots of Resistance*, 47.
31. Laura Gómez, *Manifest Destinies*, 120.
32. Magnaghi, "Plains Indians in New Mexico," 92.
33. See José Angel Hernández, "From Conquest to Colonization," 291–322.
34. Sando, *Pueblo Nations*, 83.
35. Avery, "Into the Den of Evils," 86. Avery writes, "Despite the offering of full citizenship and, in theory, full acceptance in the Hispanic society under the new Mexican government, most genízaros considered themselves Indians well into the nineteenth century. Officially genízaros had gained social equality, but in practice New Mexicans continued to hold them in low standing. Rather than try to break past this social barrier, the genízaros found it was in their own self-interest to 'perpetuate their Indian identity'" (85). See also Gonzales, "Si eres Genízaro"; Horvath, "The Social and Political Organization of the Genizaros."
36. Avery, "Into the Den of Evils," 86.

37. For the historiography of Spanish and Mexican land grant dispossession in New Mexico, see the following: Briggs and Van Ness, *Land, Water, and Culture*; Ebright, *Land Grants and Lawsuits in Northern New Mexico*; Gonzalez. "Struggle for Survival," 293–324; and Montoya, *Translating Property*.
38. Dunbar-Ortiz, *Roots of Resistance*, 106–7.
39. See deBuys, *Enchantment and Exploitation*; see also Forrest, *The Preservation of the Village*; Weigle, *Hispanic Villages of Northern New Mexico*.
40. Quintana, "Land, Water, and Pueblo-Hispanic Relations in Northern New Mexico," 296.
41. Klein, "Treaties of Conquest," 210.
42. Klein, "Treaties of Conquest," 216.
43. Klein, "Treaties of Conquest," 203.
44. See Nieto-Phillips, *The Language of Blood*. See also Montgomery, *The Spanish Redemption*; Rodríguez, "The Tourist Gaze, Gentrification, and the Commodification of Subjectivity in Taos," 105–26.
45. See Wade, *Race and Ethnicity in Latin America*.
46. Applebaum, Macpherson, and Rosemblatt, "Racial Nations," 1–31.
47. See Graham, *The Idea of Race in Latin America*; Bonilla-Silva, "We Are All Americans!," 3–16.
48. See Chang, *Chino: Anti-Chinese Racism in Mexico*; Knight, "Racism, Revolution, and *Indigenismo*."
49. Tarica, "Indigenismo," n.p.
50. Alberto notes that "Indigeneity, in the form of indigenism and through the logic of nationalism, functioned as succor for Chicanos within a U.S. ethnoracial framework that had enacted a long history of violence against Mexican Americans, including mass deportation, lynching, quotidian racism, land dispossession, language elimination, nativism, and police abuse." "Nations, Nationalisms, and *Indígenas*," 110.
51. Marez, "Signifying Spain," 267.
52. See Anaya and Lomeli, *Aztlán*; Pérez-Torres, "Refiguring Aztlán."
53. See Pérez-Torres, *Movements in Chicano Poetry*; Limón, *Mexican Ballads, Chicano Poems*. Pérez-Torres articulates the significance of the poem in the following terms: "The sense of pride and connection, rebirth and respect implied in the term Chicanismo is nowhere made more manifest than in Rodolfo Gonzales's *opus classicus Yo Soy Joaquín*. The poem manifests a Chicanismo comprised of cultural nationalism and connectivity to Mexican history and culture. It prefigures both the empowerment and contradictions inherent to Aztlán as a concept central to Chicano consciousness" (68).
54. See Romero and Harris, *Feminism, Nation and Myth*.
55. See Paz, *The Labyrinth of Solitude*.
56. Valdez's play *Los vendidos* stages these contradictions vividly. See Valdez, *Early Works*, 40–52.
57. See Alarcón, "Traddutora, Traditora"; Emma Pérez, "Sexuality and Discourse"; del Castillo "Malintzin Tenepal."

58. Qtd. in Tice, *Rhetoric of La Raza*, 18.
59. Mariscal, *Brown-Eyed Children of the Sun*, 187.
60. Bebout, "Hero Making in El Movimiento," 116.
61. Bebout, "Hero Making in El Movimiento," 113.
62. Ramón Gutierrez states that part "of the New Mexicans' hostility to the term 'Mexican' stems from its association with Mexico and Mexican nationalism. New Mexico was always marginal to Spanish imperial politics and just as isolated from Mexico City." "Unraveling America's Hispanic Past," 380. Phillip Gonzales argues that while "Mexican independence sought to uproot Castilian identification, . . . on the dominant Anglo side, the Spanish nomenclature thus originally served to herd Latinos within a civic fold while leaving the foreign and threatening sense of 'Mexican' to operate on a negative plane of social control." "The Political Construction of Latino Nomenclatures in Twentieth-Century New Mexico," 163. See also Mitchell, *Coyote Nation*; Montgomery, *The Spanish Redemption*; Nieto-Phillips, *The Language of Blood.*
63. Bebout, "Hero Making," 113. See also Muñoz, *Youth, Identity, Power*, 80; Marilyn Grace Miller, *Rise and Fall of the Cosmic Race*; Pérez-Torres, *Mestizaje*. Although each work occupies a distinct disciplinary position, they all nonetheless compress Chicanx acquisitions of mestizaje to the single history of Mexican Mestizo nationalism.
64. Muñoz, *Youth, Identity, Power*, 7–8.
65. Saldívar-Hull, *Feminism on the Border*, 64.
66. Arrizón, *Queering Mestizaje*, 4.
67. Arrizón, *Queering Mestizaje*, 55.
68. Saldaña-Portillo, "Who's the Indian in Aztlán?," 409.
69. Saldaña-Portillo, *Indian Given*, 232.
70. Saldaña-Portillo, *Indian Given*, 232.
71. Contreras, *Bloodlines*, 33.
72. Contreras, *Bloodlines*, 33.
73. Reid Gómez, "The Storyteller's Escape," 159.
74. Gómez, "The Storyteller's Escape," 161.
75. Silko, *Almanac of the Dead*, prefatory map.
76. Silko, *Almanac of the Dead*, 133. Such an account resonates with the rejection of state recognition in Indigenous Canada. See Coulthard, *Red Skin, White Masks.*
77. Barker, *Native Acts*, 11.
78. Brigham, "Productions of Geographic Scale and Capitalist-Colonialist Enterprise," 305.
79. Silko, *Almanac of the Dead*, prefatory map.
80. Romero, "Envisioning a 'Network of Tribal Coalitions,'" 625.
81. All passages from this reading are quoted from Silko, *Almanac of the Dead*, 245–53.
82. Nicole Guidotti Hernandez, *Unspeakable Violence*, 21.
83. Nicole Guidotti Hernandez, *Unspeakable Violence*, 19.
84. Nicole Guidotti Hernandez, *Unspeakable Violence*, 18.
85. Nicole Guidotti Hernandez, *Unspeakable Violence*, 18.

86. Nicole Guidotti Hernandez, *Unspeakable Violence*, 288.
87. Nicole Guidotti Hernandez, *Unspeakable Violence*, 252.
88. O'Meara, "The Ecological Politics of Leslie Marmon Silko's *Almanac of the Dead*," 66.
89. Silko, *Almanac of the Dead*, 569.
90. Rabasa, *Tell Me the Story of How I Conquered You*, 194.
91. Silko, *Almanac of the Dead*, 129.
92. Silko, *Almanac of the Dead*, 570.
93. Silko, *Almanac of the Dead*, 570.
94. Silko, *Almanac of the Dead*, 174.
95. Silko, *Almanac of the Dead*, 130.
96. Silko, *Almanac of the Dead*, 136.
97. Silko, *Almanac of the Dead*, 578.
98. Forbes, *Aztecas del Norte*, 73.
99. See Rodríguez, *The Matachines Dance*; Reséndez, *Changing National Identities at the Frontier.*
100. Brown, *Pueblo Indians and Spanish Colonial Authority in Eighteenth-Century New Mexico*, 19.
101. Ortiz, "Popay's Leadership," 113.
102. Córdova, *Abiquiú and Don Cacahuate*, 19.
103. Córdova, *Abiquiú and Don Cacahuate*, 10.
104. Córdova, *Big Dreams and Dark Secrets at Chimayó*, 218–219.
105. Gómez, "The Storyteller's Escape," 151, 150.

CHAPTER 3

1. Tijerina, *Mi lucha por la tierra*, 32, 30. All translations from the original Spanish are the author's own.
2. Tijerina, *Mi lucha por la tierra*, 31.
3. Tijerina, *Mi lucha por la tierra*, 30.
4. Tijerina, *Mi lucha por la tierra*, 31.
5. Tijerina, *Mi lucha por la tierra*, 31.
6 Tijerina, *Mi lucha por la tierra*, 31, 32.
7. Jenkinson, *Tijerina*, 22.
8. Tijerina, *Mi lucha por la tierra*, 32.
9. Gardner, *¡Grito!*, 29; González, *The Spanish-Americans of New Mexico*, 99.
10. González, *The Spanish-Americans of New Mexico*, 99–100.
11. For accounts of La Alianza's role in the Chicana/o movement, see Arturo F. Rosales, *Chicano!*; Gómez Quiñones and Vásquez, *Making Aztlán*. For La Alianza's formation within Spanish and Mexican land grants, see Correia, *Properties of Violence*; Swadesh, *Los Primeros Pobladores*; Knowlton, "Violence in New Mexico," 1054–84. For biographical accounts of Tijerina, see Oropeza, "Becoming Indo-Hispano"; Busto, *King Tiger*.

12. González, *The Spanish-Americans of New Mexico*, 99. Chakrabarty, *Provincializing Europe*, 76.
13. Chakrabarty, *Provincializing Europe*, 74.
14. González, *The Spanish-Americans of New Mexico*, 99.
15. González, *The Spanish-Americans of New Mexico*, 99. She further argues that La Alianza's more "excessive demands for the return of the landgrants and the expulsion of the Anglos" were "unrealistic and impractical" (106, 183).
16. See Maciel and Peña, "La Reconquista," 269–99; see also Griswold de Castillo, *The Treaty of Guadalupe Hidalgo*.
17. As Rudy Busto argues, accounts of La Alianza within Chicana/o and Latina/o studies remain dependent on the narratives contained within the four book-length biographies of Tijerina. These biographies are written by Anglophone writers and appeared within four years of the 1967 courthouse raid. "Their immediate goal," Busto writes, "is to provide the reader with an image of Tijerina at the height of his militant action and the Alianza's visibility and potential successes in the land grant effort." Busto, *King Tiger*, 16, 142.
18. Busto, *King Tiger*, 172.
19. Chakrabarty, *Provincializing Europe*, 76.
20. See Meir and Rivera, *The Chicanos*.
21. Busto, *King Tiger*, 26. Busto continues to note that the "four horsemen" perspective "organized and united four distinct and only tenuously related movements" under the banner of a unified Chicana/o civil rights struggle: César Chávez's United Farm Workers in California, Rodolfo "Corky" Gonzales's Crusade for Justice in Denver, José Angel Gutiérrez's La Raza Unida political party in Texas, and Tijerina's land grant movement in New Mexico. Busto further argues that "each of the four movements (there were others) represented by the horsemen spoke to particular issues and to specific Mexican descent populations. It was only when they were viewed in relationship to one another through a nationalist frame that the power of the horsemen ideal (and so the power of the Chicano Movement) could be fully articulated" (25).
22. Bebout, "Hero Making in El Movimiento," 116.
23. See Swadesh, "The Alianza Movement of New Mexico," 53–84.
24. Gardner, *¡Grito!*, 290. Tijerina's "Letter from Santa Fe Jail" is reprinted in Zaragosa Vargas, ed., *Major Problems in Mexican American History*.
25. The few direct engagements with *Mi lucha* include Antonio Márquez, "Self and Culture," 51–66; Graciela Phillips, "La gesta de un pueblo entre dos mundos," 113–16; Rosales, "En busca de la verdadera tierra amarilla," 141–63.
26. Busto, *King Tiger*, 144.
27. Busto, *King Tiger*, 145.
28. Busto, *King Tiger*, 164.
29. Anzaldúa, *Borderlands / La Frontera*; Richard Rodriguez, *Hunger of Memory*.
30. Busto, *King Tiger*, 170.
31. Busto, *King Tiger*, 164.

32. Busto, *King Tiger*, 204.
33. Busto, *King Tiger*, 170; emphasis in original.
34. Busto, *King Tiger*, 172.
35. The name change to Pueblos Libres occurred on May 24, 1967, in response to a court order filed by district attorney Alfonso Sanchez for a list of all members of the Alianza Federal de Mercedes. Unwilling to turn over such a list, Tijerina resigned as Alianza president, disbanded the organization, and renamed the group with the Pueblos Libres affix.
36. Swadesh, "The Alianza Movement of New Mexico."
37. The story behind Tijerina's papers speaks to the pivotal role that writing played as a tactic for La Alianza's movement. In 1994 Tijerina's library and home in Coyote, New Mexico, burned to the ground. His papers—which included scattered Alianza documents; news articles from national, international, and local papers; photographs; and court and FBI files—were the only documents to survive the fire. To preserve this archive, Tijerina buried the remaining records in plastic bags at an undisclosed location before providing them to the University of New Mexico's library in 1999.
38. Tijerina, *They Called Me "King Tiger,"* 20.
39. Correia, "'Rousers of the Rabble' in the New Mexico Land Grant War," 578.
40. In March 1969, a bomb destroyed the car of Alianza vice president Santiago Anaya. The same month that Tijerina was finalizing plans for his departure to the Poor People's encampment in Washington, D.C., William Fellion, an off-duty sheriff's deputy, blew off his own hand while attempting to plant a bomb at the Alianza's Albuquerque headquarters. See Gardner, *¡Grito!*, 259; Correia, "'Rousers of the Rabble,'" 199; Rosales, *Chicano!*, 167.
41. Knowlton, "Reies Tijerina and the Alianza Federal de Mercedes," 136.
42. Busto, *King Tiger*, 67; Tijerina, *They Called Me "King Tiger,"* 72–73.
43. Rosales, *Chicano!*, 160.
44. Stang, "Reies Tijerina," 6.
45. Meléndez, *Hidden Chicano Cinema*, 156.
46. Miller, *Reies Tijerina.*
47. Miller, *Reies Tijerina.*
48. Paredes, *With His Pistol in His Hand*, 16.
49. Paredes, *With His Pistol in His Hand*, 17.
50. One however wonders, in a similar vein as Paredes, "what his opinion might have been when he was in a less scholarly mood" and not looking at Tijerina and the people of the land grant from the "objective point of view" of liberal television journalism. Paredes, *With His Pistol in His Hand*, 20.
51. Qtd. in Busto, *King Tiger*, 165.
52. Busto, *King Tiger*, 165. See also Tijerina, *Mi lucha*, 531–35.
53. Tijerina, *Mi lucha*, 147.
54. Busto, *King Tiger*, 220.
55. Busto, *King Tiger*, 357.

56. Busto, *King Tiger*, 355.
57. Busto, *King Tiger*, 175, 177.
58. Boaventura de Sousa Santos, *Epistemologies of the South*. See also Grosfoguel, "The Structure of Knowledge in Westernized Universities," 73–90.
59. Alianza Federal, *The Spanish Land Grant Question Examined*, pamphlet, box 2, folder 8, Reies Tijerina Papers, University of New Mexico Center for Southwest Research, 1966, 2, 3.
60. Alianza Federal, *The Spanish Land Grant Question Examined*, 10, 16.
61. Alianza Federal, *The Spanish Land Grant Question Examined*, 14. This pamphlet, which is available in archives, was reprinted eight years later in a collection on land grant historiography by Carlos Cortés, *Spanish and Mexican Land Grants*.
62. Blawis, *Tijerina and the Land Grants*, 7.
63. Nancie González, *Spanish-Americans of New Mexico*, 103.
64. Nancie González, *Spanish-Americans of New Mexico*.
65. Alianza Federal, "The Great Land Robbery," flyer, box 2, folder 3, Reies Tijerina Papers, University of New Mexico Center for Southwest Research, 1970.
66. Alianza Federal, "El robo del siglo," folder 3, Eduardo Chávez, Alianza, and Chicano Movement Collection, National Hispanic Cultural Center, Albuquerque, 1970.
67. "The Great Land Robbery," *El Grito del Norte*, November 27, 1968, 5–6. This version also states that the "story that follows is largely based on articles by Professor Clark Knowlton at Texas Western College and Dr. Frances Swadesh of Santa Fe, N.M."
68. Alianza Federal, "The Great Land Robbery."
69. Alianza Federal, "The Great Land Robbery."
70. On the question of coalition, George Mariscal, in *Brown-Eyed Children of the Sun*, notes that one of the novelties brought by Tijerina's insertion into land grant politics was an emphasis on interracial and transnational alliances. Witnessing the gains made by the Southern Christian Leadership Conference under the leadership of Dr. Martin Luther King Jr., Tijerina made frequent use of their tactics of civil disobedience and also frequently invoked commonalities between the African American and Indohispanx struggles. In addition to Tijerina's border crossings to and from Mexico, his rise to southwestern regional president of the 1968 Poor People's Campaign enabled multiple ties with the American Indian Movement (AIM) and the Puerto Rican independence movement.
71. Alianza Federal, "An Immediate Demand from the Alianza Federal to the State Department of the United States," box 31, folder 27, Reies Tijerina Papers, University of New Mexico Center for Southwest Research, 1968.
72. Alianza Federal, "The Alianza: What, Where, Why," flyer, box 1, folder 1, Reies Tijerina Papers, University of New Mexico Center for Southwest Research, 1968.
73. Alianza Federal, "The Alianza: What, Where, Why."
74. Alianza Federal, "The Alianza: What, Where, Why."
75. Alianza Federal, "The Alianza: What, Where, Why."
76. Alianza Federal, *Spanish Land Grant Question Examined*, 19.

77. The English version of Alianza Federal's "The Great Land Robbery" claims, "The laws of the Recopilación clearly prohibited the sale of any of the common lands of the pueblos."
78. Alianza Federal, *Spanish Land Grant Question Examined*, 2.
79. Alianza Federal, "The Great Land Robbery."
80. "The Great Land Robbery" is representative of a number of flyers and pamphlets that deploy the same trickster logic. Examples found in the Reies Tijerina Papers at the University of New Mexico Center for Southwest Research include the following: "Constitución Nacional de La Alianza Federal de Mercedes," box 1, folder 1, 1963; "News Release by Reies López Tijerina," box 1, folder 1, 1967; "Demands of the Indo-Hispano to the Federal Government," box 1, folder 1, 1967; "Aztlán: Porque?" (preliminary draft), box 2, folder 2, 1969; "El Tratado Olvidado," box 2, folder 3, 1970; "El Texto de Artículo 27 de la Constitución de la República Mexicana de 1917," box 2, folder 6, n.d.; "Las Mercedes y La Corte Suprema de Los Estados Unidos," box 2, folder 6, n.d.
81. Oropeza argues that, over the courthouse raid, the Echo Amphitheater occupation is representative of the full range of La Alianza's repertoire of protest. See Oropeza, "The Heart of Chicano History," 49–67. See also Kosek, *Understories.*
82. Alianza Federal, "U.S.A. Is Trespassing in New Mexico."
83. Tijerina, *Mi lucha*, 73.
84. Tijerina, *Mi lucha*, 72.
85. Tijerina, *Mi lucha*, 73.
86. Marez, "Signifying Spain," 269.
87. Anzaldúa, *Borderlands / La Frontera*, 103.
88. He would subsequently come to serve as his own defense in the trials stemming from the raid the following year and would acquit himself of all charges.
89. See Nabokov, *Tijerina and the Courthouse Raid*, 108; Blawis, *Tijerina and the Land Grants,* 90; Gardner, *¡Grito!*, 161.
90. Nabokov, *Tijerina and the Courthouse Raid*, 13.
91. Elizabeth Martínez, "*Social Justice* Salutes Beverly Axelrod," 186–87.
92. Tijerina, *Mi lucha*, 135.
93. Tijerina, *Mi lucha*, 416–17.
94. Rabasa, *Without History*, 44.
95. Rabasa, *Without History*, 2.

CHAPTER 4

1. Castillo, *So Far from God*, 32–33.
2. Castillo, *So Far from God*, 33.
3. Castillo, *So Far from God*, 33.
4. Castillo, *So Far from God*, 77.
5. Espinosa, "New-Mexican Spanish Folk-Lore," 400–401.

6. A number of scholars have explored *la malogra*'s appearance in *So Far from God* at the intersection of the novel's nonrealist narrative techniques and its critical reevaluation of the modes of gender violence, nationalism, ecological devastation, and colonial territoriality that regulate Indigenous and Chicana/o racialization. Cooper Alarcón connects "La Malogra's attack on Caridad to the destructive conquest of the indigenous peoples of New Spain" to argue that "Castillo situates this specific act of violence within a 'centuries old' pattern of violent oppression and genocide against indigenous peoples and suggests that the attack on Caridad is not an isolated event nor, regrettably, should it be viewed as a historical anomaly." In a similar vein, Danizette Martínez claims la malogra, with "its amorphous shape, its tools and mined minerals, and its brittle parchment of old maps . . . embodies colonial impact, imperialistic violence, and the effects of war resulting in redistribution of property that speaks to Tomé's history as a land grant." See Cooper Alarcón, "Literary Syncretism in Ana Castillo's *So Far from God*," 146; and Danizete Martínez "Teaching Chicana/o Literature in Community College with Ana Castillo's *So Far from God*," 216–25.
7. Weigle, "Sharecropping with Sheep," 213.
8. Forrest, *The Preservation of the Village*, 21.
9. Américo Paredes, "The Folk Base of Chicano Literature," 4–17.
10. Saldívar, *Chicano Narrative*, 47.
11. Schmidt Camacho, *Migrant Imaginaries*, 156.
12. Norma Alarcón, "Chicana Feminism," 250, 251.
13. Schmidt Camacho, *Migrant Imaginaries*, 166.
14. See Alexander and Mohanty, *Feminist Genealogies, Colonial Legacies, Democratic Futures*; Arvin, Tuck, and Morrill, "Decolonizing Feminism," 8–34; Briggs, *Reproducing Empire.*
15. Lubiano, "Black Nationalism and Commonsense," 246.
16. Schmidt Camacho, *Migrant Imaginaries*, 169.
17. Chatterjee, "More on Modes of Power and the Peasantry," 358.
18. Chatterjee, "More on Modes of Power and the Peasantry," 358. Chatterjee elaborates a wide range of coercive labor relations that constitute feudal power. Production through slavery, "where both the life-processes of the producers as well as the labour-processes itself are controlled by the master," occupies one extreme. At another, "one can think of a free peasantry which is only required to make a . . . regular tribute to the agent of an external state." In between, a variety of relations of "serfdom" and "degrees of control over the life-processes of the peasantry" can collect "part of the social product as rent." What joins the multiplicity of these forms of production under the feudal mode of power is the way that "political domination" operates as "the prerequisite of rights or claims on the social product." In other words, the presumption of entitlement to rent, property, and class protection is directly tied to the imposition and superiority of physical force.
19. Chatterjee, "More on Modes of Power and the Peasantry," 359.
20. Chatterjee, "More on Modes of Power and the Peasantry," 359.

21. Chatterjee, "More on Modes of Power and the Peasantry," 358.
22. Marx, qtd. in Chatterjee, "More on Modes of Power and the Peasantry," 371.
23. Chatterjee, "More on Modes of Power and the Peasantry," 372.
24. Chatterjee, "More on Modes of Power and the Peasantry," 363.
25. Chatterjee, "More on Modes of Power and the Peasantry," 357.
26. Chatterjee, "More on Modes of Power and the Peasantry," 357.
27. Chatterjee, "More on Modes of Power and the Peasantry," 357.
28. Within our epoch of late capitalist modernity, Spivak notes, "unlike the case of European social relations under the feudal mode of production, it is the *woman* who confronts this structure doubly: at home and at work." In this "new feudalization under electronic capitalism," there is no need for the production of individualized subjects that attend the ascendancy of bourgeois modes of power. "No legal structure need be laid down for the army of 'permanent casuals,'" she writes; "only the circumventing of rudimentary labor and safety regulations is on the agenda." In this context, the bourgeois mode of power in which "upward class mobility may mean woman's access to individualism" is foreclosed. And unlike the communal mode of power where women are inscribed in the social order through consanguineous notions of kinship, tribe, and clan, the asynchronicity of feudal modes of power and production in postindustrial capitalism ensures that the "men are set against the women." Under these conditions, Spivak minces few words: "The woman is worst off under the feudal mode of power" ("The Political Economy of Women," 226–27).
29. All previous quotes from Alarcón, "Chicana Feminism," 253.
30. Hong, "Fun with Death and Dismemberment," 247.
31. E. S. Martínez, *The Youngest Revolution*.
32. Elizabeth (Betita) Martínez, "A View from New Mexico: Recollections of the Movimiento Left."
33. "To Our Readers," *El Grito del Norte* (Española, N.Mex.), August 24, 1968.
34. Sylvia Rodriguez, "Land, Water, and Ethnic Identity in Taos," 322.
35. Martínez, "A View from New Mexico: Recollections of the Movimiento Left."
36. Blackwell, *¡Chicana Power!*, 155.
37. Blackwell, *¡Chicana Power!*, 149.
38. Knowlton, "Patron-Peon Pattern Among the Spanish-Americans of New Mexico," 15.
39. Correia, *Properties of Violence*, 61.
40. Knowlton, "Patron-Peon Pattern," 14.
41. Forrest, *The Preservation of the Village*, 24.
42. Acuña, *Occupied America*, 60.
43. Reséndez, *The Other Slavery*, 169.
44. Reséndez, *The Other Slavery*, 175.
45. Carlson, "Spanish-American Acquisition of Cropland," 96.
46. Knowlton, "Patron-Peon Pattern," 13.
47. Knowlton, "Patron-Peon Pattern," 13.

48. Brooks, *Captives and Cousins*, 35.
49. Forrest, *Preservation of the Village*, 20.
50. Correia, *Properties of Violence*, 35.
51. Forrest, *Preservation of the Village*, 20.
52. Carlson, "Spanish-American Acquisition," 97.
53. Taylor and West, "Patrón Leadership at the Crossroads," 75.
54. Correia, *Properties of Violence*, 62.
55. Weigle, "Sharecropping with Sheep," 213.
56. Acuña, *Occupied America*, 76.
57. Knowlton, "Patron-Peon Pattern," 13.
58. Forrest, *Preservation of the Village*, 30.
59. Correia, *Properties of Violence*, 62.
60. Gregorita Aguilar, "First Anniversary of Co-op," *El Grito del Norte* (Española, N.Mex.), April 13, 1970; Curl, *For All the People*, 205.
61. Nabokov, "Chicano Power in the Feudal West" *Nation*, October 8, 1977, 337.
62. "La Cooperativa's First Harvest," *El Grito del Norte*, November 15, 1969.
63. Nabokov, "Chicano Power in the Feudal West," 337.
64. Vasquez, "This Land Is Our Land," 12.
65. Castillo, "'Taking the Fifth with Daniel Libman,'" n.p.
66. Castillo, "'Taking the Fifth with Daniel Libman,'" n.p.
67. Schmidt Camacho, *Migrant Imaginaries*, 157.
68. Chatterjee, "More on Modes of Power," 388.
69. Castillo, *So Far from God*, 10.
70. Castillo, *So Far from God*, 27.
71. Castillo, *So Far from God*, 186.
72. Castillo, *So Far from God*, 28.
73. Castillo, *So Far from God*, 186.
74. Castillo, *So Far from God*, 146.
75. Castillo, *So Far from God*, 147.
76. Castillo, *So Far from God*, 247.
77. Castillo, *So Far from God*, 130.
78. Castillo, *So Far from God*, 137–39.
79. Castillo, *So Far from God*, 139.
80. Castillo, *So Far from God*, 139.
81. Castillo, *So Far from God*, 139.
82. See Álvaro Ochoa Serrano, *Mitote, Fandango y Mariacheros*; see also Torra, "Mitote—The Dream of Reality."
83. Manríquez, "Ana Castillo's *So Far from God*," 40.
84. Unevenly analyzed in New Mexican land grant historiography, the Tomé land grant was established on July 30, 1739, after a collection of outcast genízaro families petitioned Juan Gonzales Bas, Albuquerque's chief alcalde, to establish their own settlement. Generally recognized as one of the first genízaro grants—i.e., a community grant awarded as a form of emancipation to detribalized Indigenous

slaves and captives—Tomé is more recently known for the long and divisive battle in the twentieth century between its heirs over its property status. The multiple and complex court battles that attended the adjudication of Tomé's property status pivoted around attempts in the 1950s to verify heirship and familial descent in order to facilitate the conversion of the community grant into the Tomé Land and Improvement Corporation. This controversial decision repositioned heirs as shareholders and unleashed a subsequent labyrinth of litigation over the number of heirs and the terms of their claim to the grant and their compensation, which culminated in 1985, when the Horizon corporation divested its development project in the grant, leaving the territory subdivided into ninety thousand pieces of property with thirty thousand owners, most of whom are absentee and live outside New Mexico.

85. Castillo, *So Far from God*, 146–49.
86. Castillo, *So Far from God*, 146–49.
87. Enriqueta Vasquez, "La Chicana: Let's Build a New Life," *El Grito del Norte* (Española, N.Mex.), November 15, 1969. Subsequent citations of Vasquez refer to this text.
88. Vasquez, "This Land Is Our Land," 11.
89. Vasquez, "This Land Is Our Land," 12.
90. Vasquez, "La Chicana: Let's Build a New Life."
91. Vasquez, "La Chicana: Let's Build a New Life."
92. Romero, "The Indita Genre of New Mexico," 58.
93. Brooks, *Captives and Cousins*, 34.
94. Forrest, *Preservation of the Village*, 29.
95. Nabokov, "Chicano Power in the Feudal West," 338.
96. Forrest, *Preservation of the Village*, 28–29.
97. Forrest, *Preservation of the Village*, 28–29.
98. Nabokov, "Chicano Power in the Feudal West," 339.
99. Oropeza, "*Viviendo y luchando*," xli.
100. *El Grito del Norte*, vol. 2, no. 13, September 26, 1969; emphasis in original.
101. Chatterjee, "More on Modes of Power," 388.
102. "For Machos Only," *El Grito del Norte*, August 24, 1968, 1–3.
103. See also Riddell, "Las Chicanas and el Movimiento," 155–65.
104. The conceptual tendency that marks many early and subsequently pivotal studies on land grants narrates dispossession as resulting from a failure of translation between two distinct legal regimes of property. In this narrative, the inalienable, communal, and subsistent logic of the land grants failed to translate into the individualized, corporatized, and alienable logic of land under the capitalist regime of U.S. sovereignty. A number of scholars have explored how the incommensurabilities between Spanish/Mexican and U.S. legal regimes led to several juridical strategies of dispossession. Ebright's analysis on the U.S. adjudication of the Las Vegas land grant illuminates this trend. In one view, "Las Vegas grant was a community grant whose common lands were owned by the owners of private tracts of

land within the grant and could not be sold under Hispanic law." Ebright assesses this view as benefiting the "average grant resident and is historically correct." Yet two other views came to intercede: one, that "common lands" are "not owned by the grant at all but by the United States as its public domain," a theory that presumed "anyone could acquire a piece of the former common lands as private property. This theory benefited the outsider filing a homestead entry to the detriment of the heirs of the land grant." Another view presumed "original grantees owned common lands as private property. Under this approach, a speculator purchasing one of these interests would own a fractional share of the common lands, and many lawyers and territorial administrators piecemealed control over vast swaths of grants as a result" (*Land Grants and Lawsuits in Northern New Mexico*, 209).

105. Montoya, *Translating Property*, 16.
106. Correia, "Land Grant Speculation in New Mexico During the Territorial Period," 928–29.
107. "For Machos Only," 3.
108. Swadesh, *Los Primeros Pobladores*, 23–24.
109. "For Machos Only," 1.
110. Castillo, *So Far from God*, 136–41.
111. Castillo, *So Far from God*, 216.
112. Castillo, *So Far from God*, 215.
113. Castillo, *So Far from God*, 214–18.
114. Castillo, *So Far from God*, 26, 27.
115. Castillo, *So Far from God*, 211.
116. Romero, "The Indita Genre of New Mexico," 58.
117. Allen, *The Sacred Hoop*, 15.
118. Allen, *The Sacred Hoop*, 15.
119. Silko, "Interior and Exterior Landscapes," 28, 29.
120. Castillo, *So Far from God*, 214.
121. *El Grito del Norte*, August 1973, xliii.
122. Blackwell, *¡Chicana Power!*, 135.

CHAPTER 5

1. Le Bot, *El sueño Zapatista por Subcomandante Marcos*, 6. https://www.iberopuebla.mx/sites/default/files/bp/documents/el_sueno_zapatista.pdf.
2. EZLN, "First Declaration of the Lacandón Jungle," 51.
3. EZLN, "First Declaration of the Lacandón Jungle," 54.
4. Subcomandante Marcos, *Professionals of Hope*, back cover.
5. Taylor, "Death of the Political 'I'," 13.
6. Stephen, Speed, and Hernández Castillo, "Indigenous Organizing and the EZLN in the Context of Neoliberalism in Mexico," xvi.
7. See Oikonomakis, "Farewell Marcos, Long Live Subcomandante Galeano."
8. Subcomandante Marcos, "Between Light and Shadow," 217.

9. Subcomandante Marcos, "Between Light and Shadow," 219.
10. See Bennett, *Colonial Blackness*; Chang, *Chino*.
11. Marcos, "Between Light and Shadow," 226.
12. Marcos, "Between Light and Shadow," 225.
13. Marcos, "Between Light and Shadow," 226.
14. Marcos, "Between Light and Shadow," 226.
15. Marcos, "Between Light and Shadow," 227.
16. Marcos, "Between Light and Shadow," 230, 231.
17. Marcos, "Between Light and Shadow," 231.
18. On February 16, 1996, after multiple rounds of negotiation between the Zapatistas and the Mexican government, the San Andrés Accords outlined institutional mandates for the recognition of Indigenous peoples in the general Constitution; broadening political participation and representation in the local, state, and federal levels; and the protection of Indigenous migrants. By April 2001, however, it became clear to the EZLN that the Mexican government had no intention of carrying out the accords. After a three-year period of silence, the Zapatistas embarked on the Other Campaign in a process to "unilaterally" implement the San Andrés Accords.
19. Bogado, "Interview with Subcomandante Marcos," 151.
20. Bogado, "Interview with Subcomandante Marcos," 151.
21. Marcos, "Between Light and Shadow," 222.
22. Stengers uses the term *cosmopolitics* to name a politics in which "cosmos refers to the unknown constituted by these multiple, divergent worlds and to the articulation of which they would eventually be capable." See Stengers, "The Cosmopolitical Proposal," 995.
23. Gómez, *Revolutionary Imaginations of Greater Mexico*, 205.
24. Gómez, *Revolutionary Imaginations of Greater Mexico*, 2.
25. Flores, "Chicano Artists and Zapatistas Walk Together Asking, Listening, Learning."
26. Holloway, "Zapatismo Urbano"; see also Dellacioppa, *This Bridge Called Zapatismo*.
27. See Bohm, *Wholeness and the Implicate Order*.
28. A conjunctural encounter between Little Bear and quantum physicist David Bohm, this initial dialogue on the nature of space, time, nature, and language included the thinkers James (Sákéj) Youngblood Henderson, David Peat, Clem Ford, and Dan Moonhawk Alford, among many others. Out of these dialogues came a series of epistemic convergences and tensions between Indigenous storytelling and language and the theories of motion, time, and perception that animate quantum theory. See Alford's web page, "Regarding Benjamin Lee Whorf."
29. Peat, *Pathways of Chance*, 133.
30. De la Cadena, *Earth Beings*, 33.
31. See Clegg, *The God Effect*, ch. 1.
32. Dussart and Poirier, *Entangled Territories*, 5–6; see also Thomas, *Entangled Objects*.
33. "Recur, v."
34. De la Cadena, *Earth Beings*, 33.

35. Roberto D. Hernández, *The Coloniality of the US///Mexico Border*, 21.
36. See Kourí, "La invención del ejido"; Gareth A. Jones "Dismantling the Ejido."
37. See Colín, *Indigenous Education Through Dance and Ceremony*, ch. 2.
38. Kourí, "Interpreting the Expropriation of Indian Pueblo Lands in Profirian Mexico," 80.
39. Kelly, "Article 27 and Mexican Land Reform," 542.
40. Hale, *The Transformations of Liberalism in Late Nineteenth Century Mexico*, 31.
41. Arturo Warman, "The Political Project of Zapatismo," 331.
42. Kourí, "La invención del ejido," 13.
43. Stern, "From Mestizophilia to Biotypology," 191.
44. Hale, *The Transformations of Liberalism*, 4.
45. Knight, "Racism, Revolution, and *Indigenismo*," 100.
46. Speed, Stephens, and Castillo, *Dissident Women*, xviii, n 2.
47. Saldaña-Portillo, "Who's the Indian in Aztlán?," 408–9.
48. Jones, "Dismantling the *Ejido*," 188.
49. Fox and Gordillo, "Between State and Market," 137.
50. Marcos, "Between Light and Shadow," 223.
51. Jung, "Race, Class, and Ethnicity in the History of Mexican Indigenous Politics," 37.
52. Jung, "Race, Class, and Ethnicity in the History of Mexican Indigenous Politics," 37.
53. Saldaña-Portillo, "Who's the Indian in Aztlán?," 409.
54. EZLN, "Sixth Declaration of the Lacandon Jungle," 63.
55. EZLN, "Second Declaration of the Lacandon Jungle," 43.
56. See Higgins, *Understanding the Chiapas Rebellion*, 158; see also Henck, *Subcomandante Marcos*.
57. Vodovnik, "The Struggle Continues . . . ," 41.
58. Holloway, "Zapatismo Urbano," 177.
59. Virilio, *The Vision Machine*, 62.
60. Holloway, "Zapatismo Urbano," 176–177.
61. Higgins, *Understanding the Chiapas Rebellion*, 158.
62. Higgins, *Understanding the Chiapas Rebellion*, 158.
63. Greenwood, "Constructing the Votán-Zapata Narrative," 47.
64. Maurer, "Tseltal Christianity," 23.
65. See Harvey, *The Chiapas Rebellion*, 41–43.
66. Le Bot, *El sueño zapatista*, 10.
67. Harvey, *The Chiapas Rebellion*, 47.
68. Rus, Mattiace, and Hernández Castillo, "Introduction," 3.
69. Rus, Mattiace, and Hernández Castillo, "Introduction," 3; Harvey, *The Chiapas Rebellion*, 52–53.
70. Rus, Mattiace, and Hernández Castillo, *Mayan Utopias*, "Introduction," 5.
71. Henry Veltmeyer, "The Dynamics of Social Change and Mexico's EZLN," 93.
72. Benjamin, "A Time of Reconquest," 427.
73. Ernesto Reyes, qtd. in Thomas Benjamin, "A Time of Reconquest," 428.
74. Marcos, "Between Light and Shadow," 217.

75. Marcos, "Between Light and Shadow," 224.
76. B. V. Olguín, "Of Truth, Secrets, and Ski Masks," 156.
77. Marcos, "Between Light and Shadow," 217.
78. Greenwood, "The Votán-Zapata Narrative," 49.
79. "Unveiling Mexico," 21n3.
80. Moonhawk Alford, "Dialogues Between Western and Indigenous Scientists."
81. Moonhawk Alford, "Dialogues Between Western and Indigenous Scientists."
82. Subcomandante Marcos, "The Story of the Questions," 413.
83. Marcos, "The Story of the Questions," 413.
84. Cited in Warman, "Plan de Ayala." Arturo Warman, in "Zapatismo as Political Practice," calls the document the "first Zapatista document."
85. Marcos, "The Story of the Questions," 414–415.
86. Apffel-Marglin, *Subversive Spiritualities*, 56.
87. Apffel-Marglin, *Subversive Spiritualities*, 57.
88. Marcos, "The Story of the Questions," 415.
89. "To my mind," Virilio writes, "this is one of the most crucial aspects of the development of the new technologies of digital imagery and of the synthetic vision offered by electron optics: the relative fusion/confusion of the factual (or operational, if you prefer) and the virtual; the ascendancy of the 'reality effect' over a reality principle" (*The Vision Machine*, 60).
90. Benjamin, "A Time of Reconquest," 420.
91. Marcos, "The Story of the Questions," 415.
92. Greenwood, "Constructing the Votán-Zapata Narrative," 51.
93. Speed and Reyes, "Rights, Resistance and Radical Alternatives," 59.
94. EZLN, "Votán-Zapata, Or Five Hundred Years of History," 20.
95. Veltmeyer, "The Dynamics of Social Change and Mexico's EZLN," 96.
96. Salcido, "Living in NAFTA," 3.
97. Salcido, "Living in NAFTA," 4.
98. Salcido, "Living in NAFTA," 4.
99. "dignity, n."
100. "mirror, n, v."
101. Holloway, "Zapatismo Urbano," 177.
102. Cadava, *Words of Light*, xvii.
103. Subcomandante Marcos, *Shadows of Tender Fury*, 57.
104. Olguín, "Of Truth, Secrets, and Ski Masks," 167.
105. Marcos, "Between Light and Shadow," 246.
106. French, "The Borderlands of *Borderlands*," 37.
107. Correia, *Properties of Violence*, 166.
108. Correia, *Properties of Violence*, 166.
109. Holloway, "Zapatismo Urbano," 177.
110. Alford, "Dialogues Between Western and Indigenous Scientists."
111. EZLN, "Women's Revolutionary Law," 3.
112. Altshuler, "Linguistic Forms as Symbols of People," 107.

113. Altshuler, "Linguistic Forms as Symbols of People," 107.
114. Rabasa, *Without History*, 42.
115. Blackwell, "Weaving in the Spaces," 148.
116. Hernández, "Coloniality of the US///Mexico Border," 26.

CODA

1. According to Rudy Busto, Tijerina's "unconventional yet unmistakable anti-Semitism" developed in the late 1970s in tandem with a revisionary legal, historical, and biblical genealogy that sought to prove that "Spanish-speakers were an ancient Biblical people, but that Jews had stolen their Israelite blood birthright." At the same time, Busto is careful to note, Tijerina's anti-Semitism is not an "Anglo-Israelist anti-Semitism that cast Jews as reprobate or even as a separate species of humanity." Rather, "Tijerina's anti-Semitism is spun out of what he perceives as the deceit promoted by Jews in their adoption of the name 'Israel' and their claim to Palestine." Thus, for Busto, "Tijerina remains faithful to Biblical prophecies that Israel and Judah will be reunited. He interprets the split between Christian-Israelites and Jews as an ancient feud between estranged brothers" (*King Tiger*, 195).
2. Voorhees, *The Law of Arrest in Civil and Criminal Actions*.
3. García Márquez, *The Paris Review Interviews*, 190.
4. "secretary, n.1 and adj."
5. Arnold and Silko, "Listening to the Spirits," 7.
6. Jones and Jones, "Secrecy," 55.
7. Jones and Jones, "Secrecy," 58.
8. See Debenport, *Fixing the Books*.
9. Rabasa, "Thinking Europe in Indian Categories," 71.
10. For an account of orature as a critical concept, see Wa Thiong'o, "Notes Towards a Performance Theory of Orature," 4–7.
11. Million, "There Is a River in Me," 37.

BIBLIOGRAPHY

ARCHIVAL SOURCES

Alianza Federal de Pueblos Libres Collection. Center for Southwest Research, University of New Mexico.

Eduardo Chávez Alianza, and Chicano Movement Collection. National Hispanic Cultural Center, Albuquerque.

Peter Nabokov Papers. Center for Southwest Research, University of New Mexico.

Reies Tijerina Papers. Center for Southwest Research, University of New Mexico.

SECONDARY SOURCES

Acuña, Rodolfo. *Occupied America: A History of Chicanos*. 3rd ed. New York: Harper Collins Publishers, 1988.

Adajania, Nancy, and Ranjit Hoskote. "The Nth Field: The Horizon Reloaded." In *On Horizons: A Critical Reader in Contemporary Art*, ed. Maria Hlavajova, Simon Sheikh, and Jill Winder, 16–32. Rotterdam, Netherlands: BAK, basis voor actuele kunst, 2011.

Alarcón, Norma. "Chicana Feminism: In the Tracks of 'The' Native Woman." *Cultural Studies* 4 (3) (1990): 248–56.

Alarcón, Norma. "Traddutora, Traditora: A Paradigmatic Figure of Chicana Feminism." *Cultural Critique* 13 (Autumn 1989): 57–87.

Alberto, Lourdes. "Nations, Nationalisms, and *Indígenas*: The 'Indian' in the Chicano Revolutionary Imaginary." *Critical Ethnic Studies* 2 (1) (Spring 2016): 107–27.

Alexander, M. Jacqui, and Chandra Mohanty, eds. *Feminist Genealogies, Colonial Legacies, Democratic Futures*. New York: Routledge, 1997.

Alford, Dan Moonhawk. "Dialogues Between Western and Indigenous Scientists: A Presentation for the 1993 Annual Spring Meeting of the Society for the Anthropology of Consciousness." hilgart.org. April 11, 1993. http://www.hilgart.org/enformy/dma-b.htm.

Alford, Dan Moonhawk. "Regarding Benjamin Lee Whorf." *hilgart.org*. Accessed July 5, 2019. https://hilgart.org/enformy/alford.htm.

Allen, Chadwick. *Blood Narrative: Indigenous Identity in American Indian and Maori Literary and Activist Texts*. Durham, N.C.: Duke University Press, 2002.

Allen, Paula Gunn. *The Sacred Hoop: Recovering the Feminine in American Indian Traditions*. Boston: Beacon Press, 1992.

Alonso, Ana María. *Thread of Blood: Colonialism, Revolution, and Gender on Mexico's Northern Frontier*. Tucson: University of Arizona Press, 1997.

Altshuler, Nathan. "Linguistic Forms as Symbols of People." *International Journal of American Linguistics* 22 (2) (1956): 106–12.

Anaya, Rudolfo, and Francisco Lomeli, eds. *Aztlán: Essays on the Chicano Homeland*. Albuquerque: University of New Mexico Press, 1989.

Anzaldúa, Gloria. *Borderlands / La Frontera: The New Mestiza*. San Francisco: Aunt Lute Press, 1999.

Anzaldúa, Gloria, ed. *Making Face, Making Soul, Haciendo Caras: Creative and Critical Perspectives by Feminists of Color*. San Francisco: Aunt Lute Books, 1990.

Anzaldúa, Gloria, and AnaLouise Keating, eds. *This Bridge We Call Home: Radical Visions for Transformation*. New York: Routledge, 2002.

Apffel-Marglin, Frédérique. *Subversive Spiritualities: How Rituals Enact the World*. Oxford: Oxford University Press, 2012.

Appelbaum, Nancy P., Anne S. Macpherson, and Karin Alejandra Rosemblatt. "Racial Nations." In *Race & Nation in Modern Latin America*, ed. Nancy P. Applebaum, Anne S. Macpherson, and Karin Alejandra Rosemblatt, 1–31. Chapel Hill: University of North Carolina Press, 2003.

Archuleta, Elizabeth. "Securing Our Nation's Roads and Borders or Re-Circling the Wagons? Leslie Marmon Silko's Destabilization of 'Borders.'" *Wicazo Sa Review* 20 (1) (Spring 2005): 113–37.

Arellano, Juan Estevan. *Enduring Acequias: Wisdom of the Land, Knowledge of the Water*. Albuquerque: University of New Mexico Press, 2014.

Arias, Arturo. "After the Rigoberta Menchú Controversy: Lessons Learned About the Nature of Subalternity and the Specifics of the Indigenous Subject." *MLN* 117 (2) (March 2002): 481–505.

Arnold, Ellen, and Leslie Marmon Silko. "Listening to the Spirits: An Interview with Leslie Marmon Silko." *Studies in American Indian Literatures* 10 (3) (1998): 1–33.

Arredondo, Gabriella F., Aída Hurtado, Norma Klahn, Olga Nájera-Ramírez, and Patricia Zavella, eds. *Chicana Feminisms: A Critical Reader*. Durham, N.C.: Duke University Press, 2003.

Arrizón, Alicia. *Queering Mestizaje: Transculturation and Performance*. Ann Arbor: University of Michigan Press, 2006.

Arvin, Maile, Eve Tuck, and Angie Morrill. "Decolonizing Feminism: Challenging Connections Between Settler Colonialism and Heteropatriarchy." *Feminist Formations* 25 (1) (2013): 8–34.

Atencio, Tomás. "The Human Dimensions in Land Use and Land Displacement in Northern New Mexico Villages." In *Indian and Spanish American Adjustments to Arid and Semiarid Environments*, ed. Clark S. Knowlton, 44–52. Lubbock: Texas Technological College, 1946.

Avery, Doris. "Into the Den of Evils: The Genízaros in Colonial New Mexico." MA thesis, Duke University, Durham, N.C., 1993.

Balibar, Etienne. "Racism and Nationalism." In *Race, Nation, Class: Ambiguous Identities*, ed. Etienne Balibar and Immanuel Wallerstein, 39–40. London: Verso Books, 1991.

Barak, Gene. *Mexico Views Manifest Destiny: An Essay on the Origins of the Mexican War*. Albuquerque: University of New Mexico Press, 1975.

Barker, Joanne, ed. *Critically Sovereign: Indigenous Gender, Sexuality, and Feminist Studies*. Durham, N.C.: Duke University Press, 2017.

Barker, Joanne. *Native Acts: Law, Recognition, and Cultural Authenticity*. Durham, N.C.: Duke University Press, 2011.

Barker, Joanne, ed. *Sovereignty Matters: Locations of Contestation and Possibility in Indigenous Struggles for Self-Determination*. Lincoln: University of Nebraska Press, 2005.

Barrera, Mario. *Race and Class in the Southwest: A Theory of Racial Inequality*. Notre Dame, Ind.: University of Notre Dame Press, 1979.

Basso, Keith. *Wisdom Sits in Places: Landscape and Language Among the Western Apache*. Albuquerque: University of New Mexico Press, 1996.

Bebout, Lee. "Hero Making in El Movimiento: Reies López Tijerina and the Chicano Nationalist Imaginary." *Aztlán: A Journal of Chicano Studies* 32 (2) (Fall 2007): 93–121.

Bebout, Lee. *Mythohistorical Interventions: The Chicano Movement and Its Legacies*. Minneapolis: University of Minnesota Press, 2011.

Bell, Virginia E. "Counter-Chronicling and Alternative Mapping in *Memoria del fuego* and *Almanac of the Dead*." *MELUS* 25 (3/4) (Autumn–Winter 2000): 5–30.

Beltrán, Cristina. "Patrolling Borders: Hybrids, Hierarchies and the Challenge of Mestizaje." *Political Research Quarterly* 57 (4) (December 2004): 595–607.

Benjamin, Thomas. "A Time of Reconquest: History, the Maya Revival, and the Zapatista Rebellion in Chiapas." *American Historical Review* 105 (2) (2000): 417–50.

Bennett, Herman L. *Colonial Blackness: A History of Afro-Mexico*. Bloomington: Indiana University Press, 2009.

Beverley, John. *Testimonio: On the Politics of Truth*. Minneapolis: University of Minnesota Press, 2004.

Blackhawk, Ned. *Violence over the Land: Indians and Empires in the Early American West*. Cambridge, Mass.: Harvard University Press, 2006.

Blackwell, Maylei. *¡Chicana Power! Contested Histories of Feminism in the Chicano Movement*. Austin: University of Texas Press, 2012.

Blackwell, Maylei. "Weaving in the Spaces: Indigenous Women's Organizing and the Politics of Scale in Mexico." In *Dissident Women: Gender and Cultural Politics in Chiapas*, ed. Shannon Speed, R. Aída Hernández Castillo, and Lynn M. Stephen, 115–54. Austin: University of Texas Press, 2006.

Blackwell, Maylei, Floridalma Boj Lopez, and Luis Urrieta Jr. "Introduction: Critical Latinx Indigeneities." *Latino Studies* (15) (2017): 126–37.

Blawis, Patricia Bell. *Tijerina and the Land Grants: Mexican Americans in Struggle for Their Heritage*. New York: International Publishers, 1971.

Boaventura de Sousa Santos. *Epistemologies of the South: Justice Against Epistemicide*. London: Routledge, 2014.

Bogado, Aura. "Interview with Subcomandante Marcos." In *The Other Campaign*, by Subcomandante Marcos and the Zapatistas, 148–65. San Francisco: City Lights, 2006.

Bohm, David. *Wholeness and the Implicate Order*. New York: Routledge, 1980.

Bonilla-Silva, Eduardo. "We Are All Americans! The Latin Americanization of Racial Stratification in the USA." *Race and Society* 5 (2002): 3–16.

Brack, Gene M. *Mexico Views Manifest Destiny, 1821–1846: An Essay on the Origins of the Mexican War*. Albuquerque: University of New Mexico Press, 1975.

Brady, Mary Pat. *Extinct Lands, Temporal Geographies: Chicana Literature and the Urgency of Space*. Durham, N.C.: Duke University Press, 2002.

Brady, Mary Pat. "Territoriality." In *Keywords for Latina/o Studies*, ed. Deborah R. Vargas, Nancy Raquel Mirabal, and Lawrence La Fountain-Stokes, 126–37. New York: New York University Press, 2017.

Briggs, Charles L., and John R. Van Ness. *Land, Water, and Culture: New Perspectives on Hispanic Land Grants*. New Mexico Land Grant Series. Albuquerque: University of New Mexico Press, 1987.

Briggs, Laura. *Reproducing Empire: Race, Sex, Science and U.S. Imperialism in Puerto Rico*. Berkeley: University of California Press, 2002.

Brigham, Ann. "Productions of Geographic Scale and Capitalist-Colonialist Enterprise in Leslie Marmon Silko's *Almanac of the Dead*." *Modern Fiction Studies* 50 (2) (Summer 2004): 303–31.

Brooks, James F. *Captives and Cousins: Slavery, Kinship, and Community in the Southwest Borderlands*. Chapel Hill: University of North Carolina Press, 2002.

Brotherston, Gordon. *Book of the Fourth World: Reading the Native Americas Through Their Literature*. Cambridge: Cambridge University Press, 1992.

Brown, Tracy. *Pueblo Indians and Spanish Colonial Authority in Eighteenth-Century New Mexico*. Tucson: University of Arizona Press, 2013.

Busto, Rudy V. *King Tiger: The Religious Vision of Reies López Tijerina*. Albuquerque: University of New Mexico Press, 2005.

Byrd, Jodi. *The Transit of Empire: Indigenous Critiques of Colonialism*. Minneapolis: University of Minnesota Press, 2011.

Cadava, Eduardo. *Words of Light: Theses on the Photography of History*. Princeton, N.J.: Princeton University Press, 1997.

Caminero-Santangelo, Marta. "'The Pleas of the Desperate': Collective Agency Versus Magical Realism in Ana Castillo's *So Far from God*." *Tulsa Studies in Women's Literature* 24 (1) (Spring 2005): 81–103.

Carlson, Alvar, W. *The Spanish-American Homeland: Four Centuries in New Mexico's Río Arriba*. Baltimore: Johns Hopkins University Press, 1990.

Carlson, Alvar, W. "Spanish-American Acquisition of Cropland within the Northern Pueblo Indian Grants, New Mexico." *Ethnohistory* 22 (2) (1975): 95–110.

Castellanos, M. Bianet. "Introduction: Settler Colonialism in Latin America." *American Quarterly* 69 (4) (2017): 777–81.

Castillo, Ana. *So Far from God*. New York: Plume, 1994.

Castillo, Ana. "'Taking the Fifth with Daniel Libman': An Interview with Ana Castillo." By Daniel Libman. *Fifth Wednesday Journal* (10) (Spring 2012): n.p.

Castillo, Ana, and Norma E. Cantú. "A Conversation with Ana Castillo." *World Literature Today* 82 (2) (March–April 2008): 59–62.

Castillo, Ana, and Elsa Saeta. "A *MELUS* Interview with Ana Castillo." By Esla Saeta. *MELUS* 22 (3) (Autumn 1997): 133–49.

Chabram-Dernersesian, Angie. *The Chicana/o Cultural Studies Forum: Critical and Ethnographic Practices*. New York: New York University Press, 2007.

Chakrabarty, Dipesh. *Provincializing Europe: Postcolonial Thought and Historical Difference*. Princeton, N.J.: Princeton University Press, 2000.

Chang, Jason Oliver. *Chino: Anti-Chinese Racism in Mexico, 1880–1940*. Urbana: University of Illinois Press, 2017.

Chatterjee, Partha. "More on Modes of Power and the Peasantry." In *Selected Subaltern Studies*, ed. Rajajit Guha and Gayatri Chakravorty Spivak, 351–90. Oxford: Oxford University Press, 1988.

Chávez, John. *The Lost Land: The Chicano Image of the Southwest*. Albuquerque: University of New Mexico Press, 1984.

Cherniavsky, Eva. *Incorporations: Race, Nation, and the Body Politics of Capital*. Minneapolis: University of Minnesota Press, 2006.

Cheyfitz, Eric. "Balancing the Earth: Native American Philosophies and the Environmental Crisis." *Arizona Quarterly: A Journal of American Literature, Culture, and Theory* 65 (3) (2009): 139–62.

Clegg, Brian. *The God Effect: Quantum Entanglement, Science's Strangest Phenomenon*. New York: St. Martin's Griffin, 2009.

Cobos, Rubén. *A Dictionary of New Mexico and Southern Colorado Spanish*. Santa Fe: Museum of New Mexico Press, 2003.

Cochran, Stuart. "The Ethnic Implications of Stories, Spirits, and the Land in Native American Pueblo and Aztlán Writing." *MELUS* 20 (2) (Summer 1995): 69–91.

Colín, Ernesto. *Indigenous Education Through Dance and Ceremony: A Mexica Palimpsest*. New York: Palgrave, 2014.

Collier, George A. *Basta! Land and the Zapatista Rebellion in Chiapas*. Oakland, Calif.: Food First Books, 1994.

Contreras, Shela. *Bloodlines: Myth, Indigenism, and Chicana/o Literature*. Austin: University of Texas Press, 2008.

Cooper Alarcón, Daniel. "Literary Syncretism in Ana Castillo's *So Far from God*." In *Studies in Latin American Popular Culture* 23 (2004): 145–52.

Córdova, Gilberto Benito. *Abiquiú and Don Cacahuate*. Los Cerillos, N.Mex.: San Marcos Press, 1973.

Córdova, Gilberto Benito. *Big Dreams and Dark Secrets at Chimayó*. Albuquerque: University of New Mexico Press, 2006.

Correia, David. "From Agropastoralism to Sustained Yield Forestry: Industrial Restructuring, Rural Change, and the Land-Grant Commons in Northern New Mexico." *Capitalism, Nature, Socialism* 16 (1) (2005): 25–44.

Correia, David. "Land Grant Speculation in New Mexico During the Territorial Period." *Natural Resources Journal* 48 (4) (2008): 927–47.

Correia, David. *Properties of Violence: Law and Land Grant Struggle in Northern New Mexico*. Athens: University of Georgia Press, 2013.

Correia, David. "'Rousers of the Rabble' in the New Mexico Land Grant War: La Alianza Federal de Mercedes and the Violence of the State." *Antipode* 40 (4) (2008): 561–83.

Cotera, María Eugenia, and María Josefina Saldaña-Portillo. "Indigenous but Not Indian? Chicana/os and the Politics of Indigeneity." In *The World of Indigenous North America*, ed. Robert Warrior, 549–68. New York: Routledge, 2014.

Cortés, Carlos E., ed. *Spanish and Mexican Land Grants*. New York: Arno Press, 1974.

Coulthard, Glen. *Red Skin, White Masks: Rejecting the Colonial Politics of Recognition*. Minneapolis: University of Minnesota Press, 2014.

Coulthard, Glen, and Leanne Betasamosake Simpson. "Grounded Normativity." *American Quarterly* 68 (2) (June 2016): 249–55.

Cox, James H. *The Red Land to the South: American Indian Writers and Indigenous Mexico*. Minneapolis: University of Minnesota Press, 2012.

Crapazano, Vincent. *Imaginative Horizons: An Essay in Literary-Philosophical Anthropology*. Chicago: University of Chicago Press, 2003.

Cummings, Denise K. "'Settling' History: Understanding Leslie Marmon Silko's *Ceremony, Storyteller, Almanac of the Dead,* and *Gardens in the Dunes*." *Studies in American Indian Literatures* 12 (4) (Winter 2002): 65–90.

Curl, John. *For All the People: Uncovering Hidden History of Cooperation, Cooperative Movements, and Communalism in America*. Oakland, Calif.: PM Press, 2009.

Davis, Angela, Ruchell Magee, the Soledad Brothers, and Other Political Prisoners. *If They Come in the Morning: Voices of Resistance*. New York: Signet, 1971.

Day, Iyko. "Being or Nothingness: Indigeneity, Antiblackness, and Settler Colonial Critique." *Critical Ethnic Studies* 1 (2) (Fall 2015): 102–21.

Debenport, Erin. *Fixing the Books: Secrecy, Literacy, and Perfectability in Indigenous New Mexico*. Santa Fe, N.Mex.: School for Advanced Research Press, 2015.

DeBuys, William. *Enchantment and Exploitation: The Life and Hard Times of a New Mexico Mountain Range*. Albuquerque: University of New Mexico Press, 2015.

De la Cadena, Marisol. *Earth Beings: Ecology of Practice Across Andean Worlds*. Durham, N.C.: Duke University Press, 2015.

De la Cadena, Marisol. "Indigenous Cosmopolitics in the Andes: Conceptual Reflections Beyond 'Politics.'" *Cultural Anthropology* 25 (2) (2010): 334–70.

De la Cadena, Marisol. "The Production of Other Knowledges and Its Tensions: From Andeanist Anthropology to Interculturalidad." *Journal of the World Anthropology Network* 1 (2005): 13–33.

De la Garza, Rudolphe O., Z. Anthony Kruszewski, and Tomás A. Arciniega, eds. *Chicanos and Native Americans: The Territorial Minorities*. Englewood Cliffs, N.J.: Prentice Hall, 1973.

Del Castillo, Adelaida R. "Malintzin Tenepal: A Preliminary Look into a New Perspective." In *Essays on La Mujer*, ed. Rosa Martínez Cruz, 124–49. Los Angeles: Chicano Studies Center Publications, 1977.

Dellacioppa, Kara Zugman. *This Bridge Called Zapatismo: Building Alternative Political Cultures in Mexico City, Los Angeles, and Beyond*. Lanham, Md.: Lexington Books, 2009.

Deloria, Vine, Jr. *God Is Red: A Native View of Religion*. Golden, Colo.: Fulcrum, 2003.

Deloria, Vine, Jr. *Sacred Lands and Religious Freedom*. New York: Association on American Indian Affairs, 1991.

Deutsch, Sarah. *No Separate Refuge: Culture, Class, and Gender on an Anglo-Hispanic Frontier in the American Southwest, 1880–1940*. Oxford: Oxford University Press, 1987.

"dignity, n." *OED Online. Oxford University Press*. March 2017. https://www.oed.com/view/Entry/52653?redirectedFrom=dignity&.

Dozier, Edward P. *The Pueblo Indians of North America*. Prospect Heights, Ill.: Waveland Press, 1983.

Du Bois, W. E. B. *Darkwater: Voices from Within the Veil*. New York: Dover Publications, 1999.

Dunbar-Ortiz, Roxanne. "Preface." In *Fight Back: For the Sake of the People, For the Sake of the Land*, by Simon Ortiz, n.p. Albuquerque, N. Mex.: Institute for Native American Development, 1980.

Dunbar-Ortiz, Roxanne. *Roots of Resistance: A History of Land Tenure in New Mexico*. Norman: University of Oklahoma Press, 2007.

Dussart, Françoise, and Sylvie Poirier. *Entangled Territories: Negotiating Indigenous Lands in Australia and Canada*. Toronto: University of Toronto Press, 2017.

Dyck, Reginald. "Indigenous Ways of Knowing in Simon Ortiz's *Fight Back*." In *Crisscrossing Borders in Literature of the American West*, ed. Reginald Dyck and Cheli Reutter, 97–115. New York: Palgrave Macmillan, 2009.

Ebright, Malcolm. *Land Grants and Lawsuits in Northern New Mexico*. New Mexico Land Grant Series. Albuquerque: University of New Mexico Press, 1994.

Ebright, Malcolm, ed. *Spanish and Mexican Land Grants and the Law*. Manhattan, Kans.: Sunflower University Press, 1989.

Ebright, Malcolm, and Charles T. Dumars. "Problems of Spanish and Mexican Land Grants in the Southwest: Their Origin and Extent." *Southwestern Review of Management and Economics* 1 (2) (Summer 1981): 177–213.

Ebright, Malcolm, Rick Hendricks, and Richard W. Hughes. *Four Square Leagues: Pueblo Indian Land in New Mexico*. Albuquerque: University of New Mexico Press, 2014.

Ebright, Malcolm, and Rick Hendricks. *Pueblo Sovereignty: Indian Land and Water in New Mexico and Texas*. Norman: University of Oklahoma Press, 2019.

Ebright, Malcolm, and Rick Hendricks. *The Witches of Abiquiu: The Governor, the Priest, the Genízaro Indians, and the Devil*. Albuquerque: University of New Mexico Press, 2006.

Edwards, Brent Hayes. "The Shadow of Shadows." *Positions* 11 (1) (Spring 2003): 11–49.

El Grito del Norte. "Taos Pueblo Gates Will Close If Blue Lake Lands Held." October 5, 1968.

El Grito del Norte. "Taos Pueblo Rebellion." March 28, 1970.

"El Plan Espiritual de Aztlán." In *Aztlán: An Anthology of Mexican American Literature*, ed. Luis Valdez and Stan Steiner, 402–6. New York: Vintage, 1972.

Eng, David L., and David Kazanjian. *Loss: The Politics of Mourning*. Berkeley: University of California Press, 2003.

Espinosa, Aurelio M. "New-Mexican Spanish Folk-Lore." *Journal of American Folklore* 23 (90) (1910): 395–418.

"eulogy, n." OED Online. Oxford University Press. March 14, 2017. https://www.oed.com/view/Entry/64986?rskey=EqoQsV&result=1#eid.

EZLN. "First Declaration of the Lacandón Jungle." In *Shadows of Tender Fury: The Letters and Communiques of Subcomandante Marcos and the Zapatista Army of National Liberation*, trans. Frank Bardacke, Leslie López, and the Watsonville, California, Human Rights Committee, 51–54. New York: Monthly Review Press, 1995.

EZLN. "Second Declaration of the Lacandon Jungle." In *Our Word Is Our Weapon: Selected Writings* by Subcomandante Insurgente Marcos, ed. Juana Ponce de León. New York: Seven Stories Press, 2002.

EZLN. "Sixth Declaration of the Lacandon Jungle." In *The Other Campaign / La Otra Campaña*, by Subcomandante Marcos and the Zapatistas, 51–54. San Francisco: City Lights Books, 2006.

EZLN. "Votán-Zapata, Or Five Hundred Years of History." *Our Word Is Our Weapon: Selected Writings* by Subcomandante Insurgente Marcos, ed. Juana Ponce de León, 19–21. New York: Seven Stories Press, 2002.

EZLN. "Women's Revolutionary Law." In *Dissident Women: Gender and Cultural Politics in Chiapas*, ed. Shannon Speed, R. Aída Hernández Castillo, and Lynn M. Stephen, 3–4. Austin: University of Texas Press, 2006.

Fischer-Hornung, Dorothea. "Economies of Memory: Trafficking in Blood, Body Parts, and Crossblood Ancestors." *Amerikastudien/American Studies* 47 (2) (2002): 199–221.

Folsom, Franklin. *Indian Uprising on the Rio Grande: The Pueblo Revolt of 1680*. Albuquerque: University of New Mexico Press, 1996.

Forbes, Jack. *Aztecas del Norte: The Chicanos of Aztlán*. Greenwich, Conn: Fawcet, 1973.

Forrest, Suzanne. *The Preservation of the Village*. Albuquerque: University of New Mexico Press, 1989.

Foucault, Michel. *The Archaeology of Knowledge and the Discourse on Language*. Trans. A. M. Sheridan Smith. New York: Pantheon Books, 1972.

Foucault, Michel. *Language, Counter-Memory, Practice*. Ed. and trans. Donald F. Bourchard. Ithaca, N.Y.: Cornell University Press, 1977.

Fox, Jonathan, and Gustavo Gordillo. "Between State and Market: The Campesinos' Quest for Autonomy." In *Mexico's Alternative Political Futures*, ed. Wayne Cornelius, Judith Gentleman, and Peter Smith, 131–72. La Jolla: University of California San Diego, Center for U.S.-Mexican Studies, 1989.

French, Lydia. "The Borderlands of *Borderlands*: Tres Vistas." In *Nakum Journal*, 37–54. San Marcos, Tex.: Indigenous Cultures Institute, 2012.

Gadamer, Hans-Georg. *Truth and Method*. 2nd ed. Trans. Joel Weinsheimer and Donald G. Marshall. London: Continuum, 2006.

Gandert, Miguel, Enrique Lamadrid, Ramón Gutiérrez, Lucy Lippard, Chris Wilson, and Helen Lucero. *Nuevo México Profundo: Rituals of an Indo-Hispano Homeland*. Santa Fe: Museum of New Mexico Press, 2000.

Gardner, Richard. *¡Grito! Reies Tijerina and the New Mexico Land Grant War of 1967*. New York: Harper Colophon Books, 1970.

Gallegos, Bernardo P. "'Dancing the Comanches': The *Santo Niño, La Virgen* (of Guadalupe), and the Genízaro Indians of New Mexico." In *Indigenous Symbols and Practices in the Catholic Church: Visual Culture, Missionization and Appropriation*, ed. Kathleen J. Martin, 203–23. Surrey, UK: Ashgate Publishing Company, 2010.

García, Mario T. *Memories of Chicano History: The Life and Narrative of Bert Corona*. Berkeley: University of California Press, 1994.

García Márquez, Gabriel. *The Paris Review Interviews*. Vol. 2. New York: Picador, 2007.

Gillman, Laura, and Stacey M. Floyd-Thomas. "Con un pie a cada lado / With a Foot in Each Place: Mestizaje as Transnational Feminisms in Ana Castillo's *So Far from God*." *Meridians* 2 (1) (2001): 158–75.

Goeman, Mishuana. "Land as Life: Unsettling the Logics of Containment." In *Native Studies Keywords*, ed. Stephanie Nohelani Teves, Andrea Smith, and Michelle H. Raheja, 71–89. Tucson: University of Arizona Press, 2015.

Goeman, Mishuana. *Mark My Words: Native Women Mapping Our Nations*. Minneapolis: University of Minnesota Press, 2013.

Goldstein, Aloysha. "On the Internal Border: Colonial Difference, the Cold War, and the Locations of 'Underdevelopment.'" *Comparative Studies in Society and History* 50 (1) (2008): 26–56.

Goldstein, Aloysha. "Toward a Genealogy of the U.S. Colonial Present." In *Formations of United States Colonialism*, ed. Alyosha Goldstein, 1–30. Durham, N.C.: Duke University Press, 2014.

Gómez, Alan Eladio. *Revolutionary Imagination of Greater Mexico*. Austin: University of Texas Press, 2016.

Gómez, Laura E. *Manifest Destinies: The Making of the Mexican American Race*. New York: NYU Press, 2007.

Gómez, Placido. "The History and Adjudication of the Common Lands of Spanish and Mexican Land Grants." *Natural Resources Journal* 25 (1985): 1035–80.

Gómez, Reid. "The Storyteller's Escape: Sovereignty and Worldview." In *Reading Native American Women: Critical/Creative Responses*, ed. Inés Hernandez-Avila, 145–69. New York: Altamira, 2005.

Gómez, Reid. "They Killed the Word." *Studies in American Indian Literatures* 15 (3/4) (Fall 2003–Winter 2004): 66–95.

Gómez-Quiñones, Juan. *Chicano Politics: Reality and Promise, 1940–1990*. Albuquerque: University of New Mexico Press, 1998.

Gómez-Quiñones, Juan, and Irene Vásquez. *Making Aztlán: Ideology and Culture of the Chicana and Chicano Movement, 1966–1977*. Albuquerque: University of New Mexico Press, 2014.

Gonzales, Gregory Paul Esteban. "Si eres Genízaro: Race, Indigeneity, and Belonging." PhD diss., University of Texas, Austin, 2017.

Gonzales, Moises. "The Genizaro Land Grant Settlements of New Mexico." *Journal of the Southwest* 56 (4): 583–602.

Gonzales, Phillip B. "The Political Construction of Latino Nomenclatures in Twentieth-Century New Mexico." *Journal of the Southwest* 35 (2) (Summer 1993): 158–85.

Gonzales, Rodolfo. "Corky." *I Am Joaquín / Yo Soy Joaquín: An Epic Poem*. New York: Bantam, 1972.

González, Nancie L. *The Spanish-Americans of New Mexico: A Heritage of Pride*. Albuquerque: University of New Mexico Press, 1969.

Gonzalez, Phillip B. "Struggle for Survival: The Hispanic Land Grants in New Mexico, 1848–2001." *Agricultural History* 77 (2). Special issue, "Minority Land and Community Security" (Spring, 2003): 293–324.

Gordon-McCutchan, R. C. *The Taos Indians and the Battle for Blue Lake*. Santa Fe, N.Mex.: Red Crane Books, 1991.

Graham, Richard, ed. *The Idea of Race in Latin America, 1870–1940*. Austin: University of Texas Press, 1990.

Greenwood, Elizabeth. "Constructing the Votán-Zapata Narrative." *Peace Review: A Journal of Social Justice* 18 (2006): 45–53.

Griswold del Castillo, Richard. *The Treaty of Guadalupe Hidalgo: A Legacy of Conflict*. Norman: University of Oklahoma Press, 1990.

Grosfoguel, Ramón. "The Structure of Knowledge in Westernized Universities: Epistemic Racism/Sexism and the Four Genocides/Epistemicides of the Long 16th Century." *Human Architecture: Journal of the Sociology of Self Knowledge* 11 (1) (2013): 73–90.

Guerrero, Andrés G. *A Chicano Theology*. Maryknoll, N.Y.: Orbis Books, 1987.

Gutiérrez, José Angel, Michelle Meléndez, and Sonia Adriana Noyola, eds. *Chicanas in Charge: Texas Women in the Public Arena*. Lanham, Md.: Altamira Press, 2007.

Gutiérrez, Ramón. "Unraveling America's Hispanic Past: Internal Stratification and Class Boundaries." In *The Chicano Studies Reader: An Anthology of Aztlán, 1970–2010*, ed. Chon A. Noriega, Eric Avila, Karen May Davalos, Chela Sandoval, and Rafael Pérez-Torres. Los Angeles: UCLA Chicano Studies Research Center Press, 2010.

Gutiérrez, Ramón. *When Jesus Came, the Corn Mothers Went Away: Marriage, Sexuality, and Power in New Mexico, 1500–1846*. Stanford, Calif.: Stanford University Press, 1991.

Hale, Charles A. *The Transformations of Liberalism in Late Nineteenth Century Mexico*. Princeton, N.J.: Princeton University Press, 1990.

Hall, G. Emlem. *Four Leagues of Pecos: A Legal History of the Pecos Grant, 1800–1933*. Albuquerque: University of New Mexico Press, 1984.

Hall, G. Emlem. "The Pueblo Grant Labyrinth." In *Land, Water, Culture: New Perspectives on Hispanic Land Grants*, ed. Charles L. Briggs and John R. Van Ness, 67–138. Albuquerque: University of New Mexico Press, 1987.

Hall, Stuart. "Cultural Studies and Its Theoretical Legacies." In *Stuart Hall: Critical Dialogues in Cultural Studies*, ed. David Morley and Kuan-Hsing Chen, 262–75. New York: Routledge, 1997.

Hall, Stuart. "For Allon White: Metaphors of Transformation." In *Stuart Hall: Critical Dialogues in Cultural Studies*, ed. David Morley and Kuan-Hsing Chen, 286–305. Routledge: New York. 1996.

Hall, Thomas. "Genizaros." In *Encyclopedia of the Great Plains*, ed. David J Wishart, 356. Lincoln: University of Nebraska Press, 2004.

Haney López, Ian F. "Protest, Repression, and Race: Legal Violence and the Chicano Movement." *University of Pennsylvania Law Review* 150 (1) (November 2001): 205–24.

Harvey, Neil. *The Chiapas Rebellion: The Struggle for Land and Democracy*. Durham, N.C.: Duke University Press, 1998.

Henck, Nick. *Subcomandante Marcos: The Man and the Mask*. Durham, N.C.: Duke University Press, 2007.

Hernández-Avila, Inés. "Relocations upon Relocations: Home, Language, and Native American Women's Writing." In *Reading Native Women: Critical/Creative Response*, ed. Inés Hernández-Avila, 171–87. Lanham, Md.: Altamira Press, 2005.

Hernández, José Angel. "From Conquest to Colonization: *Indios* and Colonization Policies After Mexican Independence." *Mexican Studies / Estudios Mexicanos* 26 (2) (Summer 2010): 291–322.

Hernández, Nicole Guidotti. *Unspeakable Violence: Remapping U.S. and Mexican National Imaginaries*. Durham, N.C.: Duke University Press, 2011.

Hernández, Roberto D. *The Coloniality of the US///Mexico Border: Power, Violence, and the Decolonial Imperative*. Tucson: University of Arizona Press, 2018.

Hernández Castillo, R. Aída. "Indigeneity as a Field of Power: Multiculturalism and Indigenous Identities in Political Struggle." In *The Sage Handbook of Identities*, ed. Margaret Wetherell and Chandra Talpade Mohanty, 379–402. London: Sage Publications, 2010.

Higgins, Nicholas. *Understanding the Chiapas Rebellion: Modernist Voices and the Invisible Indian*. Austin: University of Texas Press, 2004.

Hodgson, Dorothy L. "Introduction: Comparative Perspectives on the Indigenous Rights Movement in Africa and the Americas." *American Anthropologist* 104 (4) (December 2002): 1037–49.

Holloway, John. "Zapatismo Urbano." In *Humboldt Journal of Social Relations* 29 (1) (2005): 168–78.

Hong, Grace Kyungwon. "Fun with Death and Dismemberment: Irony, Farce, and the Limits of Nationalism in Oscar Zeta Acosta's *Revolt of the Cockroach People* and Ana Castillo's *So Far from God*." In *Strange Affinities: The Gender and Sexual Politics of*

Comparative Racialization, ed. Grace Kyungwon Hong and Roderick A. Ferguson, 241–69. Durham, N.C.: Duke University Press, 2011.

"horizon, n.". OED Online. March 2019. Oxford University Press. https://www.oed.com/view/Entry/88458?rskey=1U2fdy&result=1.

Horovitz, Deborah. "Freud, Marx, and Chiapas in Leslie Marmon Silko's *Almanac of the Dead.*" *Studies in American Indian Literatures* 10 (3) (Fall 1998): 47–64.

Horvath, Steven M. "The Social and Political Organization of the Genízaros of Plaza de Nuestra Señora de los Dolores de Belén, New Mexico, 1740–1812." PhD diss., Brown University, Providence, R.I., 1979.

Huffstetler, Edward. "Spirit Armies and Ghost Dancers: The Dialogic Nature of American Indian Resistance." *Studies in American Indian Literatures* 14 (4) (Winter 2002): 1–17.

Huhndorf, Shari M. "Picture Revolution: Transnationalism, American Studies, and the Politics of Contemporary Native Culture." *American Quarterly* 61 (2) (June 2009): 359–81.

Jackson, Shona. *Creole Indigeneity: Between Myth and Nation in the Caribbean*. Minneapolis: University of Minnesota Press, 2012.

Jarman, Michelle. "Exploring the World of the Different in Leslie Marmon Silko's *Almanac of the Dead.*" *MELUS* 31 (3) (Fall 2006): 147–68.

Jenkinson, Michael. *Tijerina: Land Grant Conflict in New Mexico*. Albuquerque, N.Mex.: Paisano Press, 1968.

Johnson, David. "Theorizing the Loss of Land: Griqua Land Claims in Southern Africa, 1874–1998." In *Loss: The Politics of Mourning*, ed. David L. Eng and David Kazanjian, 278–99. Berkeley: University of California Press, 2003.

Johnson, Kelli Lyon. "Violence in the Borderlands: Crossing to the Home Space in the Novels of Ana Castillo." *Frontiers: A Journal of Women Studies* 25 (1) (2004): 39–58.

Jojola, Theodore S. "The Legacy of the Pueblo Revolt and the Tiquex Province." In *Po'pay: Leader of the First American Revolution*, ed. Joe S. Sando and Herman Agoyo, 54–71. Santa Fe: Clear Light Press, 2005.

Jones, Gareth A. "Dismantling the Ejido: A Lesson in Controlled Pluralism." In *Dismantling the Mexican State?* ed. Rob Aitken, Nikki Craske, Gareth A Jones, and David E. Stansfield, 188–203. New York: MacMillan Press, 1996.

Jones, Gareth A., and Graham M. Jones. "Secrecy." *Annual Review of Anthropology* 43 (2014): 53–69.

Jung, Courtney. "Race, Class, and Ethnicity in the History of Mexican Indigenous Politics." In *Recognition Versus Self-Determination: Dilemmas of Emancipatory Politics*, ed. Avigail Eisenberg, Jeremy Webber, Glen Coulthard, and Andrée Boisselle, 21–46. Vancouver: University of British Columbia Press, 2014.

Karaka, Manu. *Empire's Tracks: Indigenous Nations, Chinese Workers, and the Transcontinental Railroad*. Berkeley: University of California Press, 2019.

Karno, Valerie. "Legal Hunger: Law, Narrative, and Orality in Leslie Marmon Silko's *Storyteller* and *Almanac of the Dead.*" *College Literature* 28 (1) (Winter 2001): 29–45.

Kauani, J. Kēhoulani. "Tracing Historical Specificity: Race and the Colonial Politics of (In)Capacity." *American Quarterly* 69 (2) (June 2017): 257–65.

Kelis. "Runnin.'" Recorded 2013. Track 5 on *Food.* Ninja Tune Records, 2014, compact disc.

Kelly, James J., Jr. "Article 27 and Mexican Land Reform: The Legacy of Zapata's Dream." Scholarly Works. Paper 668, 1994. http://scholarship.law.nd.edu/law_faculty_scholarship/668.

Kessell, John. *Pueblos, Spaniards, and the Kingdom of New Mexico.* Norman: University of Oklahoma Press, 2008.

Klein, Christine A. "Treaties of Conquest: Property Rights, Indian Treaties, and the Treaty of Guadalupe Hidalgo." In *New Mexico Law Review* 26 (Spring 1996): 201–55.

Knaut, Andrew L. *The Pueblo Revolt of 1680: Conquest and Resistance in Seventeenth Century New Mexico.* Norman: University of Oklahoma Press, 1995.

Knight, Alan. "Racism, Revolution, and *Indigenismo*: Mexico, 1910–1940." In *The Idea of Race in Latin America, 1870–1940*, ed. Richard Graham, 71–113. Austin: University of Texas Press, 1990.

Knowlton, Clark S. "Guerrillas of Rio Arriba: The New Mexican Land Wars." In *La Causa Política: A Chicano Politics Reader*, ed. F. Chris Garcia, 331–40. Notre Dame, Ind.: University of Notre Dame Press, 1974.

Knowlton, Clark S. "Land Grants." In *Borderlands Sourcebook: A Guide to the Literature on Northern Mexico and the American Southwest*, ed. Ellwyn R. Stoddard, Richard L. Nostrand, and Jonathan P. West, 111–15. Norman: University of Oklahoma Press, 1983.

Knowlton, Clark S. "Patron-Peon Pattern Among the Spanish-Americans of New Mexico." *Social Forces* 41 (1) (1962): 12–17.

Knowlton, Clark S. "Reies Tijerina and the Alianza Federal de Mercedes: Seekers After Justice." *Wisconsin Sociologist* 22 (4) (Fall 1985): 133–44.

Knowlton, Clark S. "Violence in New Mexico: A Sociological Perspective." *California Law Review* 58 (5) (October 1970): 1054–84.

Kosek, Jake. *Understories: The Political Life of Forests in Northern New Mexico.* Durham, N.C.: Duke University Press, 2006.

Kourí, Emilio. "Interpreting the Expropriation of Indian Pueblo Lands in Porfirian Mexico: The Unexamined Legacy of Andrés Molina Enríquez." *Hispanic American Historical Review* 82 (1) (2002): 69–117.

Kourí, Emilio. "La invención del ejido." *Nexos*, January 1, 2015.

Krupat, Arnold. "Post-Structuralism and Oral Literature." In *Recovering the Word: Essays on Native American Literature*, ed. Brian Swann and Arnold Krupat, 113–28. Berkeley: University of California Press, 1987.

Kuokkanen, Rauna. *Reshaping the University: Responsibility, Indigenous Epistemes, and the Logic of the Gift.* Vancouver: University of British Columbia Press, 2007.

Laclau, Ernesto. "Horizon, Ground, and Lived Experience." In *On Horizons: A Critical Reader in Contemporary Art*, ed. Maria Hlavajova, Simon Sheikh, and Jill Winder, 100–111. Rotterdam, Netherlands: BAK, basis voor actuele kunst, 2011.

Lamadrid, Enrique. "Los Corridos de Río Arriba: Two Ballads of the Land Grant Movement, New Mexico, 1965–70." *Aztlán: A Journal of Chicano and Chicana Studies* 17 (2) (Fall 1986): 31–62.

Lanza, Carmela Delia. "Hearing the Voices: Women and Home and Ana Castillo's *So Far from God.*" *MELUS* 23 (1) (Spring 1998): 65–79.

la paperson. *A Third University Is Possible*. Minnesota: University of Minnesota Press, 2017.

Larson, Robert W. "The White Caps of New Mexico: A Study of Ethnic Militancy in the Southwest." *Pacific Historical Review* 44 (2) (May 1975): 171–85.

Le Bot, Yvon. "El sueño zapatista por Subcomandante Marcos." iberopueblo.mx. August 29, 1996. https://www.iberopuebla.mx/sites/default/files/bp/documents/el_sueno_zapatista.pdf.

Limón, José. *Mexican Ballads, Chicano Poems: History and Influence in Mexican American Social Poetry*. Los Angeles: University of California Press, 1992.

Logan, J. R. "Blue Lake: Recollections from Taos Pueblos' Cause." *Taos News*. September 12, 2010.

Lorde, Audre. "Poetry Is Not a Luxury." In *Zami, Sister Outsider, Undersong*, 36–39. New York: W.W. Norton and Company, 1993.

Lowe, Lisa. "The Intimacies of Four Continents." In *Haunted by Empire: Geographies of Intimacy in North American History*, ed. Ann Laura Stoler, 191–212. Durham, N.C.: Duke University Press, 2006.

Lubiano, Wahneema. "Black Nationalism and Commonsense: Policing Ourselves and Others." In *The House that Race Built*, ed. Wahneema Lubiano, 233–52. New York: Vintage Books, 1998.

Lugones, Maria. "The Coloniality of Gender." In *Globalization and the Decolonial Option*, ed. Walter D. Mignolo and Arturo Escobar, 369–90. New York: Routledge, 2010.

Maciel, David R., and Juan José Peña. "La Reconquista: The Chicano Movement in New Mexico." In *The Contested Homeland: A Chicano History of New Mexico*, ed. Erlinda Gonzales-Berry and David R. Maciel, 269–301. Albuquerque: University of New Mexico Press, 2000.

Magnaghi, Russell M. "Plains Indians in New Mexico: The Genízaro Experience." *Great Plains Quarterly* 10 (2) (Spring 1990): 86–95.

Maldonado-Torres, Nelson. "Césaire's Gift and the Decolonial Turn." In *Critical Ethnic Studies: A Reader*, ed. Nada Elia, David M. Hernández, Jodi Kim, Shana L. Redmond, Dylan Rodríguez, and Sarita Echavez See, 435–62. Durham, NC.: Duke University Press, 2016.

Maldonado-Torres, Nelson. "Secularism and Religion in the Modern/Colonial World System." In *Coloniality at Large*, ed. Mabel Moraña, Enrique Dussell, and Carlos A. Járegui, 360–84. Durham, N.C.: Duke University Press, 2008.

Mallon, Florencia E., ed. *Decolonizing Native Histories: Collaboration, Knowledge, and Language in the Americas*. Selected essays translated by Gladys McCormick. Durham, N.C.: Duke University Press, 2012.

Mallon, Florencia E. "The Promise and Dilemma of Subaltern Studies: Perspectives from Latin American History." *American Historical Review* 99 (5) (December 1994): 1491–1515.

Manríquez, B. J. "Ana Castillo's 'So Far from God': Imitations of the Absurd." *College Literature* 29 (2) (Spring 2002): 37–49.

Mantler, Gordon Keith. *Power to the Poor: Black-Brown Coalition and the Fight for Economic Justice, 1960–1974*. Chapel Hill: University of North Carolina Press, 2013.

Marez, Curtis. "Signifying Spain, Becoming Comanche, Making Mexicans: Indian Captivity and the History of Chicana/o Popular Performance." *American Quarterly* 53 (2) (2001): 267–307.

Mariscal, George. *Brown-Eyed Children of the Sun: Lessons from the Chicano Movement, 1965–1975*. Albuquerque: University of New Mexico Press, 2005.

Márquez, Antonio. "Self and Culture: Autobiography as Cultural Narrative." *Discurso Literario* 7 (1) (1990): 51–66.

Márquez, Rubén Sálaz. *New Mexico: A Brief Multi-History*. Albuquerque: Cosmic House Press, 1999.

Martínez, Danizete. "Teaching Chicana/o Literature in Community College with Ana Castillo's *So Far from God*." *Rocky Mountain Review* 65 (2) (Fall 2011): 216–25.

Martínez, Elizabeth, ed. *500 Años del Pueblo Chicano / 500 Years of Chicano History in Pictures*. Albuquerque, N.Mex.: SouthWest Organizing Project, 1991.

Martínez, Elizabeth. "*Social Justice* Salutes Beverly Axelrod." *Social Justice* 29 (1/2) (2002): 186–87.

Martínez, Elizabeth (Betita). "A View from New Mexico: Recollections of the Movimiento Left." *Monthly Review* 54 (3) 2002. http://monthlyreview.org/2002/07/01/a-view-from-new-mexico.

Martínez, Elizabeth Sutherland. *The Youngest Revolution: A Personal Report*. New York: Dial Press, 1969.

Martínez Veiga, Ubaldo. *El Ejido: Discriminación, exclusión social y racismo*. Madrid: Catarata, 2001.

Maurer, Eugenio. "Tseltal Christianity." In *The Indian Face of God in Latin America*, ed. Manuel M. Marzal, Eugenio Maurer, Xavier Albó, and Bartomeu Melià, 23–66. Maryknoll: Orbis Books, 1996.

Meier, Matt S., and Feliciano Rivera. *The Chicanos: A History of Mexican Americans*. New York: Hill and Wang, 1972.

Meléndez, Gabriel A. *Hidden Chicano Cinema: Film Dramas in the Borderlands*. New Brunswick, N.J.: Rutgers University Press, 2013.

Meléndez, Gabriel A. *So All Is Not Lost: The Poetics of Print in Nuevomexicano Communities, 1834–1958*. Albuquerque: University of New Mexico Press, 1997.

Menchaca, Martha. *Recovering History, Constructing Race*. Austin: University of Texas Press, 2001.

Meyer, Doris. *Speaking for Themselves: Neomexicano Cultural Identity and the Spanish-Language Press, 1880–1920*. Albuquerque: University of New Mexico Press, 1996.

Mignolo, Walter. "Literacy and Colonization: The New World Experience." In *1492–1992: Re/Discovering Colonial Writing*, ed. René Jara and Nicholas Spadaccini, 51–96. Minneapolis: University of Minnesota Press, 1989.

Mignolo, Walter. *Local Histories / Global Designs: Coloniality, Subaltern Knowledges, and Border Thinking*. Durham, N.C.: Duke University Press, 2000.

Mignolo, Walter, and Michael Ennis. "Coloniality at Large: The Western Hemisphere in the Colonial Horizon of Modernity." *New Centennial Review* 1 (2) (Fall 2001): 19–54.

Mignolo, Walter D., and Freya Schiwy. "Transculturation and the Colonial Difference: Double Translation." In *Translation and Ethnography*, ed. Tullio Maranhão and Bernard Streck, 6–28. Tucson: University of Arizona Press, 2003.

Miller, Marilyn Grace. *Rise and Fall of the Cosmic Race: The Cult of Mestizaje in Latin America*. Austin: University of Texas Press, 2004.

Miller, Susan A. "Native Historians Write Back: The Indigenous Paradigm in American Indian Historiography." *Wicazo Sa Review* 24 (1) (Spring 2009): 25–45.

Miller, Walter. *The Most Hated Man in New Mexico*. New York: NBC News, 1969.

Million, Dian. "There Is a River in Me: Theory from Life." In *Theorizing Native Studies*, ed. Audra Simpson and Andrea Smith, n.p. Durham, N.C.: Duke University Press, 2014.

Minge, Ward Allen. *Ácoma: Pueblo in the Sky*. Rev. ed. Albuquerque: University of New Mexico Press, 1991.

"mirror, n, v." OED Online. Oxford University Press, March 2017. https://www.oed.com/view/Entry/119110?isAdvanced=false&result=1&rskey=zboRVN&.

Mitchell, Pablo. *Coyote Nation: Sexuality, Race, and Conquest in Modernizing New Mexico, 1880–1920*. Chicago: University of Chicago Press, 2005.

Molina, Felipe S., and David Delgado Shorter. "Geographies Yoeme." In *The World of Indigenous North America*, ed. Robert Warrior, 105–22. New York: Routledge, 2014.

Momaday, N. Scott. "Native American Attitudes to the Environment." In *Seeing with a Native Eye: Essays on Native American Religion*, ed. W. Capps, 79–85. New York: Harper and Row, 1974.

Montgomery, Charles H. *The Spanish Redemption: Heritage, Power, and Loss on New Mexico's Upper Rio Grande*. Berkeley: University of California Press, 2002.

Montoya, María E. *Translating Property: The Maxwell Land Grant and the Conflict over Land in the American West, 1840–1900*. Lawrence: University Press of Kansas, 2005.

Morrow, Colette. "Queering Chicana/o Narratives: Lesbian as Healer, Saint and Warrior in Ana Castillo's *So Far from God*." *Journal of the Midwest Modern Language Association* 30 (1/2) (Spring 1997): 63–80.

Moten, Fred, and Stefano Harney. *Undercommons: Fugitive Planning and Black Study*. New York: Autonomedia, 2013.

Muehlebach, Andrea. "What Self in Self Determination? Notes from the Frontiers of Transnational Indigenous Activism." *Global Studies in Culture and Power* 10 (2003): 241–68.

Muñoz, Carlos. *Youth, Identity, Power: The Chicano Movement*. London: Verso, 1989.

Nabokov, Peter. "Chicano Power in the Feudal West." *Nation*, October 8, 1977.

Nabokov, Peter. *A Forest of Time: American Indian Ways of History*. Cambridge: Cambridge University Press, 2001.

Nabokov, Peter. *Tijerina and the Courthouse Raid*. Albuquerque: University of New Mexico Press, 1969.

Ng'weno, Bettina. "This Land That Diaspora: Indigeneity, Nation-States, and Afro-Latin America." In *Comparative Indigeneities in the Americas*, ed. M. Bianet Castellanos, Lourdes Gutiérrez Najera, and Arturo Aldama, 198–212. Tucson: University of Arizona Press, 2012.

Nichols, Robert. "Disaggregating Primitive Accumulation." *Radical Philosophy* 194 (2015): 18–28.

Niemann, Linda. "New World Disorder." *Women's Review of Books* 9 (6) (March 1992): 1 and 3–4.

Nieto-Phillips, John. *The Language of Blood: The Making of Spanish American Identity in New Mexico*. Albuquerque: University of New Mexico Press, 2004.

Nostrand, Richard L. *The Hispano Homeland*. Norman: University of Oklahoma Press, 1992.

Oboler, Suzanne. *Ethnic Labels, Latino Lives: Identity and the Politics of (Re)Presentation in the United States*. Minneapolis: University of Minnesota Press, 1995.

Oikonomakis, Leonidas. "Farewell Marcos, Long Live Subcomandante Galeano." *ROAR Magazine*, May 26 2014.

Olguín, B. V. "Of Truth, Secrets, and Ski Masks: Counterrevolutionary Appropriations and Zapatista Revisions of Testimonio." *Nepantla: Views from the South* 3 (1) (2002): 145–78.

Olmedo, Rebeca Rosell. "Women's Earth-Binding Consciousness in *So Far from God*." *Label Me Latina/o* 2 (Fall 2012): 1–22.

Olmstead, Jane. "The Uses of Blood in Leslie Marmon Silko's *Almanac of the Dead*." *Contemporary Literature* 40 (3) (Autumn 1999): 464–90.

O'Meara, Bridget. "The Ecological Politics of Leslie Marmon Silko's *Almanac of the Dead*." *Wicazo Sa Review* 15 (2) (Fall 2000): 63–73.

Oropeza, Lorena. "Becoming Indo-Hispano: Reies López Tijerina and the New Mexican Land Grant Movement." *Formations of United States Colonialism*, ed. Alyosha Goldstein, 180–206. Durham, N.C.: Duke University Press, 2014.

Oropeza, Lorena. "The Heart of Chicano History: Reies López Tijerina as a Memory Entrepreneur." *The Sixties* 1 (1) (2008): 49–67.

Oropeza, Lorena. *¡Raza Sí! ¡Guerra No! Chicano Protest and Patriotism During the Viet Nam War Era*. Berkeley: University of California Press, 2005.

Oropeza, Lorena. "*Viviendo y luchando*: The Life and Times of Enriqueta Vasquez." In *Enriqueta Vasquez and the Chicano Movement*, ed. Dionne Espinoza and Lorena Oropeza, xix–liii. Houston: Arte Público Press, 2006.

Oropeza, Lorena, and Dionne Espinoza, eds. *Enriqueta Vasquez and the Chicano Movement: Writings from* El Grito del Norte. Houston: Arte Público Press, 2006.

Ortiz, Alfonso. "The Dynamics of Pueblo Indian Survival." In *North American Indian Anthropology: Essays on Society and Culture*, 296–306. Norman: University of Oklahoma Press, 1994.

Ortiz, Alfonso. "Popay's Leadership: A Pueblo Perspective on the 1680 Revolt." In *Telling New Mexico: A New History*, ed. Marta Weigle with Francis Levine and Louise Stiver, 107–13. Santa Fe: Museum of New Mexico Press, 2009.

Ortiz, Alfonso. *The Pueblo*. New York: Chelsea House Publishers, 1994.

Ortiz, Alfonso. "The Pueblo Restoration of 1680." In *Po'pay: Leader of the First American Revolution*, ed. Joe S. Sando and Herman Agoyo, 2–4. Santa Fe: Clear Light Press, 2005.

Ortiz, Simon. *Fight Back: For the Sake of the People, For the Sake of the Land.* Albuquerque, N. Mex.: Institute for Native American Development, 1980.

Ortiz, Simon. "Towards a National Indian Literature: Cultural Authenticity in Nationalism." In *American Indian Literary Nationalism*, ed. Jace Weaver, Craig S. Womack, and Robert Warrior, 253–60. Albuquerque: University of New Mexico Press, 2006.

Ortiz, Simon. *Woven Stone.* Tucson: University of Arizona Press, 1992.

Padilla, Genaro M. *My History, Not Yours: The Formation of Mexican American Autobiography.* Madison: University of Wisconsin Press, 1993.

Paredes, Américo. "The Folk Base of Chicano Literature." In *Modern Chicano Writers: A Collection of Critical Essays*, ed. Joseph Sommers and Tomás Ybarra-Frausto, 4–17. Englewood Cliffs, N.J.: Prentice Hall, 1979.

Paredes, Américo. *With His Pistol in His Hand: A Border Ballad and Its Hero.* Austin: University of Texas Press, 2003.

Partido Constitucional Popular (PCP). *El Grito del Norte* 1 (4) (October 31, 1968): 2–3.

Paz, Octavio. *The Labyrinth of Solitude.* New York: Grove Press, 1985.

Peat, F. David. *Pathways of Chance.* Grosseto, Italy: Pari Publishing, 2007.

Pelaez López, Alan. "The X in Latinx Is a Wound, Not a Trend." *Efniks*, September 13, 2018.

Peña, Devon, ed. *Chicano Culture, Ecology, Politics: Subversive Kin.* Tucson: University of Arizona Press, 1998.

Pérez, Emma. *The Decolonial Imaginary: Writing Chicanas into History.* Bloomington: Indiana University Press, 1999.

Pérez, Emma. "Sexuality and Discourse." In *Chicana Critical Issues*, ed. Norma Alarcón, Rafaela Castro, Emma Pérez Beatriz Pesquera, Adaljiza Sosa Riddell, Patricia Zavella, 45–69. Berkeley, Calif.: Third Woman Press, 1993.

Pérez-Torres, Rafael. *Mestizaje: Critical Uses of Race in Chicano Culture.* Minneapolis: University of Minnesota Press, 2006.

Pérez-Torres, Rafael. *Movements in Chicano Poetry: Against Myths, Against Margins.* Cambridge: Cambridge University Press, 1995.

Pérez-Torres, Rafael. "Refiguring Aztlán." In *The Chicano Studies Reader: An Anthology of Aztlán, 1970–2015*, ed. Chon A. Noriega, Eric R. Avila, Karen Mary Davalos, Chela Sandoval, and Rafael Pérez Torres, 171–90. Los Angeles: UCLA Chicano Studies Research Center Publication, 2015.

Phillips, Graciela. "La gesta de un pueblo entre dos mundos / Review of *Mi lucha por la tierra* by Reies López Tijerina." *Comercio Exterior* 29 (1) (1979): 113–16.

Pratt, Mary Louise. "Afterword: Indigeneity Today." In *Indigenous Experience Today*, ed. Marisol de la Cadena and Orin Starn, 397–404. London: Bloomsbury Academic, 2007.

Priewe, Marc. "Negotiating the Global and the Local: Leslie Marmon Silko's 'Almanac of the Dead' as 'Glocal Fiction.'" *Amerikastudien / American Studies* 47 (2) (2002): 223–35.

Quijano, Anibal. "Coloniality of Power, Eurocentrism, and Latin America." *Nepantla: Views from South* 1 (3) (2000): 533–80.

Quintana, Frances Leon. "Land, Water, and Pueblo-Hispanic Relations in Northern New Mexico." *Journal of the Southwest* 32 (3) (1990): 288–99.

Rabasa, José. "Thinking Europe in Indian Categories, or, 'Tell Me the Story of How I Conquered You.'" In *Coloniality at Large: Latin America and the Postcolonial Debate*, ed. Mabel Moraña, Enrique Dussel, and Carlos A. Jáuregui, 43–76. Durham, N.C.: Duke University Press, 2008.

Rabasa, José. *Tell Me the Story of How I Conquered You: Elsewheres and Ethnosuicide in the Colonial Mesoamerican World*. Austin: University of Texas Press. 2011.

Rabasa, José. *Without History: Subaltern Studies, The Zapatista Insurgency, and the Specter of History*. Pittsburgh: University of Pittsburgh Press, 2010.

"recur, v." March 2017. *OED Online*. Oxford University Press. https://www.oed.com/view/Entry/160083?redirectedFrom=recur&.

Reed, T. V. "Toxic Colonialism, Environmental Justice, and Native Resistance in Silko's *Almanac of the Dead*." *MELUS* 34 (2) (Summer 2009): 25–42.

Reineke, Yvonne. "Overturning the (New World) Order: Of Space, Time, Writing, and Prophecy in Leslie Marmon Silko's *Almanac of the Dead*." *Studies in American Indian Literatures* 10 (3) (Fall 1998): 65–83.

Reséndez, Andrés. *Changing National Identities at the Frontier: Texas and New Mexico, 1800–1850*. Cambridge: Cambridge University Press, 2005.

Reséndez, Andrés. *The Other Slavery: The Uncovered History of Indian Enslavement in the Americas*. New York: Houghton Mifflin, 2016.

Ricoeur, Paul. *The Rule of Metaphor: Multidisciplinary Studies of the Creation of Meaning in Language*. Trans. Robert Czernyi. Toronto: University of Toronto Press, 1977.

Riddell, Adaljiza Sosa. "Las Chicanas and el Movimiento." *Aztlán: A Journal of Chicano Studies* 1–2 (Spring and Fall 1974): 155–65.

Robinson, Cedric. *Black Marxism: The Making of the Black Radical Tradition*. Durham, N.C.: University of North Carolina Press, 1983.

Rochín, Refugio I., and Dennis N. Valdés, eds. *Voices of a New Chicana/o History*. East Lansing: Michigan State University Press, 2000.

Rodríguez, Ana Patricia. "The Fictions of Solidarity: Transfronterista Feminisms and Anti-Imperialist Struggles in Central American Transnational Narratives." *Feminist Studies* 34 (1/2) (Spring–Summer 2008): 199–226.

Rodríguez, Ileana. "Reading Subalterns Across Texts, Disciplines, and Theories: From Representation to Recognition." In *The Latin American Subaltern Studies Reader*, ed. Ileana Rodríguez, 1–32. Durham, N.C.: Duke University Press, 2001.

Rodríguez, Ralph E. "Chicana/o Fiction from Resistance to Contestation: The Role of Creation in Ana Castillo's *So Far from God*." *MELUS* 25 (2) (Summer 2000): 63–82.

Rodriguez, Richard. *Hunger of Memory: The Education of Richard Rodriguez*. New York: Bantam Dell, 1982.

Rodríguez, Sylvia. "Land, Water, and Ethnic Identity in Taos." In *Land, Water, Culture: New Perspectives on Hispanic Land Grants*, ed. Charles Briggs and John R. Van Ness. 313–403. Albuquerque: University of New Mexico Press, 1987.

Rodríguez, Sylvia. *The Matachines Dance: Ritual Symbolism and Interethnic Relations in the Upper Rio Grande Valley*. Santa Fe, N.Mex.: Sunstone Press, 2009.

Rodríguez, Sylvia. "The Tourist Gaze, Gentrification, and the Commodification of Subjectivity in Taos." In *Essays on the Changing Images of the Southwest*, ed. Richard Francaviglia and David Narrett, 105–26. College Station: University of Texas at Arlington / Texas A&M University Press, 1994.

Rodriguez y Gibson, Eliza. "Imagining a Poetics of Loss: Notes Toward a Comparative Methodology." *Studies in American Indian Literatures* 15 (3–4) (2003): 23–50.

Rosenbaum, Robert J. *Mexicano Resistance in the Southwest: "The Sacred Right of Self-Preservation."* Austin: University of Texas Press, 1981.

Romero, Brenda M. "The Indita Genre of New Mexico." In *Chicana Traditions: Continuity and Change*, ed. Narma E. Cantú and Olga Nájera-Ramírez, 56–80. Urbana: University of Illinois Press, 2002.

Romero, Channette. "Envisioning a 'Network of Tribal Coalitions': Leslie Marmon Silko's *Almanac of the Dead*." *American Indian Quarterly* 26 (4) (Fall 2002): 623–40.

Romero, Rolando, and Amanda Nolacea Harris, eds. *Feminism, Nation and Myth: La Malinche*. Houston: Arte Público Press, 2005.

Roppolo, Kimberly. "Vision, Voice, and Intertribal Metanarraive: The American Indian Visual-Rhetorical Tradition and Leslie Marmon Silko's *Almanac of the Dead*." *American Indian Quarterly* 31 (4) (Fall 2007): 534–58.

Rosales, Arturo F. *Chicano! The History of the Mexican American Civil Rights Movement*. Houston: Arte Público Press, 1997.

Rosales, Arturo F., ed. *Testimonio: A Documentary History of the Mexican American Struggle for Civil Rights*. Houston: Arte Público Press, 2000.

Rosales, Jesús. "En busca de la verdadera tierra amarilla." *Cuadernos Americanos* 55 (1996): 141–63.

Ruiz Hernández, Margarito, and Araceli Burguete Cal y Mayor. "Chiapas: Indigenous Organisation and the Indigenous Struggle at the End of the Millennium (1974–1998)." *Indigenous Affairs: International Working Group for Indigenous Affairs* 3 (August–September 1998): 26–39.

Rus, Jan, Shannan L. Mattiace, and Aida Hernández Castillo. "Introduction." In *Mayan Utopias, Mayan Lives: the Indigenous Peoples of Chiapas and the Zapatista Rebellion*. London: Rowman and Littlefield Publishers, 2003.

Salcido, Daniel. "Living in NAFTA: Settler Colonialism in the US, Mexico, and Canada; Tierra Amarilla Youth Leadership Institute Dialectics of Mexican@ Liberation." *Turning the Tide* 17 (4) (2005): 1–7.

Saldaña-Portillo, María Josefina. "Critical Latinx Indigeneities: A Paradigm Drift." *Latino Studies* 15 (2) (July 2017): 142, 138–55.

Saldaña-Portillo, María Josefina. *Indian Given: Racial Geographies Across Mexico and the United States*. Durham, N.C.: Duke University Press, 2016.

Saldaña-Portillo, María Josefina. *The Revolutionary Imagination in the Americas and the Age of Development*. Durham, N.C.: Duke University Press, 2003.

Saldaña-Portillo, María Josefina. "Who's the Indian in Aztlán? Re-Writing Mestizaje, Indianism, and Chicanismo from the Lacandon." In *The Latin American Subaltern*

Studies Reader, ed. Ileana Rodríguez, 402–23. Durham, N.C.: Duke University Press, 2001.

Saldívar, José David. *Border Matters: Remapping American Cultural Studies*. Berkeley: University of California Press, 1997.

Saldívar, Ramón. *Chicano Narrative: Dialectics of Difference*. Madison: University of Wisconsin Press, 1990.

Saldívar-Hull, Sonia. *Feminism on the Border: Chicana Gender Politics and Literature*. Berkeley: University of California Press, 2000.

Sánchez, George I. *Forgotten People: A Study of New Mexicans*. Albuquerque, N.Mex.: Calvin Horn Publishers, 1967.

Sánchez, George J. *Becoming Mexican American: Ethnicity, Culture, and Identity in Chicano Los Angeles, 1900–1945*. Oxford: Oxford University Press, 1993.

Sánchez, Rosaura. *Telling Identities: The Californio* testimonios. Minneapolis: University of Minnesota Press, 1995.

Sando, Joe S. *Pueblo Nations: Eight Centuries of Pueblo Indian History*. Santa Fe, N.Mex.: Clear Light Publishers, 1992.

Sando, Joe S. "The Pueblo Revolt." In *Po'pay: Leader of the First American Revolution*, ed. Joe S. Sando and Herman Agoyo, 5–53. Santa Fe, N.Mex.: Clear Light Press, 2005.

Sandoval, Chela, "Mestizaje as Method: Feminists of Color Challenge the Cannon." In *Living Chicana Theory*, ed. Carla Trujillo, 352–70. Berkeley, Calif.: Third Woman Press, 1998.

Satz, Helmut. *Ultimate Horizons: Probing the Limits of the Universe*. Berlin: Springer-Verlag, 2013.

Schacht, Miriam. "'Movement Must Be Emulated by the People': Rootedness, Migration, and Indigenous Internationalism in Leslie Marmon Silko's *Almanac of the Dead*." *Studies in American Indian Literatures* 21 (4) (Winter 2009): 53–70.

Schmidt Camacho, Alicia. *Migrant Imaginaries: Latino Cultural Politics in the U.S.-Mexico Borderlands*. New York: New York University Press, 2008.

"secretary, n.1 and adj." March 2017. *OED Online. Oxford University Press.* https://www.oed.com/view/Entry/174549?isAdvanced=false&result=1&rskey=ukzoDs&.

Seed, Patricia. *Ceremonies of Possession in Europe's Conquest of the New World, 1492–1640*. Cambridge: Cambridge University Press, 1995.

Serrano, Álvaro Ochoa. *Mitote, fandango y mariacheros*. 2nd ed. Michoacán: El Colegio de Michoacán, 2000.

Silko, Leslie Marmon. *Almanac of the Dead*. New York: Penguin Books, 1992.

Silko, Leslie Marmon. "Books: Notes on Mixtec and Maya Screenfolds, Picture Books of Preconquest Mexico." In *Yellow Woman and a Beauty of the Spirit: Essays on Native American Life Today*, 155–65. New York: Simon and Schuster, 1996.

Silko, Leslie Marmon. *Ceremony*. New York: Penguin, 1977.

Silko, Leslie Marmon. "Interior and Exterior Landscapes: The Pueblo Migration Stories." In *Yellow Woman and a Beauty of Spirit*, 25–47. New York: Simon and Schuster, 1996.

Silko, Leslie Marmon. Interview by Donna Perry. In *Backtalk: Women Writers Speak Out*. New Brunswick, N.J.: Rutgers University Press, 1993.

Silko, Leslie Marmon. "Language and Literature from a Pueblo Indian Perspective." In *Yellow Woman and a Beauty of Spirit*, 48–50. New York: Simon and Schuster, 1996.

Silva, Noenoe K. *The Power of the Steel Tipped Pen: Reconstructing Native Hawaiian Intellectual History*. Durham, N.C.: Duke University Press, 2017.

Silverman, Jason. "Indian Slavery: The Genízaros of New Mexico." *Native Peoples Magazine* (July–August 2011): 50–53.

Simpson, Audra. *Mohawk Interruptus: Political Life Across the Borders of Settler States*. Durham, N.C.: Duke University Press, 2014.

Simpson, Leanne Betasamosake. *As We Have Always Done: Indigenous Freedom Through Radical Resistance*. Minneapolis: University of Minnesota Press, 2017.

Simpson, Leanne Betasamosake, Rinaldo Walcott, and Glenn Coulthard. "Panel Discussion: Idle No More and Black Lives Matter: An Exchange." *Studies in Social Justice* 12 (1) (2018): 75–89.

Sirias, Silvio, and Richard McGarry. "Rebellion and Tradition in Ana Castillo's *So Far from God* and Sylvia López-Medina's *Cantora*." *MELUS* 25 (2) (Summer 2000): 83–100.

Smith, Linda Tuhiwai. *Decolonizing Methodologies: Research and Indigenous Peoples*. London: Zed Books, 2001.

Snodgrass, Mary Ellen. *Leslie Marmon Silko: A Literary Companion*. Jefferson, N.C.: McFarland and Company, 2011.

Sol, Adam. "The Story as It's Told: Prodigious Revisions in Leslie Marmon Silko's *Almanac of the Dead*." *American Indian Quarterly* 23 (3/4) (Summer–Autumn 1999): 24–48.

Spain. La Recopilación de leyes de Los Reynos de las Indias, 1681. Mexico City: M.A. Porrúa, 1987.

Speed, Shannon. "States of Violence: Indigenous Women Migrants in the Era of Neoliberal Multicriminalism." *Critique of Anthropology* 0 (0) (2016): 1–22.

Speed, Shannon. "Structures of Settler Capitalism in Abya Yala." In *American Quarterly* 69 (4) (December 2017): 783–90.

Speed, Shannon, and Alvaro Reyes. "Rights, Resistance and Radical Alternatives: The Red de Defensores Comunitarios and Zapatismo in Chiapas." *Humboldt Journal of Social Relations* 29 (1) (2005): 47–82.

Spicer, Edward. *Cycles of Conquest: The Impact of Spain, Mexico, and the United States on the Indians of the Southwest, 1533–1960*. Tucson: University of Arizona Press, 2006.

Spivak, Gayatri Chakravorty. "The Political Economy of Women as Seen by a Literary Critic." In *Coming to Terms: Feminism, Theory, Politics*, ed. Elizabeth Weed, 218–29. London: Routledge, 1989.

Stahler-Sholk, Richard. "Resisting Neoliberal Homogenization: The Zapatista Autonomy Movement." *Latin American Perspectives* 34 (2) (March 2007): 48–63.

Stanford, Ann Fowell. "'Human Debris': Border Politics, Body Parts, and the Reclamation of the Americas in Leslie Marmon Silko's *Almanac of the Dead*." *Literature and Medicine* 16 (1) (1997): 23–42.

Stang, Alan. "Reies Tijerina: The Communist Plan to Grab the Southwest." *American Opinion*, October 1967.

St. Clair, Janet. "Death of Love / Love of Death: Leslie Marmon Silko's *Almanac of the Dead*." *MELUS* 21 (2) (Summer 1996): 141–56.

Stengers, Isabelle. "The Cosmopolitical Proposal." In *Making Things Public: Atmospheres of Democracy*, ed. Bruno Latour and Peter Weibel, 994–1004. Cambridge: MIT Press, 2005.

Stephen, Lynn M., Shannon Speed, and R. Aída Hernández Castillo. "Indigenous Organizing and the EZLN in the Context of Neoliberalism in Mexico." In *Dissident Women: Gender and Cultural Politics in Chiapas*, ed. Shannon Speed, R. Aída Hernández Castillo, and Lynn M Stephen, xi–xix. Austin: University of Texas Press, 2006.

Stern, Alexandra Minna. "From Mestizophilia to Biotypology." In *Race and Nation in Modern Latin America*, ed. Nancy P. Appelbaum, Anne S. Macpherson, and Karin Alejandra Rosemblatt, 187–210. Chapel Hill: University of North Carolina Press, 2003.

Stoller, Marianne L. "Grants of Desperation, Lands of Speculation: Mexican Period Land Grants in Colorado." In *Spanish and Mexican Land Grants in New Mexico and Colorado*, ed. John R. Van Ness and Christine M. Van Ness, 22–39. Manhattan, Kans.: Sunflower University Press, 1980.

Subcomandante Marcos. "Between Light and Shadow." In *Professionals of Hope: The Selected Writings of Subcomandante Marcos*, 211–47. [No location] Song Cave, 2017.

Subcomandante Marcos. "The Fourth World War Has Begun." *Nepantla: Views from the South* 2 (3) (2001): 559–72.

Subcomandante Marcos. *Our Word Is Our Weapon: Selected Writings*. Ed. Juana Ponce de León. New York: Seven Stories Press, 2001.

Subcomandante Marcos. *Shadows of Tender Fury: The Letters and Communiqués of Subcomandante Marcos and the Zapatista Army of National Liberation*. Trans. Frank Bardacke, Leslie López, and the Watsonville, California, Human Rights Committee. New York: Monthly Review Press, 1995.

Subcomandante Marcos. "The Story of the Questions." In *Our Word Is Our Weapon: Selected Writings*, by Subcomandante Insurgente Marcos, ed. Juana Ponce de León, 413–16. New York: Seven Stories Press, 2002.

Subcomandante Marcos. *¡Ya Basta! Ten Years of the Zapatista Uprising*. Ed. Žiga Vodovnik. Oakland, Calif.: AK Press, 2004.

Suina, Joseph H. "Underestimation of Pueblo Power." In *Po'pay: Leader of the First American Revolution*, ed. Joe S. Sando and Herman Agoyo, 72–81. Santa Fe, N.Mex.: Clear Light Press, 2005.

Sullivan, Shannon, and Nancy Tuana. "Introduction." In *Race and Epistemologies of Ignorance*, ed. Shannon Sullivan and Nancy Tuana, 1–10. Albany: State University of New York Press, 2007.

Swadesh, Frances L. "The Alianza Movement of New Mexico: The Interplay of Social Change and Public Commentary." In *Minorities and Politics*, ed. Henry J. Tobias and Charles E. Wodehouse, n.p. Albuquerque: University of New Mexico Press, 1969.

Swadesh, Frances Leon. *Los Primeros Pobladores: Hispanic Americans of the Ute Frontier*. Notre Dame, Ind.: University of Notre Dame Press, 1974.

Swann, Brian, and Arnold Krupat, eds. *Recovering the Word: Essays on Native American Literature*. Berkeley: University of California Press, 1987.

Taos Pueblo—Blue Lake. Hearings Before the Subcommittee on Indian Affairs of the Committee on Interior and Insular Affairs. May 15–16, 1969, 65–69.

Tarica, Estelle. "Indigenismo." *Oxford Research Encyclopedia of Latin American History*. May 15, 2019. https://oxfordre.com/latinamericanhistory/view/10.1093/acrefore/9780199366439.001.0001/acrefore-9780199366439-e-68.

Taylor, Diana. "Death of the Political 'I': Subcomandante Marcos Is Dead, Long Live the Subcomandante." In *Dancing with the Zapatistas*, ed. Diana Taylor and Lorie Novak. Durham, N.C.: Duke University Press. http://scalar.usc.edu/anvc/dancing-with-the-zapatistas/marcos-declares-himself-dead.

Taylor, William B., and Elliott West. "Patrón Leadership at the Crossroads: Southern Colorado in the Late Nineteenth Century." In *The Chicano*, ed. Norris Hundley Jr., 73–95. Santa Barbara, Calif.: Clio Books, 1976.

Teale, Tamara M. "The Silko Road from Chiapas or Why Native Americans Cannot Be Marxists." *MELUS* 23 (4) (Winter 1998): 157–66.

Thomas, Nicholas. *Entangled Objects: Exchange, Material Culture, and Colonialism in the Pacific*. Cambridge, Mass.: Harvard University Press, 1991.

Tice, Robert. "Rhetoric of La Raza." Unpublished Book Manuscript, Hayden Library, Arizona State University, Tempe, 1971.

Tijerina, Reies López. *Mi lucha por la tierra*. Mexico City: Fondo de Cultura Económica, 1978.

Tijerina, Reies López. *They Called Me "King Tiger": My Struggle for the Land and Our Rights*. Trans. and ed. José Angel Gutiérrez. Houston: Arte Público Press, 2000.

Tillett, Rebecca. "'The Indian Wars Have Never Ended in the Americas': The Politics of Memory and History in Leslie Marmon Silko's *Almanac of the Dead*." *Feminist Review* 85 (2007): 21–39.

"Tomé Land Grant History: 1739–1967." *Wetherill: A History of Discovery*. Accessed April 7, 2013. http://wetherillfamily.com/tome_new_mexico.htm.

"Tomé, A Spanish Village, The Founding, 1739." *History of Tomé and Immaculate Conception Parish*. Accessed April 7, 2013. http://www.icchurchtome.org/History.html.

Torra, Marc. "Mitote—The Dream of Reality." mastay.info. Accessed May 14, 2019. https://mastay.info/posts/2/mitote-the-dream-of-reality/#fnref:fn1.

Torrez, Robert. "Tierra Amarilla Grant and Thomas B. Catron." New Mexico Office of the State Historian Website. Accessed June 9, 2019. http://dev.newmexicohistory.org/filedetails.php?fileID=21549.

Tsing, Anna Lowenaupt. *The Mushroom at the End of the World: On the Possibility of Life in Capitalist Ruins*. Princeton, N.J.: Princeton University Press, 2015.

Tuck, Eve, and K. Wayne Yang. "Decolonization Is Not a Metaphor." *Decolonization* 1 (1) (2012): 1–40.

Tyler, Daniel. "Ejido Lands in New Mexico." In *Spanish and Mexican Land Grants and the Law*, ed. Malcolm Ebright, 24–35. Manhattan, Kans.: Sunflower University Press, 1989.

UN General Assembly. "United Nations Declaration on the Rights of Indigenous Peoples: resolution / adopted by the General Assembly." A/RES/61/295, refworld. October 2, 2007. https://www.refworld.org/docid/471355a82.html.

"Unveiling Mexico." Zapatista communiqué. In *Our Word Is Our Weapon*, ed. Juana Ponce de León, 21n3. New York: Seven Stories Press, 2001.

U.S. General Accounting Office. *Treaty of Guadalupe Hidalgo: Definition and List of Community Grants in New Mexico.* Report to Congressional Requesters. Washington, D.C., 2001.

Valdez, Luis. *Early Works: Actos, Bernabé and Pensamiento Serpentino.* Houston: Arte Público Press, 1994.

Valdez, Luis, and Stan Steiner, eds. *Aztlan: An Anthology of Mexican American Literature.* New York: Knopf, 1972.

Van Dyke, Annette. "From Big Green Fly to the Stone Serpent: Following the Dark Vision in Silko's *Almanac of the Dead.*" *Studies in American Indian Literatures* 10 (3) (Fall 1998): 34–46.

Van Ness, John R. *Hispanos in Northern New Mexico: Development of Corporate Community and Multicommunity.* New York: AMS Press, 1991.

Van Ness, John R., and Christine M. Van Ness, eds. *Spanish and Mexican Land Grants in New Mexico and Colorado.* Manhattan, Kans.: Sunflower University Press, 1980.

Vargas, Zaragosa, ed. *Major Problems in Mexican American History.* Boston: Houghton Mifflin Company, 1999.

Vasconcelos, José. *La raza cósmica.* Los Angeles: California State University Press, 1979.

Vasquez, Enriqueta. "This Land Is Our Land." In *Enriqueta Vasquez and the Chicano Movement: Writings from* El Grito del Norte, ed. Dionne Espinosa and Lorena Oropeza, 11–13. Houston: Arte Público Press, 2006.

Vassberg, David E. "The Spanish Background: Problems Concerning Ownership, Usurpations, and Defense of Common Lands in 16th Century Castile." In *Spanish and Mexican Land Grants and the Law*, ed. Malcolm Ebright, 12–23. Manhattan, Kans.: Sunflower University Press, 1989.

Veltmeyer, Henry. "The Dynamics of Social Change and Mexico's EZLN." *Latin American Perspectives* 27 (5) (2000): 88–110.

Vigil, Ernesto B. *Crusade for Justice: Chicano Militancy and the Government's War on Dissent.* Madison: University of Wisconsin Press, 1999.

Villa, Pablo. "The Limits of American Border Theory." In *Ethnography at the Border*, ed. Pablo Vila, n.p. Minneapolis: University of Minnesota Press, 2003.

Vinson, Ben. *Before Mestizaje: The Frontiers of Race and Class in Colonial Mexico.* Cambridge: Cambridge University Press, 2017.

Viramontes, Helena María. "The Writes Ofrenda." In *Máscaras*, ed. Lucha Corpi, 124–31. Berkeley, CA: Third Woman Press, 1997.

Virilio, Paul. *The Vision Machine*. Bloomington: University of Indiana Press, 1994.

Vizenor, Gerald. *Fugitive Poses: Native American Scenes of Absence and Presence*. Lincoln: University of Nebraska Press, 1998.

Vizenor, Gerald. *Narrative Chance: Postmodern Discourses on Native American Indian Literatures*. Norman: University of Oklahoma Press, 1993.

Vodovnik, Žifga. "The Struggle Continues . . ." In *Ya Basta: Ten Years of the Zapatista Uprising*, ed. Žiga Voldovnik, 25–49. Oakland, Calif.: AK Press, 2003.

Voorhees, Harvey Cortlandt. *The Law of Arrest in Civil and Criminal Actions*. Boston: Little, Brown and Company, 1915.

Wade, Peter. *Race and Ethnicity in Latin America*. New York: Pluto Press, 2010.

Walter, Roland. "The Cultural Politics of Dislocation and Relocation in the Novels of Ana Castillo." *MELUS* 23 (1) (Spring 1996): 81–97.

Warman, Arturo. "Plan de Ayala." In "Zapatismo as Political Practice." December 11, 2011. college.cengage.com. Accessed June 9, 2019. http://college.cengage.com/history/world/keen/latin_america/8e/assets/students/sources/pdfs/55emilianozapataplandeayala.pdf.

Warman, Arturo. "The Political Project of Zapatismo." In *Riot, Rebellion, Revolution: Rural Social Conflict in Mexico*, 321–37. Princeton, N.J.: Princeton University Press, 1988.

Warrior, Robert. *Tribal Secrets: Recovering American Indian Intellectual Traditions*. Minneapolis: University of Minnesota Press, 1995.

Wa Thiong'o, Ngũgĩ. "Notes Towards a Performance Theory of Orature." *Performance Research* 12 (3) (2007): 4–7.

Weber, David J., ed. *Foreigners in Their Native Land: Historical Roots of the Mexican Americans*. Albuquerque: University of New Mexico Press, 2003.

Weber, David J. "Pueblos, Spaniards, and History." In *What Caused the Pueblo Revolt of 1680?*, ed. David Weber, 3–18. Boston: Bedford St. Martin, 1999.

Weigle, Marta, ed. *Hispanic Villages of Northern New Mexico*. Santa Fe, N.Mex.: Lightning Tree 1975.

Weigle, Marta, "Sharecropping with Sheep." In *Hispanic Villages of Northern New Mexico*, ed. Marta Weigle, 213–22. Santa Fe, N.Mex.: Lightning Tree, 1975.

White, Hayden. *Tropics of Discourse: Essays in Cultural Criticism*. Baltimore: Johns Hopkins University Press, 1978.

Williams, Raymond. *Marxism and Literature*. New York: Oxford University Press, 2009.

Wilmer, Franke. *The Indigenous Voice in World Politics: Since Time Immemorial*. Newberry Park, Calif.: Sage Publications, 1993.

Wolf, Patrick. "Settler Colonialism and the Elimination of the Native." *Journal of Genocide Research* 8 (4) (2006): 387–409.

Womack, Craig. *Art as Performance, Story as Criticism: Reflections on Native Literary Aesthetics*. Norman: University of Oklahoma Press, 2009.

INDEX

Note: Page numbers in *italics* refer to illustrative matter.

ABOUT THE AUTHOR

Simón Ventura Trujillo is an assistant professor of Latinx studies in the English Department at New York University.